My
Oregon

The people, places and passion
through the stories of a native son

BOB WELCH
The Register-Guard

AO CREATIVE
Eugene, Oregon

Published by AO CREATIVE
P.O. Box 41794
Eugene, OR 97404
www.aocreative.com

Front cover: The author, at about age 3, engaged in among his first marshmallow-roasting experiences on the beach at Yachats, circa 1957. Also around the campfire: His grandfather Ben Schumacher, mother Marolyn Welch Tarrant and sister Linda Welch Crew. (Warren Welch photo.)

Back cover photo by Sally Welch

ISBN: 0-9772306-0-0

Printed in Canada

Author information:
www.bobwelch.net
info@bobwelch.net

Table of Contents

Also by Bob Welch

American Nightingale
The Things That Matter Most
Stories from the Game of Life
Where Roots Grow Deep
A Father for All Seasons
More to Life Than Having It All
Bellevue and the New East Side

To my fellow Oregonians,
blessed children of the rain.

Tell me the landscape
in which you live
and I will tell you who you are.
— José Ortega y Gasset

Author's note

Recently my eldest son and my daughter-in-law dipped the toes of their one-month-old son, Cade, into the waters of the Pacific Ocean. It happened in Yachats, within a Frisbee toss of where Ryan's mother and I had done the same with him about a quarter-century ago. And on the same beach where, another quarter-century before, I had roasted my first marshmallow. (See cover photo.)

When Cade touched that water, it marked, at least in my mind, a baptism of sorts — not a spiritual baptism but a geographic and familial baptism. To me, that moment symbolized his being an Oregonian. And marked his being the sixth generation (on my mother's side) of our family to come to this spot of land where, in 1936, my grandfather had bought, for $500, the original shake-sided cabin.

I love this state. Love the diversity; you can, without much trouble, be in five ecoregions in the same day. You can go from sea level to 10,000-plus feet and never leave Lane County. I love the weather. Love the smell of an August grass harvest, the taste of wild blackberries and the sight of sandpipers banking like air-show F-15s. I even love the word "Oregon" — mysterious, yet touched with whimsy, as opposed to, say, the nose-in-the-air "Connecticut."

And yet Oregon is more than trees and water, mountains and valleys, coast and desert. It's people.

In a sense, the two play off each other: A place helps mold the people who live there. (Given our soggy weather, helps mold us in more ways than one.) And people help mold a place.

What drives this relationship is a certain passion. From nature: the fury of winter waves, the dogged persistence of a small pine clinging to some crag high in the Cascades and the soothing percussion of valley rain on a rooftop.

And from people: a certain pride-fueled stubbornness, reflected in Bill Bowerman's defiance of the Rajneesh cult that was threatening to take over Wasco County in the '80s. A certain persistence, reflected in that wonderful *Sometimes a Great Notion* line in which Ken Kesey suggests Oregon rain is "something you must go through a winter to understand." And a certain whimsy — there's that word again — reflected in winter bicyclers thinking nothing of riding around with spray stripes on their backs.

So when it came time to choose from the 800-plus columns I've written for *The Register-Guard* since I began as a general columnist in 1999, I didn't necessarily choose what I thought were the best ones. Nor did I choose everything I'd written that had a particular "Oregony" theme, thus saving us all from a repeat of that seemed-like-a-good-idea-at-the-time disaster in which I pretended to interview Smokey the Bear. Nor did I choose a Whitman's Sampler; you'll find few "issue" stories here, for example.

Instead, I tried to find a blend of people and place stories that, to Oregonians, might reflect familiar themes. And to non-Oregonians, might offer at least a glimpse of what makes us different from, say, Iowa or Florida. (With a few wild-card columns thrown in just for fun. See insight on hindsight — my colonoscopy — on Page 272.)

Like the proverbial blind-men-and-the-elephant story, everyone sees a different Oregon. If you grew up in the John Day area, your perspective will be different from someone who grew up in Portland. If you recently moved here from California, your Oregon is different from that of a native Oregonian. If you are 80, your Oregon is different from that of someone who is 18.

That considered, what follows is a touch of the people, places and passion that resonate with me after six years as a columnist — and 51 years as an Oregonian.

These are my stories. My experiences. My Oregon. And I'm honored you've chosen to dip your toes in them.

Bob Welch
Eugene, Oregon
September 2005

1.

Where we live

Perspective

Editor's note: The following is the first column Welch wrote for The Register-Guard, *November 1, 1999.*

ONE AUGUST NIGHT in the early '90s, I was aboard a small sailboat, anchored in a cove on Fern Ridge Lake. It was about midnight. My two sons were asleep in the cabin. All was dark except for the stars above and the faint glow of light from Eugene and Springfield to the east.

I looked across the water at that faint glow of light and I thought: This is my home.

It wasn't a particularly profound thought, I realize, but profundity doesn't come easy when you're trying to sleep on an 18-inch-wide fiberglass shelf in the middle of a lake, which is why I was awake in the first place.

Still, the moment infused me with a new sense of place, like an astronaut looking at Earth from outer space for the first time and realizing what a grand scheme we're part of.

In retrospect, the significance of the moment may have been little more than this: Looking at a place from a different perspective can help us better understand that place. And help us better understand ourselves.

As a columnist, I'll offer my perspectives on this place we call home: Oregon. Specifically, Lane County.

I'll write about the nuances that make us Lane County and not Muskogee County (Okla.) or Westchester County (N.Y.).

I'll write about people, places, events, issues and trends.

I'll write with seriousness one day, humor the next and usually with a blend of the two.

I arrive at this journalistic trail head pumped and petrified. Pumped because I think it'll be fun. I come from a background as a sports editor, columnist, features writer and 20Below leader; levity, I believe, leavens a newspaper in a good and necessary way.

Petrified because I'm replacing a legend, Don Bishoff. For newcomers to the area, Bish dates so far back with *Register-Guard* readers that some still remember his first column — about the newly opened Oregon Trail and how, in Don's eyes, it was a clear violation of land-use laws.

Why couldn't I be replacing some humorless hairball from the East who complained about the rain for a year and got fired for padding his expense account? No, I'm called off the bench to replace Cal Ripken.

Bishoff and I date back to the mid-'70s, when we played on the same *Register-Guard* football team. He was an assistant city editor/columnist who played on the line; a University of Oregon student, I was a part-time sports grunt who played wide receiver.

I graduated and worked seven-year stints in Bend and Bellevue, Wash. When I landed a features job back in Eugene a decade ago, Bish began kidding me — and continued to do so until retiring in February — that I'd been hired to replace him.

Wrong. You don't replace a Don Bishoff; I won't even attempt it. We're different, and that's fine. Just as in our football days, he's the grizzled lineman who likes nothing better than to mix it up in the political trenches; I'm the guy on the outside who has different strengths, who has different weaknesses and who still has his luggage at the end of a vacation. (My retreat of choice is Yachats, meaning I don't sacrifice my baggage to the airline gods each year as Don does.)

As a columnist, I see myself as something of a tour guide. Not a Gray Line guy who drones on about postcard scenes, but someone who takes you to the nooks and crannies you might not have seen. Who puts things in perspective. Who sometimes questions the conventional thinking, if there is such a thing in a place where I recently pulled up next to a hearse that had a camouflage-painted fishing boat on top.

In Seattle, I used to read a columnist who once said the difference between a reporter and a columnist was that reporters allow readers the luxury of their own conclusions, whereas "I drag them kicking and screaming to see mine."

Frankly, I'm not interested in abusive relationships with readers.

Though I'll offer my spin on life in Lane County, I have no lock on wisdom and insight. If I'm leading this day-hike three times a week, I do so as teacher and student.

Register-Guard readers are a diverse, fascinating bunch. I feel like I'm the chef at an Eclectics International convention. I stand in front of nearly 80,000 people — young, old; urban, rural; men, women; liberal, conservative; pierced, nonpierced; and, of course, the guy driving that strange hearse with the fishing boat on top.

Man, what do I fix these folks?

Amid the challenge, I'm encouraged by the thought that no matter how different we are, we're linked by one thing: We're all human beings who call this place home — whether we live in the hustle and bustle of that faint glow of light I saw from Fern Ridge that night or in the rural places beyond.

And that, I think, is a good place to begin.

Landscape of our lives

I HAVE A LONE Douglas fir in my back yard. When visitors see it, they see a 100-foot tree. When my sons and their childhood friends see it, they see a menacing presence in right-center field that, years ago, robbed many a would-be whiffle ball home run. And when squirrels see it — well, who knows what squirrels see, but it seems as if they see a bark-and-branch playground where they come to chatter, chew and chase each other around in pursuit of knotty romance.

Me? I see a 2-year-old girl, Alison McNeese Purscelley, planting the tree one day in 1952 with her father. Like only a handful of others, I'm privileged to know this tree's history. I've learned its

story: that instead of just always "being there" — a sort of batter-
ies-not-included fixture that came with the set — it was planted,
nurtured and trimmed for decades by others long before it became,
in essence, mine.

Knowing that changes how I see this tree. It adds personal value
to me. It humbles me. It provides context. It reminds me that this
tree belongs not so much to one man and his family as it does to
one place and its people.

We rarely look at the world around us in such a way. Rarely stop
to think that we weren't always here, that people long before us
planted, nurtured and trimmed this place we call home.

Lane County is in its 150th year. It seems appropriate to find
some meaning in the milestone. Not that it demands an exhaustive
play-by-play of how we got from there to here. But like a celebratory toast, we should honor the past with a touch of reverence. And
like New Year's contemplation, consider the future with a touch of
relief for all we've learned that will guide us on the uncertain road
ahead.

Our distinctiveness as a people is inexorably linked to the distinctiveness of our land. "Tell me the landscape in which you live,"
wrote José Ortega y Gasset, "and I will tell you who you are."

Lie on your belly and look north at Lane County from its southern border — near, say, the North Umpqua River. Only two coun-
ties on the West Coast stretch from Pacific Ocean to Sierra-Cascade
mountain crest: One is the county you're lying in, Douglas; the
other is the county you're looking at, Lane.

Around here, Lane County is our landscape. Like its moist climate, the land drips with diversity — unmatched by any other Oregon county and few in America. From your left, you find surf, tide
pools and sand dunes. But there's more: beaches and bluffs give
way to coastal mountains. Rainfall here is nearly three times what
it is in Eugene, a mere 30 miles away.

From here, you gradually dip into the Willamette Valley, fed by
the Willamette and McKenzie rivers: a patchwork quilt of farm
fields and forests, sprinkled with towns and cities. Finally, the Cascades rise to the east, lava beds offering a dramatic geologic prelude
to the High Cascades. The county that started at sea level ends at
more than 10,000 feet — the Cascades summit.

So if Lane County's 316,000 residents are a diverse lot, part of it
is because we live in a diverse landscape. A Mennonite grass farmer

outside Coburg has far different needs, lifestyles and values than the leather-skinned logger outside Springfield or the motel owner in Florence. Whether their focus is tillers, trees or tourists, each is dependent on the land, though in far different ways.

"We must remind ourselves of the power of place," writes Robert Hamma in *Landscapes of the Soul.*

But if a place shapes people, so do people shape a place. Enter the element of time, the influence of people. History.

Granted, some parts of Lane County aren't much different from decades gone by. What a commercial crabber sees off Strawberry Hill in 2001 hasn't changed much from what Francis Drake saw in 1579. The county — at 4,600 square miles, larger than Delaware and Rhode Island combined — is still more than 80 percent forest land.

But if Lane County affords an almost timeless feel in certain places, in others it's been gouged, gutted and given a glitzy make-over, replete with the kind of cookie-cutter housing developments that once seemed confined to California.

The metamorphosis began about the time Lane County began in 1851 — and was as much about attitude as it was about the saws, shovels and axes that pioneers used to manipulate the earth. For thousands of years, Lane County's lone residents were American Indians whose views of the land were far different from the settlers who came west on the Oregon Trail in the 1840s. Though some Indian practices would today trigger angry letters to the editor — they routinely burned off the valley floor, for example — they were more interested in coexisting with the land than with conquering it.

Not so the settlers. For them, the West became the fulfillment of Manifest Destiny, "Westward Ho!" and "Oregon Fever." The West was a promised land with endless trees, unlimited fish and bottomless wells, all served on a platter called The Donation Land Claim Act of 1850. A year before Lane County began, the land claim law granted married couples 640 acres of free land, single people 320 acres.

"People didn't think much about limits," says Lex Runciman, a Linfield College professor and co-editor of *A Forest of Voices: Reading and Writing the Environment.* "Your only limits were your own luck, your intelligence and the strength of your back."

Eugene founder Eugene Skinner took his land claim at the foot of Skinner Butte in 1846. Five years later, Lane County formed.

In the decades to come, disease and displacement ushered American Indians off to reservations. In sickening suddenness, their centuries-old relationship with the land was severed.

Meanwhile, by 1857, nearly all of the good land west of the Cascades had been settled. Miners came. Loggers came. Trains came.

By the turn of the century, as automobiles triggered a new demand for roads, Lane County's boosters were marketing the county as "The Immigrant's Mecca." And those immigrants came. Lane County's population, from 1900 to 1910, nearly doubled to 34,000.

With the intensity of a steam-donkey engine, the interplay between people and the land — for better or worse — was pumping at an unprecedented pace.

In 1896, the Booth-Kelly Lumber Co. bought 40,000 acres of land about four miles from Marcola. It built a steam-powered mill. It built a community, a company town predicated on the same assumption that had drawn pioneers here half a century before: that the land of opportunity was limitless.

As Lane County celebrated its 50-year anniversary in 1901, the county's population was 20,000, and Booth-Kelly employed more than a thousand of them.

Half a century later, Wendling was a ghost town. The old growth timber that had been the town's lifeblood was gone. Replanted clear-cuts weren't mature enough to log.

I recently stood among those replants, now about 50 feet high. Like the lone Douglas fir in my back yard, the Wendling trees offer stories of their own — stories of dreams and broken dreams.

Indeed, Lane County's most profound lesson to us in the past 150 years might be that, depending on how we treat it, the land giveth and the land taketh away.

August 19, 2001

The way we, uh, are

RELATIVES OF GRADUATES. Track athletes, coaches and fans. Business types. Vacationers.

They arrive in the Eugene-Springfield area, particularly this time of year, knowing little or nothing about this place. So what do they find? How are they regarded? What are they told about a place that for those of us who live here is the experiential norm of brushing our teeth but for them is unfamiliar?

I decided to find out. Thursday morning, wearing sunglasses and a Boston Red Sox shirt and cap, I walked out of the Eugene Airport and slid into a cab. "Where to?" my driver asked.

"I don't know — what do you suggest?" I said.

And so began the adventure.

My rules were simple: Pretend I'd never been here and knew nothing about the area. Ask questions but don't lie, which didn't prove to be hard. Only one person, for example, asked me where I was from.

As we headed toward downtown — my driver suggested I stay at the Campus Inn between the University of Oregon and downtown Eugene — I was treated to a nearly nonstop fact-fest of the area. He told me about Eugene Skinner, the McKenzie and Willamette rivers, rafting, the Oregon Coast, lumber, the Schnitzer Museum of Art and the Saturday Market.

"What's that?"

"Guys come in and sell all kinds of crafts."

"Like what?" I asked.

"Physical stuff. Paintings. Shoes. You can buy lots of kinds of shoes."

Huh. I tried to picture a big parking lot full of homemade loafers.

I pointed to the Coburg Hills. "What mountains are those — right here, close?"

"The Cascades," he said.

He described Eugene as a "little college town," Springfield as "a small farm town."

I was let off close to the Eugene Hotel. At the nearby Zenon Cafe, I drank in Eugene — and a glass of orange juice — from an outside table. I was curious about a giant duck down the street and my waitress, friendly and efficient, explained that these art-festooned ducks were all over town, part of a charity fund-raiser.

Huh. Giant art ducks. Whimsical place, this.

While thumbing through something called the *Oregon Daily Emerald*, an "independent newspaper" — apparently of the local university, though I couldn't determine that from the front page

— I saw an ad that read "Take a Hike." At noon, there was to be a "UO Faculty/Staff Fitness Walk." "Questions?" it said. "Call Molly Kennedy."

I liked that — an actual name. And the walk sounded like a good way to see the campus and meet folks. I called. I got a recorded message. Figures.

I meandered west and saw two high school students, studying next to a statue at Broadway and Willamette. "Who's the statue of?" I asked.

"No clue," the boy said.

"I think it's that Ken 'Keh-see' guy," the girl said.

"Who was he?"

"Don't know," she said.

A man zipped by on a three-wheeled bicycle being pulled by three dogs on leashes. He was talking on a cell phone. *Hmmm.*

I told a couple of punk-looking young men I'd just come from the airport; what was there to do in this town? One suggested I go to a movie at "Gateway." He told me I'd need to take a bus; the station was a couple of blocks south. (Later, he asked if I wanted to buy some "crystals." I said no, remembering some long-lost "just-say-no-to-crystals" campaign.)

Around the block, I asked a smoky-smelling guy outside a bar called Luckey's what he recommended for me to see or do. He recommended shooting pool at Luckey's.

I walked toward the bus depot, then noticed the library and poked my head inside. A volunteer suggested I spend time here, then go see the Schnitzer Museum of Art and something called Hayward Field. Big track meet this weekend, he said.

Outside, I asked a guy who used to live in Mississippi but now lives in Eugene — "I love it here"— how to get to the university. He said I should take a bus.

Suddenly, my cell phone rang. Molly had called me back! I explained that I'd just come in from the airport, the walk looked like fun and, well, could I come? She said sure.

Is this a cool place or what?

Here's a little "or what?" At the outdoor bus station, I got lost trying to figure out what bus to take. For starters, the map needed one of those "you-are-here" arrows. (Bad signage.)

"Is it always this nice here?" I asked a young woman whom I was seated next to on the bus. She shrugged and looked the other way.

Okaaaay.

At the bookstore, I asked a clerk how to get to Hayward Field. She went out of her way to get me a map.

"Hey, I'm a Twins fan, not a Red Sox fan," said a young woman who had overhead the conversation, "but I'm heading that way. Follow me."

Heidi Erickson, a soon-to-be molecular biology grad, walked me to Hayward Field. She suggested, if I had time, to hike to the top of something called Spencer Butte.

She was nice — and sold on UO. "I'm from Minneapolis. University of Minnesota. Downtown hustle and bustle. This is an actual college campus."

I walked through a cemetery right on campus, saw solar-powered parking meters and learned the mascot here is — get this — a duck. Quirky place, this.

Inside something called the "EMU" — a building named for a bird? — I was puzzled by the odd names of meeting rooms: Alsea, Coquille, Metolius, Owyhee, Rogue and Umpqua.

"Help you find something?" a young man asked.

I asked about the names. He told me they were Oregon rivers. "There's a map over there that shows you where they're located." (Excellent signage.)

I swung by the Schnitzer Museum of Art, then to the Knight Library. I asked three students for whom the library was named. One didn't know. One said, "I think Phil Knight. He sponsors just about everything on campus." The third said Phil Knight, then a rather curt: "I thought it was common sense."

Ouch.

En route to the recreation center to start the hike, I saw a big building called "McArthur Court." A young man told me "it's like the oldest, biggest standing building in the nation — or something like that."

I saw a young man in an "I hate Beavers" shirt. I asked him why he hated beavers and he said that that was the mascot for Oregon State. Ah ha! Rivals! I get it.

It was hike time. A woman who helped me register greeted me with wide-smile gusto. She handed me a canvas bag.

Nearly 200 of us then started walking around campus. Every few hundred yards, we'd stop at a little table and — like Halloween — some nice person from a different campus department would give us gum or a granola bar or an ergonomically correct pen to put in our bags.

I walked with a 68-year-old woman who was a secretary in the — what are the chances? — molecular biology department. She chatted with me the whole way. "I love my job," she said. "The students keep me young."

With the walk over, I thanked my hosts and later called a cab to return to the airport. My driver, with uncombed hair and a pack of nonfilter Camels on the dash, looked like the kind of guy who once worked on a fishing trawler in Alaska, which he had.

The temperature was in the mid-80s. "Is it always this hot in Oregon?" I asked.

"Yeah, it gets pretty hot here," he said. "A hundred sometimes."

He didn't much like this place. "Good thing I like to travel because this place drives you nuts. It's a weird area."

"Weird in what way?" I asked.

"Lot of those anarctics here," he said. "Hippie people."

" 'Anarctics?' " I asked.

"Yeah, rioters. Coupla times the cops had to use tear gas. They were breaking windows, running across the tops of cars."

He dropped me off at the airport. Seven hours earlier, I hadn't known a thing about what the airport exit refers to as "The Gateway to Western Oregon." But now I understood. Sort of.

I got in my truck and drove off, occasionally glancing at the towering Cascade Mountains.

May 25, 2005

The sweet smells of home

I WAS WALKING across the University of Oregon campus recently when I smelled it — fresh bread from the Williams Bakery near Franklin Boulevard.

Aaaah.

In an instant, I was an 18-year-old freshman in overalls searching for (a) the meaning of life and (b) Gerlinger Hall, where I was late for a first-term lit class.

Somehow, amid my freshman lostness, that bread smelled of reassurance, as if the world wasn't quite as dark and cold as I'd come to believe.

The sense of smell does that to you. Takes you back to a time of your life that may have been profound or trivial, that may represent a highlight or heartbreak, but waits patiently for its calling — like a library book that hasn't been checked out in years.

Now that we're settling into a season of muted scents, I thought I'd compensate by offering my top 10 Lane County smells.

Nobody has begged me for such a list, but I thought mine might trigger your own; thus, if it's a little premature to be thinking cherry blossoms and campfires, this might at least offer us all the promise of sweeter smells to come.

These are, understand, public smells, smells available to all. (A private smell would be, say, your Big Boy tomatoes or your father's Prince Valiant pipe tobacco.)

These are smells chosen not for their political correctness — I confess I like the smell of field-burning smoke. And these are smells offered with the full realization that one person's perfume is another person's sinus headache.

The list, in no particular odor:

Williams Bakery. "Of all smells, bread; of all tastes, salt," wrote the 17th-century poet George Herbert. Bread, indeed, but particularly the smell of bread in such an odd context: outdoors, not in a kitchen. And a wholesome scent wafting across campus dorms — dorms that, unless they've changed since the '70s, can smell fairly unwholesome.

Your first whiff of coast air. Like seafood chowder, it's a blend of a little this and that — salt, sand, surf, seaweed and (not to spoil the alliterated mood) dead fish, birds and diatoms, those little sea creatures with an out-there odor.

Blackberries. They're the smell of childhood, of simplicity, of easily overlooked goodness — and are best enjoyed at dusk as a hot day fades to black. The smell of blackberries can almost make you forget we live in a world of political backbiting, "Survivor" spinoffs and Howard Stern.

Cherry blossoms. So easily taken for granted, but so gloriously up front — not only in your face but up your nose. And one of the few smells whose source is as wondrous to see as it is to breathe. (As opposed to say, smoke, which, visually, leans toward the oppressive side.)

While living in Bend, I arrived in Eugene for a journalism conference one April day, got out of my car and thought I'd gone to heaven — only it was 15th Avenue, just down from Mac Court. I'd been gone so long from Eugene that I'd forgotten how sweet was the smell of spring — a season that Central Oregon skips each year.

Freshly cut grass. Not unique to Lane County, of course, but noteworthy nevertheless. The best whiff comes on that false-spring day in late February when you breathe deep and think for the first time: There's life beyond an Oregon winter.

Just a touch of field-burning. No political statement, this. But I can't un-ring the bell of personal history; the smell stirs something deep within — and, unlike with some folks, it's not asthma. It's the thought of back-to-school and football and last gulps of summer.

East Broadway and Pearl Street in downtown Eugene at noon on a July day. The diners are on the sidewalks at Cafe Zenon, Hawthorne's and Ambrosia — and the smell of food is scrumptious.

Peoria Road between Corvallis and Eugene on a summer evening during grass-seed harvest. It's just so Oregon, one of those smells you won't find hardly anywhere else in the world.

The mud of a Turkey Bowl football game behind Cal Young Middle School. This smells of football at its primordial best, before the game was corrupted by artificial turf and bowl games named after potato chips. To be knocked on your face in the mud by some punk teenager is to smell your youth — while feeling your age.

Smoke from the Richardson Park campground as you moor your boat at Fern Ridge Lake after an evening sail. The perfect combination: a scent that evokes all sorts of summer memories — and the time to actually stop and consider them.

Who could ask for more in a place to live?

January 7, 2001

Eugene for dummies

WELCOME TO EUGENE, Chris, Lee and Kirk. We're honored ESPN's College GameDay has chosen to televise its daylong show of Saturday's college football highlights — and predictions — from Autzen Stadium.

Given that this is GameDay's first trip to the Northwest and given that I've talked to people at Denver International Airport who believe Oregon is bordered by Missouri, South Dakota and Michigan, thought I'd offer you a little "local knowledge."

First, a safety warning: While you're visiting, a stranger may well shout at you, "Freeze, sucker. Hands on the hood." Don't panic. It's just the gas-station attendant politely informing you to drop the nozzle; we're one of two states that don't pump their own.

Next, geography: Lee, you asked on-air a few weeks back where Eugene, Oregon, is. Officially, we're at Latitude 44 North, Longitude 123 West, according to the U.S. Naval Observatory. Unofficially, we're the center of the universe, but keep that low if you would or people will want to move here.

We're always getting listed in those best-places-to-live polls, but please don't mention that. Don't mention the internationally known Bach Festival, the 27 miles of bike paths, the zillion trees, the being only a two-CD drive from the coast or the Cascades.

The fields you see are fields, not "prairies," as a writer for the *Atlanta Journal-Constitution* once wrote. And that river just south of the stadium is the Willamette. That's will-LAM-it, not as some outsiders have referred to it, the will-uh-MEH-tee.

Speaking of language, it's youGENE, not YOUgene. And Ory-gun, not Aura-gone.

Remember, as our name suggests, there's a little "ego" in Oregon. Probably a little Northwest inferiority complex, too; you get a bit defensive when people assume the state fabric is flannel and when a Newport Beach, Calif., waiter says to you, "Is that the place where it, like, stays light all night long?"

Oh, by the way, an ABC sportscaster during the Wisconsin game called our head coach "Nick" or "Mick" Bellotti. It's Mike. Nick Aliotti is our defensive coordinator.

The state motto is Alis Volat Propiis — "She Flies With Her Own Wings." Eugene's motto is Argumenta Ad Nauseam — "We'd Rather Peck Each Other to Death."

Let's just say we're a spirited community, guys. Eugene is this odd combination of innovation and cannibalization. Where else does the city's first female city manager pressure the city's first black police chief to resign, then get fired herself by the City Council?

Where else does Julia "Butterfly" Hill, who sat in a tree for two years to protest clear-cutting, get heckled during a speech — by a masked trio who suggest she "sold out" to the logging company?

We're the political equivalent of that adage about ever-changing weather: If Eugene is calm, wait five minutes and someone will protest something, whether it's anarchists wanting to bring down corporate America.

Mother Jones magazine recently named UO the top school in the country for campus activism — We're No. 1, We're No. 1! — so don't be surprised if a few radicals chain themselves to the goalposts if the Ducks, say, get called for clipping.

Eugene can be a bit quirky. *Animal House* was filmed here. Our annual parade features a slug queen. And where else does the post-parade newspaper coverage say, "The Eugene Skinner Award was given to Planned Parenthood for its Joe Sperm entry"?

Oh, almost forgot: It's not the University of Oregon Beavers, as some outsiders have said. To call UO the Beavers would be to call Democrats Elephants. It's Oregon Ducks, Oregon State Beavers.

Originally, Oregon was the Webfoots, named for Willamette Valley pioneers who slogged through winter mud, but sportswriters thought the name too long. As for Oregon winters, well, some say they're too long, too.

Feel free to mention those long, rainy, gloomy, pathetically-dark-and-dank-go-crazy winters. Just, remember, they're Ory-gun winters, not Aura-gone winters.

September 22, 2000

A Eugene Christmas wish

'TWAS THE NIGHT before Christ — winter solstice —
when all through Eugene
Letter writers were furiously venting their spleens
Ashcroft was hung by the lefties with spite
In hopes that such effigy would rankle the right.

The hard-core "conserves" were all snuggled to Bush
While visions of air raids danced and went "whoosh."
Like the Gang of 9 artist dropping his load
Not even hanging around to see it explode.

When at the Wayne Morse Plaza there rose such a clatter
I sprang from my slumber to see what was the matter
Away to downtown, I drove with surprise
The Sixth Street lights, for once, synchronized.

The cops in their riot gear in the new-fallen rain
Suggested our protesters were at it again
Afghanistan? Parkway? Trees that need love?
Assisted suicide? Mocked turtle doves?

Ozone depletion? Christmas trees? Gun play?
BCS? Sweat shops? Or what was formerly Hyundai?
Any, I suspected, could account for this rally
Even leftover bile from the Gore-Bush vote tally.

But what to my wondering eyes should appear
But a woman in red, spreading holiday cheer
With fairy wings and Birkies, she was oh-so-Eugene
I knew in a moment it was the Santa Slug Queen.

More rapid than eagles her subjects they came
And she whistled and shouted and called them by name:
"Now Torrey, Bettman, Papé and Rayor
On Nathanson, Kelly, Farr, Meisner and Taylor.

"On, peaceniks and writers of letters so preachy
On U of O, PeaceHealth, on Musumeci
Gang of 9, CEOs, Red Guard and Weekly
And all of the citizens who entwine us uniquely."

And then, in a twinkling I heard snorts and shouts
And realized the "rain"-deer were all duking it out
They were prancing and pawing, out to divide
The sleigh was bogged down by political pride.

All full of strength, vision and passion to fly
But the energy was wasted on hoofs held up high
And so it is with Eugene's citizen masses
Some of them jewels and some of them — not jewels.

But, said Santa Slug, as she positioned her sleigh
"How high could we fly if we all pulled the same way?
How high could we fly if we chucked the self-interest
If we set aside tags like left, right and centrist.

"We could soar higher, if we learned compromise
If we listened more, talked less, seldom despised
If we took a cue from my merrymaking elves
And sometimes broke down and laughed at ourselves.

"For beneath all the rancor, fighting and fear
We all are part of this community here
You and I, he and she, each make this place
Reps, Demos, Greenies and some lost in space.

"Christians, Muslims, Sikhs, atheists and Jews
Some driving Beemers, some sporting tattoos
There's intelligent life, don't beam us aboard, Scotty
Good folk live in Eugene, including Bellotti.

"I know it's far-fetched, like a Rodney King song
That despite ourselves, we might all just get along
But it's a season for dreaming so dreaming I'll do
In the land of the buttes where the rivers run through."

Then done with her message, Santa Slug started her route
Filling stockings with Gore-Tex and organically grown sprouts
Frog joke books and coupons for bike-parking valet
And Nutcracker *tickets to Eugene's own ballet.*

Fiesta Bowl packages and stuff that is free
Like gentle rain, seasons and Douglas fir trees
Blackberries, running trails, Williams Bread whiffs
Boaters' Fern Ridge and climbers' Skinner Butte cliffs.

Then she sprang to her sleigh, to her team gave a whistle
And away they all flew like an LTD missile
But I heard her exclaim, high above the Pioneer Mother
"Happy Christmas to all, and take care of each other."
December 16, 2001

Angels in the snow

HE SHOWED UP seemingly out of nowhere, like a sort of guardian angel in logger's jeans, baseball cap and suspenders. He was lugging a Husky 288 chain saw, 36-inch bar. Someone around here call for help?

That would be the frantic folks at Child Care Inc., a hole-in-the-wall day care just west of Skinner Butte. They'd had a tree crash down, blocking their entrance, in Thursday's roof-smashing, fence-shattering, power-cutting windstorm. A parent of one of their tots had heard some guy on KKNU radio volunteering his services. Have chain saw, will travel.

So there was Jon Millard, 26, silhouetted in the headlights of his Subaru Forester, bucking up a tree so a couple of dozen ankle-biters could come to preschool the next morning and their parents wouldn't be frantically looking for baby sitters. No charge.

"We're just a small nonprofit," says Michelle Lang, the school's administrative director. "I don't think we'd have been opening the next morning without his help."

"I'm just a sucker for helping people out, I guess," Millard says.

For all the headaches and havoc they cause, storms remind us of something that gets lost in our pursuit of rugged Northwest individualism: We still need each other.

Crisis breeds character and by Monday, as the smoke settled from downed-limb fires dotting Lane County's rural areas, this community had shown plenty of it. Oh, I know there's a flip side. I heard about drivers avoiding midstreet branches by ripping through people's lawns and about motels that bumped up their rates to exploit the demand.

But I'd rather tell you about how the Doubletree Hotel on Gateway Street offered storm-stricken folks a $49 special instead of its standard $94 rate. "I sensed they were genuinely concerned," says Ray Hodson, who showed up with his wife, Linda, after their Fall Creek house lost power. The Ramada Inn on Coburg Road lowered its rates from $77 to $50.

I'd rather honor all the folks who had electricity, but who strung extension cords across the street to bring light and heat to their neighbors who didn't.

I'd rather brag about Vicki, a woman who, in gathering darkness

Thursday, handed her cell phone to Jerry Swartz of Swartz Brothers Select Market in Walterville and said, "It's yours for as long as you need it."

Sure, I could tell about people who think the EWEB folks have been sitting around on their transformers, watching the geese land on the Willamette instead of restoring power lines.

But I'd rather tell you about the dead-tired utility guys who showed up at Karen Ory's west Eugene house at 7 a.m. Sunday to get the neighborhood reconnected.

I'd rather tell you about how her neighbors were helping each other clear debris. "There was a sense of community that doesn't normally exist — and suddenly it's just there," she says. "We tend to be so afraid of each other because of our political beliefs or religious beliefs, but something like this strips us of our opinions, and we're down to the bare necessity of just all being human beings."

I'd rather tell you about the Bascoms out in Pleasant Hill — Nancy and John — who, after two days without power, had to head for Portland and forgot about their freezers. And how their neighbors drove their motor home over and hooked up the freezers to their generator to save the Bascoms' food.

I'd rather tell you about how those Swartz Brothers — Jerry and Larry — donated more than $30,000 worth of frozen food to FOOD for Lane County. How, when their scanners went dead and the lights went out Thursday, they handed out flashlights and pencils to customers, and trusted that folks wouldn't fudge on the prices they wrote down. How they gave away ice cream and how customers brought them hot coffee and sandwiches.

"It just brought out the best in people," Jerry says. "I don't ever remember the store being so relaxed, where we were just talking with each other, everybody sharing their experiences.

"It's like when you jerk away our electricity it takes people back down to the stuff that really matters: their hearts and souls. It changes everything. Suddenly we don't have TV or VCRs. All we have is each other."

I could leave you with the image of angry people demanding that their power be restored, but you can read that elsewhere. I'd prefer to leave you with the image of those extension cords going across neighborhood streets, connecting people with far more than electricity.

February 12, 2002

2.

Seasons

In praise of rain

YACHATS — It came as if on cue. A friend and I had just finished hauling, cutting and splitting a winter's worth of firewood for the cabin. I had a cup of hot chocolate in my hands. A fire burned lazily from across the room.

Then, I heard it on the window: rain.

Not just the scattered-drop sort of rain, but the going-through-a-carwash sort of rain. The kind of rain that, for a devotee of downpours like me, is long overdue.

I confess, I like the stuff. As much as I enjoyed November's rare cold-and-dry spell — through Sunday, we had only 1.11 inches of precipitation compared to our normal 7.12 inches — I'm ready for the winter rains to set in. And there's reason to believe that those rains will soon arrive, in earnest, at a gutter near you.

Traditionally, December is the wettest month and the first weekend in December the wettest week of the year. During that week, there's a 67 percent chance rain will fall on any given day. And current weather patterns suggest this year will follow statistical suit.

"It looks like Thursday it gets wet and stays wet," says state climatologist George Taylor.

Bring it on, I say. I've made peace with precipitation. It's just something soaked into the fabric of the state.

It's why we have frothy rivers to float, lakes to fish, forests to fight about. It's why we have only one-fifth the population of Los Angeles.

It's why we read more than most people. Why we have so many writers and artists and cappuccino philosophers.

Rain turns us inward, not only to homes and cafes, but to ourselves. In *Northwest Passages,* Charles Johnson refers to rain as "a perfect externalization of the brooding inner climate of the creative imagination."

It's rooted in our history. In 1875, a *Roseburg News Review* reporter visited Eugene and wrote, "The mud is as thick as boarding house custard."

In the winter of 1805-1806, Lewis and Clark recorded only a dozen rain-free days, one entry sounding very much like a Waldo Lake vacation our family once had: "Some rain all day at intervales (sic), we are all wet and disagreeable."

Though rain can make people disagreeable, it also can give us a common consciousness as well.

It falls, after all, on the just and the unjust, Republicans and Democrats, aristocrats and anarchists, men and women, Beavers and Ducks.

As such, the umbrella symbolizes whatever oneness we might have left. Regardless of who we are, we all must deal with rain, which, records show, will fall on slightly more than half our winter days.

But lest we saturate ourselves in "poor-us" cynicism, hear the words of a Haida Indian I met last summer in Ketchikan, Alaska, where residents not only have learned to live with 180 inches of rain per year — Eugene gets 49 — but apparently thrive on it.

"If we get too many days without rain," sculptor Lee Wallace told me, "people get cranky."

I admire such adaptability. And I see a good deal of it here.

I think of a couple I saw sitting in front of the Adobe Motel in Yachats earlier this fall, enthralled with the pounding waves, seemingly oblivious to a downpour that blurred the difference between land and sea.

I think of a man playing a piano on the mall a few years ago, an umbrella lashed to his keyboard-on-wheels like a sailboat mast.

I think of 50 people playing Turkey Bowl football at Cal Young

Middle School last Thursday morning as rain fell like bullets.

Rain steels us to the purpose at hand, whether it's watching waves, playing music or reaching for gridiron glory. It separates the wheat from the chaff, genuine fans from fair weather fans, true Oregonians from Oregonian wannabes.

Indeed, the Oregon rain tests and tries us. It dares us to improvise, to buck up, to persevere. A while back, when Mac Court sprang a leak during a concert by soprano Eileen Farrell, someone handed her an umbrella and she simply sang on.

One April, I asked a builder friend of mine if it was dry enough to sink fence posts. "Hey, this is Oregon," he said. "If you want, you can wait until the ground's dry enough — but, then, you'll never build a fence."

Which is why, during rainstorms, I've seen Oregonians mowing their lawns, walking their dogs, fishing, golfing, running, skateboarding, protesting, caroling, reading, kissing and selling goods at the Saturday Market.

Winter is coming. Time to build fences. Or a fire.

November 28, 2000

Spring tease

SPRINGTIME IN OREGON arrives like my father's old Johnson 35-horsepower outboard motor used to start on opening day: fitfully, crankily and — when all hope seemed gone — gloriously.

My mother, my sister and I would breathe a collective sigh of relief. My sweat-soaked dad would start with his "What, me worry?" routine. And, as we fastened our life jackets for the journey, the engine would rev up like a neighing horse — then sputter and die.

Sort of like waking up to Monday morning's rain after Oregon's first truly spectacular weekend of the New Millennium.

We never learn, do we? We never learn about this state's annual Spring Tease.

After months of better-than-usual-but-still-fairly-dismal weather, we awaken to see this strange glowing ball low in the eastern sky. Cautiously, we walk out of our houses, like people who have been holed up in bomb shelters for months. We talk quietly, compare notes and hold up our hands to shade our eyes.

Could it be?

In only moments, we shift from hibernation to hallucination. Everywhere we look, we see hope, promise, possibilities.

We begin thinking outlandish thoughts — thoughts about planting gardens and building Adirondack chairs and watching baseball games without being wrapped in blankets.

It gets worse. We wonder if this might be the year for the rock wall we've been talking about since '92. We ponder pruning the backyard apple tree that once was planted safely in foul territory but now has taken over right field. We think about fixing the electricity in the back shed, a thought that passes quickly since we "fixed" it only two years ago.

Thoughts turn to talk. We could paint the house. We could replace all of the shrubbery that came with the house a decade ago. We could add on to the front porch.

Then comes that inevitable Oregon-esque comment that someone makes every year about this time: "Man, it must be, like, 60 out here," which always makes me think of a Californian saying the same thing — in disgust, while shivering beneath polar fleece.

Could it be?

Talk turns to action. We gather our shop tools with the urgency of someone on a supermarket shopping spree. We call the rental place to reserve a sod-cutter. We pound stakes in the front lawn to mark the rock wall that, deep down in the footing of our soul, we know will be one of those why-did-I-ever-start-this projects but that we can't resist.

We're Oregonians. Like scuba divers desperate to leave the depths of darkness, we know there's a price to pay for surfacing too fast — the bends — but we've seen the light and need it like a battery-low laptop needs a charge. So we flutter-kick like crazy, higher and higher, regardless of the consequences.

We find ourselves inventing work, just to stay outside. The Kindling Guy has dropped off the annual load of shingles, so we use that as an excuse to rearrange the outdoor wood shed.

We're not alone in our thirst to do as much work or have as much fun as possible. We're Oregonians, so we try too hard. We try to fly kites even though there's no wind. We turn up our music too loud. We stay in the sun too long.

Could it be? Could it be spring? We desperately want to believe so.

As Oregonians, we're winter's orphans, wanting desperately to be taken home to live with Dry and Warm.

We've somehow come to believe that if we think, talk and act as if it's spring, it will somehow stay this time, that we can influence the season by embracing it with such gusto that the weather gods will reward our faithfulness.

But Monday comes and with it the sulky skies of winter.

Like zombies, we walk around as if suffering from expectation hangovers. As I write Monday afternoon, the rain is falling so hard that from our building's west windows, it looks as if we're going through a giant car wash.

Executive Editor Jim Godbold has left for home, having hurt his back Sunday while falling off a ladder during a tree-cutting venture. Some Eugene fans who sat through a Saturday double-header are nursing sunburns.

Other people are bummed that the weekend weather — Sunday's high of 64 equaled our millennium high — came and went, leading us on with the sweet seduction of cherry blossoms and tulip trees and newborn lambs on velvet green hills and bicyclists on country roads and outside dining and Frisbees flying.

Spring doesn't come to Oregon in a single weekend. It comes in fits and starts, over a few months' time, teasing us along the way.

And though it may ask a price, it also offers a dividend: a chance for Oregonians to learn patience, perseverance and all of that other good stuff that steels our collective character.

Even if we'd happily trade it all for another day like Sunday.

March 28, 2000

Children of the rain

I'M AWASH IN GUILT — all because of the coming drought. You see, I even feel guilty about using the verb "awash" in that first sentence, its literal meaning being "flooded with water." Now that we're on the brink of the state's worst drought in 70 years, I feel like the shipwreck survivor who mentions a Snickers bar to his starving companions.

I wake up in the morning and the sun is shining. It's one of those feel-good-all-over days so perfect I want to mentally press Command-C so I can copy and paste it again and again. And then I remember: I must not think this way — and quickly hit the delete key.

Me bad. Sun bad. Rain good.

In a weather story a few weeks ago, *Register-Guard* reporter Susan Palmer nailed it. "Sun guilt," she called it. "That feeling evoked when pleasure over yet another cloudless day collides with the bald truth that right now sun is bad, very bad."

For Oregonians, it's a hard truth to absorb — if I can use the word "absorb," which is often used in water-related ways — but we need rain. Usually by this point in the year we have about 17.5 inches. As of Friday, we had 4.29.

That's not much of a problem now, but this summer it will be. Without water, crops can't grow, fish can't swim, boats can't float. Farm animals go thirsty; forest fires lick their chops.

But who wants to give up this unexpected glimpse of heaven we've been afforded?

It's Spock's human side doing battle with his Vulcan side: emotion vs. logic.

It's the classic clash between instant gratification — breathing deep a cherry-blossom day — and ultimate consequences: yellow lawns, muddy reservoirs and charred timber.

As a native Oregonian, this unexpected dryness goes against everything I stand for (usually while in a mud puddle).

As Oregonians, we natives were brought up as rain-numbed defeatists, sodden Cinderellas destined to clean gutter sludge while our California friends and relatives traipsed merrily off to some beach blanket bingo party.

Suddenly, we find ourselves not only invited to the party, but winning the limbo contest and dancing the frug along with Annette Funicello and Frankie Avalon.

Temperatures soar into the mid-60s. Frisbees soar into the air. The soil isn't its usual quicksandy self. Uncaught fly balls actually take a hop or two instead of imbedding like stones in Jell-O. Runners forget they own rainsuits.

People take umbrellas in their hands — as during this weekend's rainy aberration — and say: Now tell me again: How do these work?

Everyone's doing the frug on the beach.

Then it happens: The music stops with the suddenness of a jukebox cord ripped from the wall. There, standing in a wintry dark suit, is Gov. John Kitzhaber, the look on his face so dour he makes the guy in "American Gothic" look like your crazy uncle with the joy-buzzer handshake.

"Hope for rain," says Kitzhaber, as if a character from *The Grapes of Wrath*. "Prepare for drought."

In other words, the party's over, folks. Go back to your homes and raise the wheels on your lawn mowers and take short showers and repair your leaks so nary a drop is wasted.

In Cinderella speak, the clock has struck midnight. It's time to remember who we are: not sun gods or goddesses, but rusty relics of James Cloutier's Hugh Wetshoe cartoons.

Go back and somberly contemplate a summer without sailing, the Thursday night races replaced, perhaps, by team mud wrestling.

Go back to your homes and remember that we are Children of Rain, and that that yellow glow in the sky is only a temporary temptress.

Go back to your homes and brood. Contemplate. Philosophize. And, of course, feel the guilt swirl around you like the Floods of '96.

I know it's not the governor's fault; he's just the bearer of bad news. Still, I'm climatalogically confused.

I look at my trees and shrubs and garden remnants, which, in a normal year at this time, would be melded together in a concoction that looks like beef stew, and think: This is not right. They look too good.

Enjoy, enjoy it, whispers the Devil of Drizzle. You have paid your penance in springs gone by, like the year you lost your Kidsports shortstop in the bog at second base.

Every rainless day means a deeper drought this summer, harrumphs the Angel of Clear Skies. You must not give in to such temporal pleasures, even though, I confess, in moments of weakness, I, too, dance the frug.

So there you have it — a story of one man's drought. It isn't pretty. But that's how it is when we Oregonians get too much sun — and find ourselves feeling so bad for feeling so good.

March 25, 2001

Summer sounds

LONG STORY short: Because of a cowboy-singing friend of mine, I recently wound up staying in the West Texas ranch house of a guy named Billy Ray something.

I was almost asleep — it was about 1 a.m. — when Billy Ray himself suddenly appeared and told my friend and me to throw on some clothes and get outside.

"I want ya'll to hear the pertiest summer sound you'll ever hear," said Billy Ray, the apparent model for those one-tooth-missing-cowboys you see in the $8.95 gift-shop paintings. He guided us out beneath a Texas sky glittering with stars to a pond where frogs were croaking happily away.

"Ain't nothin' better than bullfrogs makin' music, Hoss."

On my Top 25 Summer Sounds, bullfrogs don't even make my "also-receiving-votes" list, but I was impressed that Billy Ray called them to my attention at 1 a.m. (even if I never understood why he kept calling me "Hoss").

One man listens to bullfrogs and hears a symphony while another man listens to bullfrogs and scratches his head, hoping this concert will end soon so he can go back to bed.

Such is the way of the world when it comes to summer sounds.

Now if Billy Ray came to Oregon — unlikely because Texans don't seem to think there's life beyond their state — I'd want him to hear what I think are the best sounds of summer.

I'd want him to hear the rumble of the Pacific Ocean as you lie on the beach, just before you drift off to sleep, cocooned in blankets, a paperback discarded in the sand.

I'd want him to hear the whistle of one of those night trains that come through Eugene, the sound that irks so many folks at the Ya-Po-Ah Terrace but makes me, just for a moment, think I'm living in Lake Wobegon.

I'd want him to hear squirrels chattering high up in a Douglas fir. And 4,000 people at Civic Stadium singing *Take Me Out to the Ball Game* during the seventh-inning stretch. And the final, sweet note of a Bach Festival concert. And cold, clear McKenzie River water tumbling down from Clear Lake.

Summer sounds are the best sounds of the year. They beckon you to contemplate life, to appreciate the moment, to think back.

Late on summer nights, a kid down the street skateboards in the dark — I never see him, I only hear him — and it takes me back to Draper Court, where I remember a sound I haven't heard in decades: baseball cards fluttering in the spokes of a Schwinn bike, having been clothespinned there by those of us who imagined ourselves driving Little Deuce Coupes.

I like "kid sounds" in summer: water fights, whiffle-ball banter, sprinkler play. I particularly like the sounds of those ch-ch-ch sprinklers — Rainbirds? — that you don't hear much anymore, replaced, as it were, by the steady shhhhh of automatic sprinklers. (Lawn irrigation is losing all its romance.)

I like camping sounds in summer, especially at dusk: the sizzle of a fire that's down to the embers, an ax splitting a log far away, the dipping of a canoe paddle, quiet voices across a lake. Goodness, there's even something deep within me — Suttle Lake as a 6-year-old? — that welcomes the sound of an outhouse door banging shut half-a-mile away.

Of course, not all summer sounds are pleasant. The worst, I believe, is a toss-up between the personal watercraft and the jet boat, which are like lone mosquitoes in your tent: small and seemingly insignificant, but enough to ruin the night. Runner-ups include motel/hotel air-conditioning units and squawking crows.

But good summer sounds abound: I like that thu-THUNK swimming-pool sound of a "cannonball" jump — knees tucked, hands grasping legs — and its artsier cousin, the "can-opener" — leaning back, hands grasping one bent knee.

I like the sizzle of a barbecue, the first bite of corn and, while on a walk, the quiet exchange of people on a back deck.

At the beach, a squawking California gull rarely disappoints, nor does that Newport radio station's morning sell-it-on-the-air show, which is always a good reminder that you're on vacation. ("So we have a regular-bed pickup canopy, $250, and a Winchester 12-gauge, $600 or best offer ... ")

The summer rarities are nice, too — thunder, fireworks (one night is enough for me) and the first rain after weeks of drought, preferably at night.

Finally, there is the ice-cream truck. Is there anything better than hearing its back-in-time jingle on a summer evening?

And after 131 times of it, anything worse?

June 26, 2001

Dog days of summer

HARRISBURG — In this, the first full week of summer, a windless morning locks the Willamette Valley's grass fields in photo-like stillness.

Beside the farmhouses that dot Coburg Road, American flags lie as lethargic as tired dogs.

The softball diamond at Lake Creek Mennonite School is awash in knee-high dandelions; beyond the backstop, birds in their oak-tree bleachers sing a lonely national anthem, a lament to a season now gone.

And yet if there's a certain sadness — and a definite blandness — to this brief intermission between school-end excitement and summer proper, there's also a sense of expectation. Of a season that's about to burst forth in fireworks, grass-seed harvest and ripe Royal Ann cherries. Of events anticipated, such as Timothy Bunnell's summer vacation that he's marked on the grease-board calendar at Harrisburg City Hall — the annual camping trip to Fall Creek.

Bunnell's business card says he's the city's "community development superintendent," but most people around here know him as the city's maintenance guy and, more importantly, as the one responsible for seeing to it that some 800 chickens get barbecued to perfection at Harrisburg's Old-Fashioned Fourth of July celebration.

"I wear a few hats around here," he says, as an oscillating fan cools a City Hall office accented with red, white and blue bunting.

Around here, folks stuff dollars in a fireman's boot at Serena's Diner to raise money for the fireworks. A waitress spots Joe Morneau of Ag West Supply and says to him, just to make sure he hasn't had a sudden change of taste after six years of lunchtime orders:

"Chicken sandwich and macaroni salad?"

"Yep."

Some of life's best-anticipated things are the ones rooted in the seeming mundanity of tradition. In different versions of a repeating event or holiday or lunch order. Minutes later, as Morneau bites into his traditional meal, an advertisement on an "oldies" radio station touts season tickets for Oregon State football.

Anticipation.

These may be summer's early dog days, the dormant days, the six-weeks-till-football-practice days, but they are also days gathering themselves up for more.

Some things come and go as part of no particular rhythm; by September, Harrisburg will install its first traffic light ever — at the intersection of Third Street and Territorial Road. Meanwhile, the final pieces of the town's dismantled water tower are expected to be hauled off today.

But what makes seasonal fruit so scrumptious is that it is part of a rhythm, a rhythm that allows you access to it only once a year. And, let's face it, it's the 11 months of not having fresh strawberries that make fresh strawberries so inviting.

Nearly lost in a waist-high field, 12-year-old Lisa Bowers clips clumps of ryegrass out of acres of fescue belonging to her grandparents.

She's not only immersed in a few square miles of grass, but the task of preparation — much less exciting than the harvest, though no less important. Her sacrifice now means a better yield come harvest in a few weeks, not to mention $6.50 an hour.

Meanwhile, summer's intermission hangs in these parts like the dust of a pickup truck on a gravel road. A kidless tire swing hangs from a maple tree. A kidless above-ground pool awaits warmer weather. Both are reminders of a necessary pause in the seasonal rhythm, the down time that speaks of up times to come.

In Coburg, a cross-road banner reminds passersby that the town's annual Golden Years celebration is the third weekend in July.

South of Harrisburg, sprinklers nourish the fruits of summer; by now, the strawberries have all but come and gone. But at Detering Orchard off Coburg Road, cherries are almost ready, and July 10 is the anticipated ripening date for peaches.

North of Harrisburg, Veldon Kropf — around here, about every third farmer is a Kropf — stands next to his John Deere windrower, an implement that cuts grass and leaves it in a row. For farmers such as Kropf, expectation is all part of the game. And this week marks the shift from sowing to reaping; cutting and combining will begin any day.

"We want blue skies every day from now till September," he says.

He will, of course, not get those blue skies every day. Nor will our vacations or reunions or weddings or Fourth of July celebrations or all the other stuff of the season be quite as sweet as we hope for now.

But, then, isn't dreaming what the dog days of summer are all about?

June 25, 2002

Post-summer sigh

SUMMERS FLY BY like *Classical Gas,* that song-and-film collage by McKenzie River musician Mason Williams in which hundreds of split-second images flash by in four minutes — in Williams' case, major news events of 1968; in my case, memorable moments of June, July and August 2004.

When it's over, you find yourself thinking: Did all that really happen?

Did I really wrestle a 5-pound steelhead, barehanded? Did I really find myself as the only non-Jewish person at a barbecue in Attleboro, Mass.? Did I really see a Eugene World War II veteran weep at being reunited with a tent mate nearly 60 years after their war ended?

Summers, I've found, are best appreciated after they've happened. Because while they're happening, we're too busy living them to put them into any sort of perspective.

My summer of 2004 — much like yours, I assume — is scattered all over the place: in plane ticket stubs, in mosquito bites, in thousands of digitized pixels in a computer's photo archive.

There I am, with friends who introduced us to whitewater rafting last summer, introducing them to sailing — and the kind of rail-grilled chicken you don't get on a rubber raft. There he is, a big-hearted usher at Baltimore's Camden Yards telling a friend of mine about Babe Ruth being born only a few blocks away. There they are, my nephew kissing his bride, my niece's newborn son in killer shades and my two feet, silhouetted — beyond my book — against Washington's Olympic Mountains.

Of such pixels are one man's summer made. No better than yours. No worse. But mine.

In the end, our seasons — some glorious, some bitter, some boringly routine — link to one another to comprise whatever picture our lives become.

Last Thursday, at a memorial service for the 52-year-old wife of a friend, I watched the man and his four children — hands locked, faces wet — celebrate and agonize over this woman claimed by cancer.

I know what the "Summer of 2004" will always mean to them. In a few minutes' time, photos of her life flashed on two large screens, showing us who she was, what she valued and why she was so loved.

All those seemingly insignificant clicks of the camera — the make-a-wish birthday photos, the walks on the beach, the quick group shots taken over the objections of eye-rolling teenagers — are the stuff we will remember in the end.

Not our business titles. Not our stock portfolios. Not our honors. But the pixels of each picture, the pictures of each season, the seasons that come and go like bullet trains.

In the summer of 2004, I sailed on the sheen of a full moon for the first time. I spent a day proving I was man enough to be a Girl Scout. And I was reminded how soothing is the sound of late-summer rain.

I learned courage from a friend dying of cancer, conviction from a son who believed in himself when I did not, and the brevity of life from too many young people — drowned, shot, killed in wrecks — who will never know another summer.

They go by fast, these summers of our lives. We dare not miss whatever wonder they might offer.

September 5, 2004

The kind of September

I'VE SEEN them each morning for the past few days — more than a hundred Canada geese gathered in a crew-cut field just north of Belt Line Road. Like passengers waiting in an airport terminal, they mill around, grab a bite here and there but they have an anxious look about them, as if waiting for their flights to be called.

And so it is with us. September is about saying goodbye and leaving for somewhere else.

It's about quick glances back — does anyone ever have time to actually look at family videotapes they've taken? — and long looks forward.

It's about going from days ruled by sea tides to days ruled by school bells, from vacations to vocations.

It's about the sweetness of summer giving way to the fickleness of fall, a season much less predictable than its predecessor, which, until the surprising rain of last week, seemed to unfold in one blue-sky day after another.

Who and what will win in the elections? At Autzen Stadium? In the Eugene Celebration parade?

Does this early rash of rain portend — as the supermarket tabloid warns — the worst winter in decades?

And, in the afterglow of "Survivor," what will TV executives dream up next to remind us how shipwrecked we've become as a culture?

But first, we savor the season that was.

I play summer like a game of Yahtzee, trying desperately to meet my scorecard goals, predetermined by me and my penchant to work way too hard at relaxing. Alas, September arrives and I'm still missing my "large straight" (camping at Waldo Lake) and "full house" (not only going to Seattle's Safeco Field, which I did, but snagging a batting-practice ball, which I did not.)

Still, my summer was rich: I'm sailing at Fern Ridge Lake shortly before sunset and a wicked wind has the boat leaning so far to starboard that I can wake up and smell the coffee — meaning that, among the plates, cups and silverware that have clattered to the cabin floor, so has a spilled jar of Taster's Choice.

Not one normally wowed by technology, I'm watching sprinkler heads pop up for the first time to water my lawn at the precise moment I've programmed them to. After 10 weeks of time and 12 tons of bricks on this relandscaping project, it's like a suburban Old Faithful experience. Free hot dogs for the neighbors!

I'm listening to a Filipino quartet, the Rosario Strings, play *Try to Remember* while the Veendam cruise ship streams south alongside Vancouver Island. In my mind, I can hear the words I first heard long ago after going to *The Fantasticks*.

Try to remember the kind of September
When life was slow and, oh, so mellow

Try to remember the kind of September
When grass was green and grain so yellow ...

I'm picking blackberries on Old Coburg Road early one Sunday morning when a man walking his dog points me to a gold mine he'd earlier hacked a pathway to. With generosity like this, who says we're shipwrecked as a culture?

I'm watching a Challengers baseball game and realize that a Roosevelt/St. John's batter has swung with only one arm. Then I realize — as the crowd realizes too — that his other arm is withered and unusable. He strikes out on three straight pitches but I'm left thinking that in a media-mad world that trumpets the trivial, this young man was no made-for-TV "survivor," but the real thing. We applaud loud and long.

I'm playing a self-made, 7-mile-long golf hole with one of my sons and his friend at sunrise — Waldport to Yachats, par 72 — when I see not only the usual seagulls and sandpipers, but an unusual sight for the Oregon Coast: a flock of Canada geese. They are ghostly and graceful in the morning mist, plying the waters of a sand-locked lagoon. Like me, lost in summer.

But now comes September, the letting-go month. The starting-up month. The now-boarding-Flight-804 month. Service to autumn and beyond.

Never mind that fall doesn't officially begin until Sept. 22. Our apples have all been picked, fallen or ravaged by The Worms of Summer.

Fall is here. It's time to migrate. Time for kids to leave for college. For tucking in gardens for the winter. For a final look back at sailboats and sprinklers, beaches and blackberries, one-armed swings and Rosario Strings.

The geese are heading south. And so, too, must we leave for new seasons, our suitcases stuffed with sandals, T-shirts and photos that will remind us of what the Strings' song reminded me: it's the going home that makes the having-been-there all the better.

Deep in December, it's nice to remember
Although you know, the snow will follow
Deep in December, it's nice to remember
Without a hurt, the heart is hollow.

— September 5, 2000

The great leaf panic

NOVEMBER ARRIVES and I find myself musing over Shelley's *Ode to the West Wind,* particularly the lines:

O wild West Wind, thou breath of Autumn's being,
Thou, from whose unseen presence the leaves dead
Are driven, like ghosts from an enchanter fleeing ...

I'm not sure, but I surmise the English Romantic poet was saying something profound about overzealous individuals and their gas-powered leaf blowers.

I confess, this is a hard time of year for me: Just as the Willamette Valley comes ablaze in a collage of color, The Leaf Brigade hits the yards and streets to vanquish that "breath of Autumn's being."

The brigade comes in two forms: the armed-to-the-teeth citizens who attack with a sort of guerilla-warfare approach, a blitzkrieg with blowers, and the city of Eugene's 1st Infantry Division, which launched its annual all-out assault Monday after dividing the battleground into five sectors.

(Oregonians live in such a benign state that, beyond feeling slightly ashamed at our good climatological fortune, we subconsciously pine for weather-related adventure. And if no such adventure exists, we, being the same imaginative people who invented the Phillips screw and the Fosbury Flop, make believe — in this case, that there's an actual threat out there that we must vanquish.

DREADED LEAVES THREATEN STORM DRAINS.

Give an assist to guilt, too. Implanted deep in our Beaver State souls is what I call a g-chip, or guilt chip, triggered by the realization that we don't know what real weather is. Witness the five pairs of gloves I saw on people Thursday afternoon on the University of Oregon campus, where the temperature at the time was an unglovely 51.

We look to the north and note that Washington recently endured massive flooding — at a time when we were basking in record-breaking highs and baby blue skies.

We look to the south and note that Southern California crews are desperately trying to put out wind-whipped fires that have spread faster than Hollywood rumors — at a time when grim-faced city of Eugene crews are mobilizing for their, ahem, Annual Leaf Pickup.

We look to the northeast and note that, beyond terrorist attacks and power failures, last February's blizzard killed 59 people. And to the southeast, where twisters and hurricanes arrive with the menacing regularity of unwelcome relatives over the holidays.

And, feeling guilty about our wimpy weather in comparison, we compensate by taking the path of leaf resistance: Maples. Dogwoods. Birch. They become our Goliaths. Take that, you measly Acer macrophyllum! Onto the compost pile, you dreaded Fraxinus latifolia!

My dilemma in all this is the collision between practicality and aesthetics. I understand that, left unattended, leaves can kill grass, makes bicyclists and pedestrians slip, add pollutants to our stream system and — who knows? — perhaps cause teenagers to turn to lives of crime.

But what bothers me is that this attack comes in what's an otherwise enjoyable lull in the year. It is a quiet season, save for one presidential candidate who wants to turn the country into Texas and another so intent on chest-strutting that I expect sometime before Tuesday he'll announce he invented The Wave and was The Fifth Beatle.

It is a season to clean up from summer and batten down for winter. A season for quiet and contemplation. A season for — if it absolutely, positively has to be done — rakes.

Then, with no warning, they strike: The leaf blowers, under whose command "leaves dead are driven" from lawn to street. Not once. Not twice. But over and over, as if every fallen leaf were an enemy paratrooper that must be snuffed upon landing.

(Years ago, in downtown Eugene, I actually saw a guy aim his blower on leaves still attached to trees, knocking them down so he could blow them away. Doesn't this sort of defeat the purpose of a tree? It's like a man shaving his head because he figures he'll go bald someday anyway.)

I am pro-choice when it comes to power tools; I use some myself. But what bothers me about leaf blowers is the sheer duration of the drone; they're like leaving your electric sander all day.

Some people's obsession with leaf-sanitized lawns, I theorize, is rooted in Oregon's relatively wimpy winters. Because the state faces so little in the way of harsh winter weather, some Oregonians have adopted leaf-blowing as a surrogate struggle, a stand-in for snow-blowing.

What we see from afar is someone in goggles and ear protectors — an engine mounted on his back — blowing leaves while new ones fall where he just blew. What the blower sees is a Suburban Rocketeer, individual and machine melded as one to gallantly protect Yard and Family from the beastly onslaught of, say, a pink flowering dogwood.

Once these foot soldiers have softened up the enemy, the city troops swoop in to mop up with their trucks and loaders, not to mention their giant, leaf-sucking vacuum cleaner.

These are seasoned troops, soldiers who have seen the horrors of war — the sidewalk stain of oak leaves that overstayed their welcome, the pile of big leaf maples hiding a missing VW, the European birches clogging a storm drain.

Last year, these troops — call them the Brown Berets — picked up nearly 4,000 tons of leaves in Eugene, virtually all them recycled back into the community in the form of mulch, fertilizer or garden covers.

"We do our darnedest," says Sgt. Richard Zucker, more commonly known as the city's maintenance crew supervisor. "We have our battle maps and go into each of the five sections and get as much as possible."

One by one, millions of leaves — like "ghosts from an enchanter fleeing" — will be captured and redeployed in the next 10 weeks, and I understand the whys behind this offensive.

Still, there's much to be said for a quiet Sunday afternoon, a good book — Shelley perhaps — and a lawn of untouched leaves.

November 2, 2000

The snowflakes cometh

HAVING HAD A week of storms on which to base evidence, I hereby offer the five personality types Oregonians fit when it comes to our rare winter guest, snow:

Snowaholics. In relation to snow: Love it. Can't get enough of it. Get annoying when they've had too much of it. Characteristics: Giddiness. Don't make snowmen, but entire snow families, including step-cousins, generally by the time the rest of us are just getting up. Keep telling anyone who will listen — and some who won't — the latest forecast, the current temperature and snow depth to the nearest quarter-inch. Cross-country ski to work. Pet phrase: "How much do you have?" Dress: Eddie Bauer sweaters (moose, deer or snowflake patterns) and monster boots, even if the snow depth is roughly the thickness of this newspaper. Likely fits: Kid-hearted grown-ups (many of whom organized their high school's spirit weeks) and school teachers hoping for a day off. Heroes: Mary Tyler ("you got spunk; I hate spunk") Moore, Clark Griswold and the Campbell Soup TV commercial kids.

Snowgrumps. In relation to snow: Hate it. Characteristics: Cynical. Glass is always half-frozen. Hate shoveling. Hate slipping. Hate flight delays. Call snow lovers "flakes." Pet phrase: "We love snow — in the Cascades, where it belongs." Dress: Any fabric or design bloodied by knuckles torn up while putting on tire chains. Likely fits: Seniors, retailers, travelers and transplants from warm-weather states. Heroes: Andy Rooney, Scrooge and the "before" guy in the Preparation H ads.

Snowblowers. In relation to snow: Self-described experts in dealing with it. Characteristics: Their snow is deeper, their commute more courageous and their 4-wheel-drive vehicle more reliable than anyone else's. Think Snowaholics are "weak," snowgrumps whiners. Pet phrase: "This is nothin." Dress: Anything from REI or any outdoorsy, gadget-fueled Web site. Likely fits: Males adrift — get it? — in midlife crises, shadow guys who suddenly see spotlight opportunities ("stand aside, ma'am, while I hook your bumper to my 16-strand, heavy duty poly tow rope") and transplants from cold-weather states who think Oregonians are soft. Heroes: Arnold Schwarzenegger, Walter Mitty and the pint-sized cop on the old "Newhart" show who always acted as if Vermont was facing one giant crisis and he was the only guy who could save it.

Snowdevils. In relation to snow: Muck it up for others. Characteristics: Penchant for pushing over snow forts, driving across lawns and doing 65 on black ice. Guys with the big-wheeled trucks and the small-wheeled minds. (See "Mr. Smart" on NW Cable News who tried to stop a car sliding into another car by attempting to fend it off with his own two hands ... while standing on ice. Note: The car won.) Pet phrase: "Outta my way, pal!" Dress: Anything distinguished by Skoal rings on back pockets. Likely fits: Young males with less brain mass than Frosty's. Heroes: Phil Hendrie, the two bad guys in *Fargo* and an array of super-intellects, like whoever created the "Insured by Winchester" bumper sticker.

Snowangels. In relation to snow: Allow the rest of us to get on with our lives despite it. Characteristics: Willingness to work round the clock. Tough, confident, dedicated — your basic NASA astronaut with a chain saw, sanding-truck steering wheel and your life in his hands. Pet phrase: "What seems to be the problem?" Dress: Anything with a fluorescent-vest accent. Likely fits: Cops, firefighters, utility workers, street maintenance workers, garbage collectors or maybe even the neighbor you've always been leery of — until he volunteered to buck up that fir tree blocking your driveway. Heroes: Who needs 'em when you're already one yourself?

January 6, 2004

Back to our soggy selves

THE BLESSED SOUND came from the basement, the first time I'd heard it in seemingly forever: The sump pump had kicked in.

We live in a house built in 1939, a house with a "wet basement." When enough water soaks down to a certain level in the ground, it seeps into the basement and collects in a concrete corner trough. That triggers a mechanism like the floating ball in the back of your toilet and — whoosh — the water is pumped up and out to the street.

I love that sound. It's a reassuring sound suggesting that things are as they ought to be.

When I heard the whoosh of the sump pump the other night, I felt like the Dust Bowl farmer who had finally felt a drop from the sky.

I felt like Oregon was Oregon again. All was well with the world. In terms of rain, you see, we just haven't been ourselves lately. And I've missed us.

If it feels the same way to you, there's good reason: Eugene got more rain in November than in any month since January 2000

— 22 months ago.

"Everybody's coming up to me and saying how wet it is all of the sudden," says George Taylor, the state climatologist. "It's been so long since we had a normal winter — basically two years — that we've forgotten what it's like. This is what is supposed to happen."

In essence, we're returning to the way we were, to our Oregonesque selves after traipsing around the last couple of years like a band of normal, sun-fed people.

Why be normal when you can be an Oregonian?

In Los Angeles, it sprinkles and people cancel their trips to the spa. Last Saturday, in a seemingly endless downpour, I saw a guy washing his car and a woman running — and said to myself: Is this a great place or what?

I recently received an e-mail from a Snow Bird. "We'll be watching (the Civil War) from down here in Tucson where we're basking in the sun now," she wrote.

I imagined that — basking in the sun in late November — and thought: There but for the grace of rain go I. Indeed, without our changing weather and seasons, I, too, could be condemned to the dreary life of sunshine, day in and day out. Fine for others — to each his own — but a year of sunshine would turn me into a bitter, brooding, basking man.

To bask, you see, means "to warm oneself pleasantly." I admit, I have basked before and I will probably bask again. But continually basking would parch my soul.

I need seasons. I need change. I need that look toward the Coast Range and seeing the dark clouds and wondering what's in them — then, half an hour later, getting a thunder-clapping, hail-zapping answer.

Oregonians, you see, have the privilege of not only basking come summer, but — now that we've returned to our normal climatological programming — burrowing come winter.

To burrow means "to take refuge ... to delve or search ..." It conjures up the huddled masses, yearning to read a good book in front of a fire. It suggests a turning inward to self and others, as opposed to just lying there in the sun, basking — as if you were nothing more than a french fry under a fast-food heat lamp.

Rain, on the other hand, offers challenge. Rain offers resistance, not ease. And just like exercise breeds stamina, resistance builds character.

You run across a parking lot, dodging puddles, getting soaked and throwing yourself into a suddenly steaming car, and you're a stronger person because of it. You come home to a problem child and think: I can get through this crisis because I made it to my car without drowning.

That's why I'm glad the rain is back. Because rain is the Oregonian's solar energy; it's what empowers us, steels us, makes us who we are. You might not like some of your fellow Oregonians, but you have to admit: They rarely lack character.

All because of the rain. Because they run across parking lots and because they improvise ways to do things outside when it's wet and because they burrow. They throw themselves into an indoor project and appreciate the snap of a fire and consider how soothing is the sound of rain on a roof.

So on this first Sunday of December — statistically, the best chance for rain in any given year — I'm glad we're back where we belong, back to our normal, soggy selves.

The winter rains have come. The sump pump is sounding. Time to delve and search.

December 2, 2002

3.

State of mine

Tom McCall's legacy

ON A MAY morning in 1967, two helicopters landed on the sand near Seaside. In one of them was Oregon Gov. Tom Mc-Call. After a beachside motel owner had erected a fence, McCall had, in essence, come to take back the beach, to say to Oregonians: This sand is your sand, from Astoria to Brookings.

Vintage McCall: Bold. Media-centered. And born of the man's genuine love for this state and a bedrock belief that it should be protected for use by all.

But now, almost 25 years to the day that he stepped down as governor, you wonder about his legacy. You wonder if, like the names etched in the sandstone banks along the coast, time has eroded the name of Tom McCall.

"If you stop the average citizen on the Eugene Mall and mention the name of Tom McCall, most people are probably going to say they've heard the name but can't remember why," says Bill Lunch, a professor of political science at Oregon State University and political analyst for Oregon Public Broadcasting.

Nearly a fourth of today's Oregonians have moved here since 1975, according to the Census Bureau. "And, remember," says Lunch, "you have 25-year-old people who weren't even born when McCall was governor."

All the more reason Lane County should name something in his honor — to help breathe life into a legacy nearly lost.

We'll soon open the (Peter) DeFazio Bike Bridge, which will honor the Oregon 4th District representative whose political clout helped make it possible. And DeFazio himself is spearheading a $150,000 fund-raiser to erect a memorial for the late U.S. Sen. Wayne Morse.

Good ideas, both. But what about McCall? Portland has Tom McCall Waterfront Park. Wasco County has McCall Point. "But McCall's name hasn't been chiseled in a lot of buildings," says Brent Walth, author of *Fire at Eden's Gate: Tom McCall and the Oregon Story.*

Something in Lane County — perhaps on the coast, which benefited from the 1967 Beach Bill he pushed so passionately — should be named for the man. And not just because he was a 1936 graduate of the University of Oregon.

Some believe McCall has been Oregon's greatest governor, that had he been 10 years younger, it might have been him walking down — rather than Gerald Ford stumbling down — the steps of Air Force One as president.

"A lot of governors in the last 25 years have lived in the shadow of Tom McCall," says Walth, a former *Register-Guard* reporter who now covers environmental issues for *The Oregonian.* "Whether he was the best or not, he was probably the most overall effective governor in terms of policies that had a long-lasting effect."

McCall was an environmentalist before it was cool. The Willamette River made the cover of *National Geographic* in 1972, largely because McCall led the charge to clean up what he once called "an open sewer." (Never one to mince words, he even publicly skewered fellow Republicans Ronald Reagan and Spiro Agnew.)

As governor from 1967 to 1975, he was the impetus behind land use planning to prevent runaway growth. Though others planted the seed, he championed what became the nation's first returnable-bottle law.

"In terms of visibility, McCall had a fair amount to do with establishing a national reputation of Oregon being environmentally conscious," says Lunch.

And yet for many, McCall's legacy begins and ends with the trademark words, "Come visit us again and again. This is a state of excitement. But for heaven's sake, don't come here to live."

Indeed, McCall had a flare for the dramatic; he never backed off the visit-but-don't-stay comment, though the words would return to haunt him, especially in the recession-racked '80s. Some blamed McCall for discouraging out-of-staters from moving to Oregon, which some think hurt an already-hurting economy.

"I believe it had the opposite effect," says Walth. "I believe there were people who came to Oregon because of McCall. Blaming McCall for the economic problems was unfair."

Regardless, Lane County should find a way to commemorate what he gave to this state — by putting his name on something more weighty than a wayside and something less ironic than a welcome center.

McCall, who died in 1983, would probably hate the idea. Not that he lacked ego. But he once said that "heroes are not giant statues framed against a red sky. They are people who say: This is my community, and it's my responsibility to make it better."

Rather than naming something for him, he'd probably think the more meaningful tribute would be for each of us to simply be good stewards of the land he loved.

How about a compromise? Let's do both.

January 16, 2000

Relish the obscurity

PERHAPS YOU'VE seen the illustration: "How New Yorkers View the World" above a map that pretty much shows a world of New York and nothing else.

As a native Oregonian who lives in that "rest of the world," I'm suffering from an East Coast-induced inferiority complex.

Maybe you think this stems from my emotional anguish after Oregon's NCAA basketball loss Friday to an East Coast team at an East Coast site on national TV. No, no, no; I'm over that. In fact, my therapist says with a few more sessions, I'll soon be talking again.

No, my sense that Oregon isn't taken seriously by those on the Right Coast goes deeper than a silly game of basketball. It's reflected in much more profound ways, such as in how CBS announcer Jim Spanarkel, in an otherwise surprisingly well-balanced broadcast, made the same mistake that countless announcers make — referring to us as "Ore-GAWN."

It's reflected in how the East Coast media project election winners long before Oregonians have had a chance to go to the polls.

And in how Oregon's primary election has become essentially meaningless, like having a wedding while the bride and groom are honeymooning in Hawaii.

And in how if you're at a national conference in Washington, D.C., some people will think you arrived at the Regency on a stagecoach.

And in how East Coast sportswriters confuse the Beavers and Ducks.

And in how The Weather Channel spends all its time yammering about states east of the Mississippi and mentions Oregon only if they've run out of footage of little kids sledding.

You think I'm the only one who feels this way?

"Oregon is continually ignored by the weather forecasters on The Weather Channel," writes reader Nancy Simpson of Veneta. "It's as if Oregon is an invisible state."

Preach it, sister.

Sara Spettel, a former 20Below writer who attends Barnard College in New York, recently wrote of a roommate of hers who had no clue Oregon abutted the Pacific Ocean. And when hearing that the Eugene area had nearly 200,000 people, replied, "Really! How cute."

A "really-how-cute!" attitude is almost as bad as a "don't-bother-me-with-whatever-your-state-is-called" attitude. Perhaps you remember a column I did in December after spending a couple of hours at Denver International Airport asking people what they thought of Oregon.

A woman from New York — a well-educated professional who travels the globe — not only said Oregon brought no images to mind, but acted as if I were somehow pretentious for suggesting it should.

When I asked if she'd ever heard of Bill Bowerman — and explained who he was — she replied, "People who jog in Central Park don't give a damn who invented jogging."

Okaaaaay.

Faris Cassell, who writes about books for *The Register-Guard*, has long railed against an East Coast literary establishment that gives Northwest writers a "cursory down-the-nose- and-over-the-shoulder" glance. In 1997, she pointed out, *The New York Times* listed 324 notable books for the year; eight were by Northwest authors.

That the East Coast gets so much attention doesn't bother me. Let's face it, cities such as New York, Washington, D.C., and Boston are impressive places. And the lopsided population base suggests the East Coast should get more attention; heck, New York, in 1900, had twice as many people as Oregon has now.

What bothers me isn't so much that they mispronounce the name of our state, but that they seemingly don't care about repeating the mistake.

What bothers me isn't that they dwell on our state's dark side — the Hardings, Packwoods and New Carissas of our lore — but don't dwell on us, period.

So what's the answer here? Do we need to try harder? Educate Easterners on how great we are? Beat the Seton Halls of the world to earn respect?

Naw. The solution is to avoid getting all worked up about it like I just did. (Somebody slap me with a technical foul to ease my guilt.)

The solution is to not rely on other people to validate our worth as a state, but to simply relax and enjoy what we have.

The other day, I was standing on a bluff above the Pacific Ocean near Bandon watching endless waves as a late-afternoon sun played on the froth. Not a single person was in sight. And I remember thinking: What a place.

No matter how you pronounce it — or whether anyone on the other coast knows it even exists — what a place.

March 19, 2000

Thoreau weekend

CAMP SHERMAN — Henry David Thoreau went to the woods because he wished to live deliberately, to "live deep and suck out all the marrow of life, to live so sturdily and Spartan-like as to put to rout all that was not life... ."

Me? I wanted the same basic program but with the added luxury of perhaps picking up a fuzzy radio broadcast of the Oregon-Arizona State men's basketball game Saturday night.

Given this juxtaposition of hoops and Henry David, my weekend on the Metolius River might be aptly called a "free Thoreau" — an attempt at the philosophical foul line to compensate for the injustices inflicted upon me by deadlines, phone solicitors, freeway sounds and other urban culprits that I'd like to put to rout (Webster's: "to defeat and throw into confusion").

A "veg-out" weekend, if you will, to ponder, sleep and read.

Thoreau learned enough in his two years on Walden Pond to write a 200-plus page book; someone else, given time in the woods, might learn nothing more than the effects of poison oak.

Me? While holed up in — and venturing forth from — a circa-1940s cabin about the size of your average two-car garage, I was reminded how much hotter and faster pine burns than does the washed-up driftwood in Yachats. How wonderful is the sound of a maul splitting pine. And how there are few better moments in life than two people, side by side, reading two good books on a Saturday afternoon.

I was reminded what "quiet" really is — when, after running down a snowy road at the base of Black Butte, I stopped to read a sign and could hear the pounding of my heart in my ears. Nothing else.

I was reminded how different a fire-burned forest looks in winter than in summer. The results of the B and B Complex Fire, which burned to within 2 1/2 miles of Camp Sherman's western edge last August, certainly were obvious six months ago. But now, with charred conifers against a background of snow, the damage appears far more drastic, like the black-on-white etchings of a Richter scale.

But, mostly, I was reminded of the power of place, how if you've had some experience at some point on earth, returning to that point unlocks memories you only thought were gone.

For example, as I watched the riffles of the river — nearly mesmerized by the pattern of repetition — I half expected to look up and see him there: my father, wet to his knees, tying a fly, his sunglasses propped on the end of his nose.

It would be inaccurate to say we fished the Metolius together; better to say he cast his fly line while sometimes pausing to untangle mine. But when I was a boy, we were here together. And seven years ago, on the other side of Black Butte, we were there together. For the last time. Anywhere.

These are the stories unlocked by a weekend in the woods. You don't come to the place as much as it comes to you — in visions of the past.

While running, I crossed Lake Creek, and it dawned on me that this was the same creek that flows from Suttle Lake, where we camped each summer. The same creek at whose mouth we had found our homemade motorboat — a mile from where it had been moored the night before, by me. ("Please, Dad, I can tie it up!")

As I ran in truck-rutted snow to where the Metolius gurgles out of the ground from a natural spring, I thought of my boys and their cousins feeding chipmunks on a hot summer day here in the late 1980s.

Now, all was quiet, the clouds casting what's usually a postcard scene in stark black and white. Mount Jefferson was missing in action. I hadn't seen a person since I'd left.

I watched the riffles and wondered, in a way that Thoreau probably would not have, how long it might take a drop to get from here to the ocean — and if any of those molecules might wash ashore at Yachats.

Then, I headed back to the cabin, to the now, to the other book reader, to a basketball game sounding as if it were being broadcast from Mars.

And to all the live-deep memories yet to come.

February 24, 2004

Obscure Oregonians

IT'S OREGON'S birthday — we're 143 today — so I'm celebrating by recognizing Obscure Oregonians Whom We Mustn't Forget (If We Ever Knew of Them to Begin With):

Carolyn Davidson, designer of the Nike "swoosh" logo. It was 1972. Davidson, 32, was a graphic design student at Portland State. Phil Knight, 34, was teaching an accounting class and launching a fledgling running-shoe company. In a hallway, he overhead her mention something about not being able to afford an oil-painting class. Would she like to take on a project? The rest is history,

so intriguing I'll save the details for another column tha
story justice. But here's a teaser: Davidson billed Nike $
design.

The victims of the only Japanese attack on the mainland United States that proved deadly. During World War II, the Japanese released hundreds of bomb-bearing balloons that landed in Western states. On May 5, 1945, people on a church picnic outside Bly — 60 miles east of Klamath Falls — triggered such a balloon bomb. The explosion killed a woman and five children.

Richard Chambers, the father of Oregon's Bottle Bill. Chambers, a logging equipment salesman from Salem, hated seeing litter while he hiked Oregon's trails and beaches. One morning in 1968, he returned from a hike on Nestucca Spit, opened the newspaper and suddenly yelled, "That's it! That's the answer!" Chambers called Paul Hanneman, the local state representative, and showed him an article about a British Columbia lawmaker who had proposed banning nonreturnable cans and bottles. Why not do that in Oregon? Give people money back for returning their empties. Hanneman liked the idea. He introduced a bill at the next legislative session, and in 1971, with Gov. Tom McCall as its biggest champion, the "Bottle Bill" became the nation's first such law. No legislation during McCall's years did more to turn Oregonians toward environmentalism — and to anger grocery-store owners. Chambers died in 1974.

Bellfountain's 1936-37 boys' basketball team. The team was Oregon's version of *Hoosiers*, the movie about a "David" farm school beating a "Goliath" urban school for the state title. Back in the days before schools were segregated by size for athletic events, Bellfountain smote Portland's Franklin and Lincoln high schools to finish No. 1. The school had two teachers and 29 students.

Abigail Scott Duniway, women's suffrage advocate. In 1871, the Yamhill County woman founded *The New Northwest* newspaper, through which she championed the right of women to vote. Despite her decades of persistence, the Oregon Legislature continually turned down the idea, in part because of opposition from her brother, *Oregonian* editor Harvey Scott. He died in 1910. Two years later, *The Oregonian* changed its stance. And on Nov. 12, 1912, Oregon became the ninth state to recognize the right of women to vote. Duniway died at age 80 — but not before casting numerous ballots.

Buzz Holmstrom, a Coquille service-station attendant who, in 1937, became the first person to navigate the Colorado River alone. Holmstrom made headlines nationwide when he survived 1,100 miles of river, including 365 major stretches of rapids, in a homemade boat — then returned to pumping gas. At 37, he was found dead beside the Grande Ronde River.

Robin Holmes, an African-American man from Salem whose court case, in 1852, opened the door for the end of slavery in the Oregon Territory. Slavery was illegal in the Oregon Territory, but original census records prove that it still existed. Holmes, his wife, Polly, and their three children had come West as "property" of Nathaniel Ford. After releasing the parents from their status as slaves, Ford kept two of the children and gave one to his daughter and her husband. Robin Holmes then went to court to gain his children's freedom and won. His children were given back to him and their status as slaves ended. This not only opened the door for the end of slavery in the Oregon Territory, it established that a black man could freely sue in Oregon courts.

Walter Umenhofer, the guy in Florence whose car was crushed by blubber from an exploding whale in 1970. When a 45-foot dead — and very smelly — whale washed ashore south of Florence, the state Highway Division decided the practical thing to do was blow it up with dynamite. Umenhofer, who lived in Springfield at the time, didn't find their solution all that practical. A 3-foot piece of whale meat crashed through the roof of his brand new Oldsmobile Regency 98, assuring Umenhofer of a lifetime of regional fame.

February 4, 2002

Greenhorn: Population 0

GREENHORN — I visited Oregon's smallest — and highest — incorporated city Monday.

Greenhorn sits 6,271 feet up in the Blue Mountains, about 50 miles west of Baker City.

It's a place of awesome beauty: ponderosa pines, steep ridges, dramatic views. The people of Greenhorn, well, that's another matter.

It's not that I found them rude or ornery or peculiar. It's that I didn't find them at all. That's because Greenhorn doesn't have any people.

None. Zip. Zilch.

Oh sure, the latest *Oregon Blue Book* shows that Greenhorn has a population of three, which ranks it 222nd out of 222 cities in terms of size. But those three have died, though city officials — yes, Greenhorn has them — have admittedly been slow in letting anybody know.

"The last one to go, Mrs. Potter, died about 10 years ago, but I guess we never got around to taking her and the others off the rolls," says Brad Poyser, Greenhorn's city recorder.

Poyser lives nearly 300 miles away in Oregon City, which you'd think would make it tough to attend City Council meetings. But the last council meeting — they have one or two a year — was at a Portland-area fire hall because the mayor, George Massinger, lives in Beaverton. The councilor closest to Greenhorn is a guy in Prairie City, 25 miles away.

Here's the catch: Greenhorn is the only municipality that exists under Oregon's "ghost town" law, which, not surprisingly, was championed by friends of Greenhorn in the early '70s. The law allows an incorporated city to remain incorporated as a "historic ghost town" even if its population drops below the number of people needed to provide enough elected city officials.

"It's kind of a tangled web to explain how Greenhorn got to where it is today," says the 48-year-old Poyser, who, like other city officials, stays involved because his family owns property — and a bare-bones cabin — here.

The city was founded in 1891 as a gold-mining town, replacing nearby Robinsville, which burned to the ground. (Robinsville was also home of a guy known as "49" Jimmie, who had worked the gold mines in California and was reputed to be able to swear in seven different languages.)

Greenhorn was incorporated in 1912. In a strange municipal twist, the U.S. government granted the town a patent for 53.58 acres, in effect making the town a law unto itself; President William Taft signed the trust himself.

WIth the gold mines humming, some 500 people lived here — that's about the size of present-day Monroe — and 2,000 miners worked its mines. It had five saloons, a red-light district and

a newspaper, all of which apparently necessitated one more thing
— a jail.

By 1919, though, the mines had given all they had; Greenhorn
became a ghost town. More than a half-century later, the legislative
bill in the '70s, in essence, "reactivated" it as an incorporated city.

"This was done primarily for protection against land specula-
tors who might turn the colorful old camp into a tourist area with
gaudy donut shops and hamburger stops," wrote Miles Potter,
author of *Oregon's Golden Years* and Greenhorn's first mayor after
the redesignation.

I wouldn't say there's much of a threat of golden arches coming
to Greenhorn. To get here, you need to climb a seven-mile gravel
road that rises more than a thousand feet in elevation. No burger
is worth that.

Once you're here, you find a handful of old houses that have
been converted to vacation homes, though Sunriver this is not. You
find a few rotting structures, a few outhouses, some rusty cans and,
well, a fiber-optic cable system.

Say what? Yup. Greenhorn is also the only Oregon city that
doesn't have electricity, but does have a fiber-optic phone line,
which some places in Eugene don't even have.

Seems Pine Telephone Co. had a line laid to the nearby me-
tropolis of Granite — population 25 — and decided to go ahead
and connect Greenhorn. "We're thinking of the future," says Rick
Miller of Pine Telephone.

Poyser says he's heard there's a guy who might move to Greenhorn year-round; in fact, there's a new cabin being built in the city's
eastern "suburbs." For now, it's mainly an elk-hunting and snow-
mobile destination.

I ask Poyser about the two residents who died before Lillian Potter. "That would have been Guy Miller, also our sheriff. He'd take a
six-month vacation twice a year — in Medford and here, where he
lived in a tent. The third would have been Miles Potter, the mayor
who got Greenhorn up and running again in the '70s.

"He actually died sitting in a rocking chair on his porch. Had a
massive heart attack. Went right where he wanted to go: in Greenhorn."

The way this place operates, though, I'll bet Potter still gets a
vote on the council.

August 28, 2001

Oregon must-dos

IN HONOR of the state's 142nd birthday, I offer my 75 quintessential Oregon experiences:

1. Hike the Pacific Crest Trail from California to Washington. 2. Watch the Rose Festival Parade. 3. Be your 1967 self again at the Oregon Country Fair. 4. Stand at the Oregon-California border where Gov. Tom McCall's sign once told newcomers to visit, but not stay. 5. Watch Shakespeare in Ashland. 6. Drive the li'l dogies across the expansive ZX Ranch near Paisley. 7. Go skiing or snowboarding. 8. Drive a grass-seed combine. 9. Cheer civilly at a Civil War football game. 10. Cut down some trees.

11. Protest the cutting down of some trees. 12. Drive to the top of Steens Mountain on Oregon's highest road — 9,720 feet. 13. Run the Hood-to-Coast Relay. 14. Ride Portland's rapid-transit MAX. 15. Tour the Tillamook Cheese Factory. 16. Hunt fossils near the Painted Hills, near John Day. 17. Train your binoculars on a bald eagle in the Klamath Basin, home to the largest wintering concentration of that bird in the Lower 48. 18. Picnic at Champoeg Park, Oregon's birthplace. 19. Fish a lake that's not accessible by road. 20. Watch for California gray whales from atop 800-foot high Cape Perpetua, a view so spectacular, you'll forget about the lack of whales.

21. Down a bowl of clam chowder at Mo's original restaurant in Newport. 22. Soak your bod at Breitenbush Hot Springs. 23. Run or walk the Portland Marathon. 24. Watch a Blazers game, live. 25. Time-travel at Fort Rock, where 7,000-year-old bark sandals were found. 26. Fly-fish the North Umpqua River, then chow down with a dozen strangers at the Steamboat Inn. 27. Listen to the Sophisto-Kats play *Sentimental Journey* at the Gold Beach Fish Fry. 28. Whoop and holler at a Pendleton Roundup. 29. Have your photo taken in front of Haystack Rock. (Everybody else has.) 30. Run a mile in a pair of Nikes. (Timed.)

31. Sit beside what used to be Celilo Falls on the pre-dam Columbia River — and imagine what once was. 32. Descend into the Sea Lion Caves. 33. Ascend Mount Hood, the tallest point in the state — 11,239 feet. 34. Go deep-sea fishing out of Depoe Bay, just as they did in the movie version of Ken Kesey's *One Flew Over the Cuckoo's Nest.* 35. Stare a snake in the eye at the Oregon High

Desert Museum. 36. Take the tour boat at Crater Lake and ponder what lies beneath. 37. Play golf at Bandon Dunes — Pebble Beach without the pretense. 38. Listen to Bach in the Silva Concert Hall, look at that ceiling and imagine you're sitting beneath the world's largest lawn chair. 39. Stand on Cape Blanco, the state's westernmost point. 40. Look up in the Capitol's rotunda and see the state's history through art.

41. Somersault down a sand dune at Honeyman State Park. 42. Kick a Les Schwab tire in Prineville. 43. Spend an afternoon browsing at Portland's Powell's Books. 44. Watch a sunrise from Crown Point above the Columbia Gorge. 45. Track Bigfoot. 46. Understand true darkness in the Oregon Caves. 47. Ride the Green Tortoise, the I-5 alternative to Greyhound. 48. See the New Carissa's stern before it gets carted off to a courtroom as "Exhibit A." 49. Run to the top of Hendricks Hill, pausing briefly at the unofficial Pre memorial. 50. See the house in Yamhill where children's author Beverly Cleary grew up.

51. Wind-sail at Hood River. 52. Spend a winter at Fort Clatsop, just like Lewis and Clark did in 1805-06. 53. Lick a double-scooper at K&R Drive-In at Rice Hill. 54. Listen to the Sunriver Music Festival in that wonderfully woodsy Great Hall. 55. Imagine living in the house next to Heceta Head Lighthouse. (Everybody else has.) 56. Groove at the Mount Hood Jazz Festival. 57. Ride the weeklong CycleOregon tour. 58. Climb Smith Rock. 59. Raft the Rogue. 60. Do Bend's Pole, Pedal & Paddle event.

61. Look down at Hells Canyon, the deepest gorge in the United States. 62. Look up — 350 feet up — at redwoods in Brookings. 63. Explore a tidepool. 64. Visualize world peace at Eugene's Saturday Market. 65. Visualize Bill Bowerman at a Hayward Field track meet. 66. Walk the McKenzie Pass lava fields. 67. View the classic Christmas light displays in Albany's historic district. 68. Visit Oregon's Alps — the Wallowa Mountains. 69. Walk under — and over — creatures of the deep at the Oregon Coast Aquarium. 70. Tour Portland's Japanese Gardens, so splendid a Japanese ambassador called them the finest landscape of its kind outside Asia.

71. Float the Willamette. 72. Toss a Frisbee in Oregon State University's quad. 73. People-watch at UO's bookstore corner. 74. Feel the spray of Multnomah Falls. 75. Do something — anything — in a driving rainstorm.

February 13, 2001

Renaming Oregon

BOSTON (AP) — With the state facing a $3 billion deficit, Massachusetts lawmakers are considering selling corporate sponsors the naming rights to parks and forests, including the Walden Woods immortalized by Henry David Thoreau.
—From the April 9 *Register-Guard*

SITTING IN THE SKYVIEW terrace of the Oregon Convention Center in Portland, I had a bad feeling about this meeting. I'd been invited here by state budget officials to meet with a New York ad team for an "exclusive" story — some idea to save the state's financial bacon.

"Mount Hood looks great from here, doesn't it?" I said, making small talk.

"You mean Mount Hoody Peanut Butter," said the lead New Yorker, a woman named Medusa.

"Huh?"

"That's among the name changes we're proposing," she said. "We're one-upping Massachusetts. We're not only selling naming rights to Oregon's parks and forests, but all its geographic features. Sort of David Douglas meets Mr. Goodwrench."

"Shoulda seen it coming," I said, thinking of our changing state. "People swiping their Visa cards to get into day-use areas ... the Mount Pisgah pay-to-hike travesty ... "

"Uh, uh, uh, there you go again," Medusa said. "You mean 'Mount Pisgah Presented by Pepsi.' "

My knees felt weak, like when I heard Luke Ridnour was gone for good. "Bob, dream with me a moment," said Medusa, sweeping her hand toward the window. "Oregonians will hike the Dr. Scholl's Pacific Crest Trail. They'll climb the Kellogg's Frosted Mini-Wheats Three Sisters. Stroll the Ocean Spray beaches. Wade in the Pacific Source Ocean. Watch a sunset from atop Cape Pepto-Bismol. And waterski right here below us on the Waremart Willa-Metty River."

"That's Wil-LAM-ette," I said.

"Whatever ... Don't you understand? This is your state's financial salvation! You sell your assets. We're working on a deal with Prudential; why pay list price for Gibraltar when we can give them Haystack Rock for a song? The Visine folks want Clear Lake. Ore-

Ida Potatoes is a natural for the Snake River Canyon. And we're having some serious talks with the Tidy Bowl folks for Crater Lake. It's just soooo blue — and, of course, from what I hear, so is the lake.

Somewhere, *Oregon Geographic Names* author Lewis McArthur rolled over in his grave.

"You don't understand Oregonians," I said. "We have our faults — funding education comes to mind — but we have our pride, too. Tell some Prineville cowboy that he now lives in the shadows of the Oscar Mayer Wiener Ochocos and you're likely to find your BMW branded with a boot spur."

"We're one step ahead of you," Medusa said. "We've done market surveys. We'll customize the names to fit the kind of people who frequent those areas. Sahalie Falls will become Aquafresh Falls; I'm sure your little earth muffins in Eugene will go for that. And with their quirky good humor, the folks there should love that landmark near downtown, Snickers Butte. And those rugged Eastern Oregon elk hunters will be hunting Hungry-Man Ridge, Camel Filters Canyon and Budweiser Butte."

"As I said, you don't understand us. A lot of our elk hunters eat salads, don't smoke and like a good merlot with dinner. Oregonians are an independent lot. Our state motto is 'She Flies With Her Own Wings.'"

"Nope, sold that, too," she said. "Your state motto is 'She Flies With Her Own Wings Into the Friendly Skies of United.'"

April 18, 2003

It all began here

OREGON IS TAKING a lot of heat lately from Oregonians who are unhappy with budget cuts, politicians and schools that are, according to some, underfunded and, according to others, overstaffed.

So as the state turns 144 let's remember the good stuff about this place. In particular, the stuff that's been invented here — and not just the Nikes/jogging/bottle-bill mainstays. For example:

The hand-cranked pencil sharpener, 1874. It was the idea of Albany resident William E. Howell — and the sharpeners still sell.

The Erector Set, 1913. A.C. Gilbert of Salem invented this metal build-what-you-want toy. He also became the first toy manufacturer to advertise in national magazines. The risk paid off. Thirty million sets sold.

The gas tax, 1919. Property owners were complaining about having to pay the cost of roads for well-heeled joy-riders, so they helped usher in this idea. Within a few years, every state in the country had one.

The maraschino cherry, 1925. Oregon State's Ernest H. "Prof" Weigan became known as "the father of the maraschino cherry" after crossbreeding led to this variety.

The newspaper delivery tube, late '20s, early '30s. Glenn Cobb, a newspaper delivery boy in the tiny town of Jefferson, just northeast of Albany, got tired of slogging up muddy farm lanes to leave papers under dry porches, so he built roadside wooden boxes. His brother, Clair, upgraded the idea by making sheet-metal tubes.

The Phillips screw, 1936. Henry F. Phillips of Portland originally designed these for automakers.

The View-Master, 1940. William Gruber of Portland invented the hand-held 3-D slide-viewing gizmo after a trip to the Oregon Caves in Southern Oregon.

The marionberry, 1956. If, like me, you love marionberry pie and cobbler, thank George Waldo. In 1935, the Salem-based USDA horticulturist began experimenting with crossbreeding loganberries, blackberries and olallie berries. The result was "U.S. Oregon No. 928," released to the public in 1956. It was named for Marion County.

The Fosbury Flop high-jump style, 1963. Medford High sophomore Dick Fosbury invented it out of desperation. Fosbury was a pathetic high jumper using the "scissor" and "western roll" methods. Then one day he flung himself over the bar as if a couple of shot-putters had taken his hands and legs and tossed him off a dock. He perfected the style at Oregon State, won a gold medal in the '68 Olympics and inspired the world to convert.

The computer mouse, 1968. David Engelbart, OSU class of '48, first demonstrated what we now know as a "mouse" at a conference.

The self-cleaning house, '70s. OK, so it didn't exactly take off as a Jetson-esque step into the future, but Frances Gabe of Newberg not only got an "e" for effort, but got attention from NPR, *People* magazine and Erma Bombeck's column.

Hacky Sack, '70s. Oregon City residents Mike Marshall and John Stalberger Jr. invented the footbags — and sold millions.

The Wave, 1981. OK, OK, so everyone knows it started at the University of Washington in 1981. What everyone doesn't know is that co-creator Bill Bissel, then the Husky band director, got all his rah-rah spirit at Willamette University in Salem, where he was a student. So at the very least, we get an assist.

Desktop publishing, 1985. University of Oregon graduate Paul Brainerd invented Aldus PageMaker software, which revolutionized publishing.

The vandal-proof mailbox, 1998. Tired of having teenagers bash his box with baseball bats — and riddle it with shotgun blasts — Bruce Elliot of Creswell invented "Vandalgard." The box is supposedly tougher than bats and bullets.

Take that, Any Other state.

February 16, 2003

Ken Kesey's Oregon

WHAT I LIKED best about Ken Kesey has nothing to do with psychedelic buses or LSD or Merry Pranksters.

What I liked best about Kesey was his words. Specifically, the way those words brought to life Oregon, the state he loved and in whose cool, moist soil his body was lowered Wednesday afternoon. The Oregon author, icon and '60s guru died Saturday at age 66 after surgery to remove a tumor on his liver.

Kesey loved this land with an odd blend of respect and irreverence that showed up best in his 1964 book, *Sometimes a Great Notion.* It's about a bitter strike in a small lumber town near the Oregon Coast and, in particular, the involvement of one family — Henry Stamper's family.

Early on, Kesey describes the return of one of the Stamper boys, Leland, to Oregon:

"... as the bus — a different bus, rickety and uncomfortable — began the climb from Eugene into the long range of mountains that separates the coast from the Willamette Valley and the rest of the continent, he found himself becoming more alert and excited. He watched the green stand of mountains build before him, the densening of ditch growth, the clear, silver-shrouded clouds moored to the earth by straight and thin strands of autumn smoke, like dirigibles ..."

You can't read this book without realizing Kesey was alert and excited about Oregon, not in a jump-up-and-down sense but in a quiet, almost mysterious sense, like someone who knew things others did not. Like someone who understood this place — at least the old, rural, pre-factory outlet version — better than most.

Kesey's was no Johnny-come-lately love of the land; he moved to a farm near Springfield in 1943. Nor was it the stuff of Ray Atkeson coffee-table books or tourism brochures whose photographs never show rain. It was more honest and objective and deeply rooted than such varieties.

"You must go through a winter to understand," he writes. Is there a better description of trying to comprehend Oregon's rain? Or, for that matter, Oregon itself?

It was as if Kesey and Oregon were one, like saltwater and freshwater at a river's mouth, nothing to define where one started and the other ended but clearly part of one another.

Kesey had to be from Oregon, had to emerge from the primordial valley mud, as if his ilk could survive nowhere else.

As you look at the photograph in last Sunday's *Register-Guard* — Kesey, the moss-draped bus and his farm's dense woods — what strikes you is that all three seem somehow organic, as if alive and part of one another. It's an earth-tone collage of things grown old, memories mulched by time, change as the proverbial constant.

Kesey considered both people and place actors on life's stage; to him, Oregon wasn't just a state in the union, it was a living, breathing character all its own. And so, then, were its trees, waters and weather.

"She's a brute, she is," says an old-timer in *Notion* about the Wakonda Auga River. "She got my house last winter an' my barn this, by gum. Swallered 'em up."

In Kesey's Oregon, nature was alive. He wrote of how "unruly mobs of young clouds gather in the bright blue sky, riotous and surging, full of threat that convinces no one."

In Kesey's Oregon, fog couldn't simply be some meteorological term. Instead, "(fog) creeps down the river and winds around the base of the house, eating at the new yellow-grained planks with a soft white mouth."

Kesey's Oregon was much like Kesey himself: full of independence, rough-hewn realness and a brooding darkness known to explode, at winter's end, into Day-Glo delight.

With his death, Kesey leaves an Oregon far different from the one he found in 1943. The population has more than tripled. The customer in the "Sea Breeze Cafe" is less likely to be a logger in suspenders ordering coffee — "black" — than a mountain-biker in REI shorts ordering a vanilla latte.

But for all of Hank Stamper's Never-Give-A-Inch defiance, Kesey understood that nature bats last — even in matters of life and death. Dust to dust. Ultimately, the earth takes us back.

"I say there was no permanence," wrote Kesey in a passage that twines life in general with the Oregon he loved. "Even the town was temporary. I say it. All vanity and vexation of the spirit. One generation passeth away, and another cometh: but the earth abideth forever, or as forever as the rain lets it."

November 15, 2001

4.

The coast

A clash of waves

YACHATS — Never mind its official December 22 start date. Winter wakes me at 4:15 Sunday morning. The roar outside the beach cabin sounds more like Dallas-Fort Worth than Yachats. A jet? Coast Guard helicopters? What?

"Tsunami?" asks my wife.

No, I soon realize, just the changing of seasons. Looking north from the porch, I see it in the dim light of a half moon: a frothy sea blasting against the bank. Outgoing waves clashing with incoming waves and spewing a zipper line of white into the air. Whip-cream water surging up Starr Creek, then rolling back rocks as it retreats.

I like this about Oregon. I could never be happy in, say, Arizona. Yuma gets 242 clear days a year, but such monotony would bore me. I need storms. I need seasons. I need change.

"The fortunate people of the planet," John Kenneth Galbraith once wrote, "are those who live by the seasons. This means that people who live where the seasons are good and strong have no need to travel; they can stay at home and let change come to them."

But here's the rub: Some of us are a lot more accepting of nature's changes than of our own — or of those around us. I was reminded of this after a Thanksgiving weekend on the coast.

A party of six, we arrived in two vehicles: Two adults. One semi-adult son with semiadult girlfriend. One teenage son with teenage friend. And, looking back, lots of different expectations.

I envisioned a full weekend of the Traditional Stuff: reading and sleeping and wave-watching, followed by more of the same. Semiadult Son and girlfriend, I learned, envisioned a much shorter stay: one night, then back to where the action was. Teenage Son envisioned a weekend marathon of playing video football on his pal's portable TV/video player.

Whatever happened to the good old days when we all knew what we were supposed to do — stay the entire weekend and quietly enjoy the splendor of surf, solitaire and each other?

In a 67-year-old cabin not much larger than your average Java Hut, the thought of two days of grunting and groaning football players wasn't working for me. When the video game itself wouldn't work, I thought perhaps Generation Next would realize videos and weekends at the coast were simply incompatible. Instead, what they realized was they needed a video store; the game might not work, but a movie probably would.

They were right. The soothing sound of distant surf was replaced by Nicolas Cage in *Snake Eyes*. In a rustic cabin whose charm lies in its not having a phone, a TV or built-in heat, this was nothing short of sacrilegious.

It was like doing the wave at the Hult following Mahler's *Symphony No. 9*, lighting up in the Sistine Chapel, selling Tupperware at Saturday Market. But like the rocks pounded by the waves outside, I quietly endured.

The young ones leave the next day, bound for home, marathon video football and whatever else; no hard feelings. The Keeper of Traditions remains, as does She Who Endures the Keeper of Traditions.

Walking the beach, we talk of children and change. How hard it is to get our varied expectations to line up. And, well, how easy it is to forget what it's like to be 20 or 17.

I begin realizing that, though I'd been coming to this cabin since birth, I couldn't recall many weekends here with my parents when I was a teenager. Hmm.

I begin realizing that, as a kid, I played endless games of "electric football" — similar to, if not as sophisticated as, video football. Years later, when I asked how she stood the noise, my mom said: "By figuring at least you weren't out stealing hubcaps." Hmm.

I begin realizing how I sometimes let tradition become more important than the people it's supposed to benefit. Hmm.

We walk to Starr Creek. Years ago, the man whose house sits next to the creek had a riprap wall built to guard his place from the surf. Now, we notice, he has resorted to inch-thick steel rods driven deep into the rock and sand to keep even the riprap in place.

No matter what we do, the seasons change. Winter comes. The ocean has its way. Already, it has washed away the sand spit at Alsea Bay. It takes sand from one beach, deposits it at another. It erodes the sandstone banks, leaving cement stairways to nowhere.

In the meantime, it confronts not only sand and shore, but us. It reminds us, as Galbraith says, that there's no need to look for change; it finds us.

And the fortunate people embrace it for what it is — the inevitable way of life.

The roar that awakened me to winter was no tidal wave. It was simply the inevitable clash of outgoing waves and incoming waves, two generations on their ever-changing journeys.

November 30, 1999

Sinking of a dream

YACHATS — High-tide waves crash and lick at a handful of beach fires. The rain pounds down. Two lone figures putter in the distant driftwood, as if part of an Elton Bennett painting.

On Wednesday, a week after being rescued from their sinking fishing boat six miles south of this coastal town, Duncan and Maggie MacDonald have come to burn the remains of the *Charlie Tuna*.

"It's like losing family," says Duncan, as he douses a fire with more diesel. "It's like burying one of your kin."

But it's necessary. Maggie, 71 and a member of The Nature Conservancy, doesn't want the beach littered with the wreckage. Duncan, who turns 73 today, just wants it behind him.

"There's some closure in this," Maggie says.

The two had bought the 43-foot wooden boat three years ago at an auction for $10,000 and plowed so much into having it rebuilt that they had nothing left for insurance.

"It had two 'Jimmy' 671 diesel engines that purred like kittens," says Duncan, who looks a little like *Cocoon's* Wilford Brimley.

He loves the sea — still. "It's the freedom to be your own boss. It's always looking for what's on the other side of the waves. We saw two whales on our way north."

Duncan joined the Navy at 16. He has toiled in the merchant marines, fished commercially and weathered typhoons — and more.

He's had quadruple heart-bypass surgery and once found his boat-building partner, Roger, dead while doing work on a fiberglass catamaran they owned together.

"Bad ticker," he says of his friend.

Duncan is full-blooded Scottish — "Is there any other kind?" he asks — while Maggie is Scottish and Irish, a fit, rosy-cheeked woman who looks at peace on a beach.

They met in Washougal, Wash. on the Columbia River, and married eight years ago — the second marriage for both. Maggie's background was farming, but she willingly made the shift from soil to sea.

The two wound up in Warrenton, at the mouth of the Columbia, living aboard a 40-foot boat they moored next to *Charlie Tuna*.

Maggie called *Charlie Tuna* "the clubhouse" because it became a gathering spot for family and friends — whether moored or underway.

On April 26, Duncan and Maggie were aboard the *Charlie Tuna*, returning to Warrenton from Winchester Bay after checking out salmon-fishing prospects near Reedsport. While crossing the bar, a rogue wave — 40-feet high, Duncan estimates — hit the boat.

After Duncan checked the engine room and saw no damage, the boat chugged north in calmer seas. But a second look, near Heceta Head, stunned him: 2 feet of water had poured in after a seam apparently split.

He radioed the Coast Guard. A helicopter and boat were dispatched to the scene. As a Coast Guard crewman came aboard and tried furiously to pump out the water, Maggie prayed the rosary.

But the sea would win this battle.

They had no choice but to leave — quickly. "When we were leaving on the Coast Guard boat, you could see the boat going down in the distance," says Maggie.

The *Charlie Tuna* sank and broke apart about half a mile off the Strawberry Hill picnic area, in about 50 feet of water.

The MacDonalds were taken to Florence, where they saw the silver lining: Betty Stocking, who was mailing some letters, saw them at a postal outlet where they were trying to have money wired to them. She loaned them $75 for bus fare and arranged for them to eat free at her son-in-law's place, The Beachcomber Tavern.

"She just took us in under her wing," Duncan says.

The Siuslaw Women's Center provided the MacDonalds with dry clothes and a motel room — ironically, at The Lighthouse Inn.

And a few days later the Newport police called to say someone had turned in a handful of Maggie's credit cards — found 20 miles north, near Waldport.

Wreckage washed ashore mainly in a quarter-mile swath at Strawberry Hill, where the MacDonalds arrived early Wednesday morning to drag splintered pieces of mainly plywood and 2x4s into burn piles and watch the *Charlie Tuna* go up in smoke.

"The rest of it's out there to stay," Duncan says. "A lot of memories lost forever. But I gotta forget it — like when Roger died."

As the rain falls harder, they climb the sandstone bluff to their car to take a break. Duncan says he's not going back down.

Meanwhile, Maggie, like a concerned mother looking into a crib, peers over the bluff's edge at the smoldering fires below.

She then looks out to sea, for what's on the other side of the waves.

May 4, 2000

While nobody's watching

YACHATS — I met her on the beach last Friday morning.

I was heading south, dragging a fishing-net float — how can you pass up such a find, complete with "Republic of China" stamped on it? She was heading north, carrying plastic sacks.

"Groceries from Yachats?" I asked.

"No," she said. "Garbage from the beach."

Meeting Marianne Moore, 71, was like breathing the first whiff of coast air after the stuffy drive from Eugene. Just what I needed: someone to remind me that, beyond the sordid headlines live everyday people who choose wisely — and make the world a better place because of it.

The previous night, I'd gone to sleep lulled by the waves of an outgoing tide — after reading *Sports Illustrated's* account of Mike Price, the coach recently swept out to sea by the Crimson Tide.

The ex-Washington State coach was fired when Alabama officials learned of a strip-joint outing that began with Price being the life of the party and ended with the bill coming due: not only $1,000 worth of hotel food charged to Price's credit card from his room by a "dancer," but his seven-year, $10 million contract.

Elsewhere, the magazine wrote of Iowa State basketball coach Larry Eustachy, a $1-million-a-year coach who parted ways with the Cyclones after photos surfaced of him partying with college-aged women.

Throw in the William Bennett revelation — the *Book of Virtues* author, it was learned last week, has gambled away nearly $8 million on slots and video poker in the past decade — and the week left me shaking my head.

No, this wasn't murder and mayhem. But to slough off such revelations with a boys-will-be-boys wink is to overlook the real victims here — wives, children and, in the case of Price and Eustachy, assistant coaches and players who suddenly find themselves shipwrecked at sea.

Suddenly, amid my contemplation, there was Marianne Moore, picking up plastic bottles, wrappers, light bulbs — the garbage left by others. She does it virtually every day, combing a stretch of sand between Yachats and Waldport with her plastic bags and dog Leo.

"I hate seeing litter," says Moore, her tan, weathered face framed with gray hair. "If it doesn't get picked up, it just stays there."

Our truest character, it's been said, isn't revealed when we're in the spotlight, when people expect us to be "on." It's revealed when nobody is watching or when we think nobody is watching — whether that place is a lonely stretch of Oregon beach or a gambling casino.

Among the selections in Bennett's *Book of Virtues* is a story called "Someone Sees You," a "folktale that reminds us that an act of dishonesty is never truly hidden."

Likewise, in a sketch called "Letter from Jim," Garrison Keillor spins a soul-searching story about a professor in a college town — ironically, it sounds like Price's old home, Pullman — who's waiting to leave for a conference in Chicago, where he expects to have an affair with a colleague.

But as he looks around at his neighborhood, "Jim" suddenly realizes — as Price did not — that a bill someday will come due. "I saw that although I thought my sins would be secret, they would be no more secret than an earthquake," he writes. "All these houses and all these families — my infidelity will somehow shake them. It will pollute the drinking water, it will make noxious gases come out of the ventilators in the elementary school ... a school teacher will say, 'What the hell,' and eliminate South America from geography ... . I just leave the story there ... except to say that we depend on each other more than we ever know ... ."

As sandpipers swooped, I bid farewell to Moore, richer for having met her. Some of us, I was reminded, leave behind garbage. Some of us pick it up. In the end, the makeup of the beach — the world where we live — rests on the sum of such choices.

May 5, 2003

Winter in summer

YACHATS — You've had it happen: You're headed west, somewhere between Mapleton and Florence.

In the rearview mirror: work, responsibility and the vacant, early-morning stares of angst-ridden urbanites, waiting for their pump numbers to be called at the AM/PM.

Ahead, through your windshield: a weekend at the Oregon Coast. Surf. Sun. A guy at the counter at Vickie's Big Wheel in Waldport who, out of the blue, starts telling everyone in the joint a joke involving water baptism.

Suddenly, you come around a bend on Highway 126 and are visually assaulted by a wall of clouds that looms like a Hollywood tidal wave.

It is August. On the Eastern Seaboard, the suntan lotion is flowing. It is sunny and hot on Southern California's coast. It is sunny and hot right out your window.

But you're in Oregon so you're about to enter The Drizzle Zone, a 65-degree summer weekend — a fifth dimension of weather beyond that which is known to man.

Officially, it's known as "marine air penetration," according to state climatologist George Taylor, a condition often triggered by extreme valley heat. Unofficially, it's known as "Coast Crud," according to non-state climatologists such as me.

It is so dark and cool at 7 p.m. in Florence that, as you head north, you half-expect the residential Christmas lights to flick on. The ocean — when you finally locate it after driving alongside it for five miles — looks like oatmeal on a morning when you've forgotten your contact lenses. It has no definition, just this battleship-gray blur of something out there that looks like it should be enhanced with whale-sized raisins.

Blessedly, that icy 20 mph wind from the north — so fierce you can start your beach fire at Tillicum Beach Campground and put it out near the Sea Lion Caves — is not blowing. Still, it's not quite what you had in mind all these weeks as you envisioned this vacation.

Silly you. You envisioned an aqua ocean the color of mouthwash, contrasted by crisp, white breakers, like the piping on a birthday cake. You envisioned blue skies that would fade to orange and pink as the ocean swallowed the evening sun.

Instead you got a weekend that not only didn't come with a sunset, but — other than a Saturday afternoon cameo appearance — didn't even come with sun. You can't tell high noon from 8 p.m. You can't tell whether it's summer or winter. At times, you can't even tell land from sea.

All you can tell is that in what was supposed to be the sweet air of summer there is moisture. Not rain, no, that would be too distinct, too defined. No, this is drizzle. Summer fog.

So what do you, as an Oregonian, do to rescue such weekends? Two things.

First, you reach deep into your recesses of rationalization and say to your Drizzle Zone Mate: "At least it's not windy."

It is one of those phrases rooted deep in our state psyche, a protective mantra — probably begun by some pioneer whose wagon was floating sideways down the Columbia — to stiffen our upper lips. And if it's windy, you remind yourself that at least it's not raining. And if it's windy and raining you remind yourself that you're relatively healthy and, after all, sun can cause skin cancer.

So first you emphasize the bad that isn't present. Then you emphasize the good that *is* present.

Last weekend — without being able to even identify, much less admire, the sea and sky — you looked at the up-close world.

The cottontail rabbits were out in record numbers; more bunnies popped out of the brambles than out-of-state RVs plodded down Highway 101, their drivers too busy chortling over not having to pay sales taxes to notice they were doing 40 mph in a 55 zone and had 23 cars behind them.

And these orange plants everywhere; everyone calls them Indian paintbrush but, technically, they're *crocrosmia*. And more vibrant than you can remember since first focusing a Nikkormat lens on them 29 summers ago.

With the rest of the coast lost in a Garfunkelian hazy shade of winter, all sorts of plants and flowers — from morning glory to daisies — seemed more spectacular than ever.

So you look at — and appreciate — the beauty you might normally overlook.

And you nap more, justifying that it's not like you're missing out on spectacular surf and sun.

A report comes from home in Eugene: hot and sunny. As you doze, the woman on the radio says look for clouds this afternoon, clouds tonight and clouds tomorrow — with a slight chance of drizzle. High 65. Low 55.

At least it's not windy.

August 14, 2001

The new coast

NEWPORT — Maybe it was watching a Depoe Bay Fish Co. forklift poke down Bay Boulevard with a red Honda CRX on its tail.

Maybe it was trying to remember what that beautiful stretch of sand dunes looked like before it was blocked by the new Fred

Meyer store in Florence.

Maybe it was driving by the usual motels along Highway 101 — the Terry-A-While variety, featuring animals made of driftwood — and then suddenly seeing "The Village@North Pointe" in Depoe Bay, a new concoction of condos starting at $380,000 apiece.

At some point during my latest escape to these parts, I was reminded — more vividly than ever — that this invigorating stretch of sand, surf and brackish smells is no longer simply a blue-collar coast.

It's a Mo's clam chowder coast trying to survive in a Martha Stewart world.

The Oregon Coast — or, for those who demand style, The Coast@Oregone — has long been blessed with a touch of tackiness. (Are there more grains of sand on the beach than Highway 101 gift stores selling Made in China shells, Roadrunner whirligigs and "I'm With Stupid" shirts?) But that traditional lack of polish has always been a comical virtue, an offshoot of unpretentious locals that added a certain ambiance to the place.

Yachats, for example, once had a gas station that called itself "Ain't-Mad-at-Nobody," which offered passers-by a sense of inclusiveness. Now, however, the Oregon Coast is increasingly being marketed for its exclusiveness.

A New Coast is emerging. And while that's not altogether bad — what's to not like about, say, the Oregon Coast Aquarium? — it could be if it obliterates the Old.

What's at stake, I think, is the very essence of this place. Can it grow and maintain that get-away-from-it-all feel or is it destined to become like all those places people left to get away from?

The tide seems to be shifting toward the latter. It seems mildly ironic, for example, that a coastline whose virtues have been vehemently protected by a public beach law is now sprinkled with private, gated communities.

And that in a place like Lincoln City, where the largest ocean on Earth laps ashore, more and more tourists find their treasures not on the beach but in a factory outlet mall and a gambling casino.

What's happening on the Oregon Coast is not unique. Spirit Mountain Casino in Grand Ronde has replaced Multnomah Falls as the state's No. 1 tourist destination. And, nationally, the country is awash in what author David (*Bobos in Paradise*) Brooks refers to as "Bourgeois Bohemians," well-heeled baby boomers who have morphed into these best-of-both-worlds creatures who may still like beachcombing but, at day's end, also like the idea of returning to, say, The Village@North Pointe for a movie at the place's 19-seat, big-screen theater.

Coast developers obviously saw the Bobos coming. Bandon Dunes Golf Course, voted by *Golf Digest* as the best new upscale course in the United States last year, is having no trouble filling its dance card — at $135 a round.

The world is changing and, with it, the Oregon Coast. Oh, parts of it remain seemingly timeless; the beach itself, beyond eroding bluffs and shifting sand, is still blessedly consistent. On Newport's Bay Boulevard, where crabbers' lines over the decades have worn hundreds of notches into the wooden rail, you can stroll across the street to the Wood Gallery and, if so inclined, spend $30,000 on a mermaid sculpture.

Of course, change in itself isn't bad. But change is best when it honors the people and environment around it. The Oregon Coast Aquarium, which highlights the very stuff that makes the coast the coast, has been a win-win for locals and tourists.

But all is not well. In Florence, Newport and Lincoln City, a wave of franchise additions have eroded the towns' distinctiveness.

I used to love seeing that sudden sweep of dunes midway through Florence; though small, it was like a visual oasis — a parenthetical pause in an otherwise run-on sentence. It's now a Fred Meyer and, architecturally, a handsome design.

But unlike one-stop shopping centers, they don't make sand dunes anymore. And if we're to preserve the Old Coast while welcoming the New, we dare not forget that.

August 15, 2000

Studying the 'coasties'

I AM A STUDENT of the Oregon Coast, just back from my latest field trip.

It was a week of "Coast Crud," that befuddling phenomenon whereby the east side of Highway 101 is 85 degrees and looks postcard-sunny and the west side is 51 degrees and looks like a good place to get hypothermia.

Despite the weather, I was able to complete my research on Oregon's seven kinds of beach people:

The Beachcomber. He hits the beach with childlike wonder, hoping to find exotic bottles thrown overboard by Russian sailors and floats from the nets of far-off Japanese trawlers.

Instead, he finds a left-footed thong, a pill box, three spent sparklers and a plastic bag from Clark's Market in Waldport. No matter. He has the perseverance of a barnacle. Each walk is an adventure.

He not only doesn't whine about Coast Crud, he relishes it. In his knee-high rubber boots and wool cap, he has the beach to himself.

The Naturalist. She is closely related to the beachcomber, but is less interested in what the sea might wash ashore than what's already here. She knows the difference between the cockle clam (clinocardium nuttalli) and the littleneck clam (venerupis staminea). She knows that the common sea star can move at a rate of 3 inches per minute. She can even correctly spell, and pronounce, "sea anemone."

She has a low-digit REI member number, carries a Nikon with a close-up lens and will be on the beach before the sea gulls have gutted their first dozen breakfast crabs.

The Doer. To him, the beach is a playground. He molds the sand. Digs in it. Runs on it. Putts on it. Draws baseball diamonds in it. Has himself buried up to his neck in it — just about the time he realizes he shouldn't have had that third Mountain Dew.

He walks on the rocks. He braves waters so cold that the feeling in certain extremities won't return until he's been back from vacation for a week. He taunts the waves. Body-surfs them. Skims the backwash. Feels the salt in his eyes.

He is 6 years old. At least in his mind.

The Dreamer. In a previous life, she was a sea gull. She's sure of it.

She doesn't walk on the beach. She walks on the sands of time. She doesn't hear the surf. She hears his voice calling her name in every wave. She doesn't look at a sunset. She ponders the meaning of life as the ocean swallows the last bites of sun, her mind drifting to lost loves — mainly '60s stuff — and whether she turned off the stove back in Eugene.

She looks out to sea and wonders why there are wars, whether any publisher will buy her handwritten haiku and if she should go back to grad school.

The Beautiful People. They never come alone, so they must be referred to in the plural.

They look as if they just walked out of a Lexus commercial. Out of place. They're used to warmer beaches in places where episodes of "Baywatch" are filmed. They don't "get" the Oregon Coast. It is, they believe, frumpy, foul-weathered and dull.

They watch a clammer and think: weird. They're mildly offended by the plastic garbage buckets on the tables at Mo's. They set up a beach volleyball net, not yet understanding that if someone serves a volleyball at, say, Waldport, the shot will wind up at Cape Blanco.

They have small dogs that yap at the waves. They stay on the beach for 20 minutes, then leave for the outlet malls in Lincoln City.

The Relaxer. Book in her lap, drink at her side, toes in the sand, she could sleep through a tsunami. Office? What office? By Day Two, she has forgotten she even has a job. By Day Four, she can only remember the names of two of her four children.

She reads paperbacks whose covers show Adirondack chairs on white-railed porches of oceanfront beach houses. Her favorite columnist is Ellen Goodman, especially when she writes about her summer vacations at Casco Bay, Maine.

When feeling particularly spunky, she walks to the ocean and cools off her feet.

The Worrier. He has come to the Oregon Coast to get away from it all, but brings it all with him: The briefcase. The laptop. The thoughts of demanding clients.

He takes a stick and, in the wet sand, absent-mindedly makes jagged lines going downward, unable to forget the carnage that once was his 401(k) plan.

"Daddy, look at me," says his daughter, who, after 18 tries, has finally gotten her kite to fly. But he doesn't hear her. It's not the surf. It's the voice on the other end of the cell phone.

In the distance, the beachcomber is celebrating madly in the shallows, holding something in his hand.

He's finally found it: an exotic bottle thrown overboard by a Russian sailor.

August 1, 2002

5.

Yesterday

The cost of freedom

ON A STORMY November day in 1880, a Waldport man got into a small wooden boat and began rowing north across white-capped Alsea Bay. Other townsfolk refused to go, believing it too dangerous. But Lou Southworth wouldn't be deterred.

He wanted to vote.

In a time when we now cast our ballots through the convenience of mail, a time when 60,000 of Lane County's 241,000 eligible voters haven't even registered, there's a lesson to be learned from Lou Southworth.

And as someone who has never had the man's electoral zeal, I confess I need that lesson as much as anyone.

I stumbled across the Lou Southworth story in Yachats, in an obscure book about the history of south Lincoln County, *The Land That Kept Its Promise*. It was written by the late Marjorie Hays, whose ancestors settled in the Yachats area soon after Southworth set out on his crossing 120 years ago, and I've paraphrased it with permission of the Lincoln County Historical Society.

Southworth, wrote Hays, was perhaps the most loyal and trusted citizen of Waldport. He and his wife, Marie, were "widely known for their happiness and hospitality." And though women wouldn't be allowed to vote in Oregon until 1912, Lou never missed an election.

That could have been despite his past. Or because of his past. For Lou Southworth was, in the eyes of the government, property — not a person — for much of his life.

He was born a slave in Kentucky, probably in the 1820s or '30s. He came West as a slave and bought his freedom with gold he'd dug in Yreka, Calif., and Jacksonville mines. He settled in Waldport in 1879, homesteading about four miles up the Alsea River from Waldport.

Above Lou Southworth's fireplace hung a single picture. It was of Abraham Lincoln, whose 1863 Emancipation Proclamation abolished slavery in rebel states and boosted the abolitionist cause; nationally, slavery wouldn't legally end until the 13th Amendment was ratified in 1865.

Southworth lived in a rugged place and in a rugged time. He was chairman of the board of Darkey Creek School — the creek was recently renamed "Southworth" to bury its racist connotation and honor Lou — and once made a motion and seconded it himself.

John Turks, a German immigrant, jumped up. "You cannot do dot. Dot is not legal."

The two stepped outside and pummeled each other in a clump of ferns. "Suddenly," wrote Hays, "yellow jackets swarmed everywhere and the meeting was hastily adjourned with everyone trying to outrun the pests and no one escaping the stings."

Such disagreements weren't uncommon, wrote Hays, but left few scars. What wounded Southworth far deeper was when the church he attended dropped him from its roll because he dared to play the fiddle in it.

Southworth pointed out that in his travels, he had often played for miners who didn't have Bibles or hymn books and so his fiddle "was most like a church of anything we had."

The church disagreed; it was the devil's instrument, leaders said.

"I inquired if there's music up in heaven and they told me that there is," Hays quoted Southworth as saying, "but when I asked them if I could play a little of it here below, they couldn't answer that to suit a fellow like me."

Southworth was a man of conviction; he wouldn't stay in a

church that wouldn't allow him to play his fiddle and he wouldn't stay home on Election Day 1880, no matter how hard the southwest winds were churning Alsea Bay.

The presidential race pitted Republican James Garfield against Democrat Winfield Hancock. The polling place was across the bay, at a store owned by the Lutgen brothers.

As he got in his boat, Southworth probably intended to vote for Garfield; for blacks who were allowed to vote in that era, any friend of The Great Emancipator's party was a friend of theirs.

Onlookers urged him not to go, but Southworth wouldn't listen.

"Boys, Abe Lincoln's on trial every time there is a big election, so I'm going to cross the bay to vote or drown in the attempt."

He fastened two large oil cans to the bow and stern of the boat for added buoyancy, then shoved off. People stood on the beach and watched until they could see him no more. The storm gobbled up Southworth. The wind whipped. The waves rolled.

Then, faintly, they later saw movement: someone standing on the dock below Lutgen's store — a man waving his hat.

In the presidential election of 1880, won by Garfield, Americans cast 8,891,083 votes.

One belonged to Lou Southworth, whose story reminds us that, in the name of democracy, others have endured far more than 360-page voter guides.

October 1, 2000

Those who shaped us

AT CENTURY'S END, some questions come to mind: As a community, who do we thank — or blame, depending on your perspective — for what we've become in the past 100 years? Who are the people whose legacies have endured? Who really helped shape Lane County, this place some 313,000 of us call home?

I've come up with 12 people who, I think, stand above the rest. For the most part, they're linked by having started long-lasting legacies. The late Steve Prefontaine, for example, didn't make my list; that's because he's a legacy of Bill Bowerman, who did.

My list of 12 includes only people alive after 1900. And it includes only people who once lived, or are now living, in Lane County.

Why 12? Hey, this is Eugene. Most people's millennium and century lists have been 10, 100 or 1,000 deep; to honor this place's penchant for nonconformity, we should be different.

Creating such a list, I realize, is a risky proposition; I'll certainly leave out worthy candidates. But better to honor some and inadvertently omit a few, I figure, than to ignore the past completely.

So here they are, 12 people who — among thousands of others — have helped shape Lane County during the 20th century:

Prince Lucien Campbell. President of the University of Oregon from 1902 till his death in 1925, he turned a fledgling school into the largest institution of higher ed in the state. He spearheaded a property tax bill that gave a cut to the university and developed the first-ever private-contribution campaign. "He came to Oregon when it was a college with a preparatory department," said UO Regent Henry McKinney. "He left it a university."

Also cool: Campbell was a member of the first party to spend a night on Mount Hood. Uncool: That he got such a dorky-looking building on campus named after him.

Robert A. Booth. He was co-founder of the Booth-Kelly Lumber Co., whose Springfield mill in 1902 gave that city an economic boom that more than quintupled its size by 1910. Booth-Kelly, which eventually sold to Georgia Pacific in 1959, along with Weyerhaeuser, was foundational in Lane County's rise as the producer of more lumber and plywood than any similar-size region in the world.

Booth was more than a businessman, however. He was a state legislator, a candidate for U.S. Senate and — ever get state funding to help you through college? Thank Bob; he founded the state student loan program.

Maude Kerns. An artist, professor and philanthropist, she graduated from the UO in '99 — and I don't mean this '99 — and headed off to study art in San Francisco and New York. She returned to Eugene in 1921 and taught for 26 years before retiring in 1947 — at age 70.

Kerns had paintings exhibited in New York, Los Angeles, San Francisco, Paris and Japan; several of her works are part of the Guggenheim Museum's permanent collection.

Besides gifts and endowments bequeathed to the UO, her gift of a house led to the creation of the Maude Kerns Art Center, which has moved locations but carries on her legacy.

Alton Baker Sr. In 1930, Baker bought the *Morning Register* and merged it with the *Eugene Guard* he already owned to found *The Eugene Register-Guard,* Lane County's largest newspaper and one of its oldest family-run businesses.

In the early '40s, Baker launched a "Community Chest" program that later became United Way of Lane County. In 1962, Alton Baker Park was opened in honor of Baker, who not only fought for land being preserved for public parks but donated a 10-acre tract west of Skinner Butte to the cause. Baker was also a staunch supporter of Boy Scouts; Camp Baker near Florence is named for him.

Bill Bowerman. More than anyone, Bowerman, who died Friday, is responsible for Eugene's reputation as a running mecca. He was UO men's track and field coach from 1949 to 1972, his teams won four NCAA titles. He triggered the nation's jogging fad after writing a book on the subject. He was a major reason Prefontaine chose Oregon and helped turn the Coos Bay runner into the best middle distance runner in the nation. He coached and later mentored Bill Dellinger, who carried on his legacy. He coached the U.S. Olympic Track & Field team in 1972. And along with Phil Knight, he helped start a mom & pop shoe and apparel company named Nike.

Cool: Behind the scenes, he helped get the Oregon Bach Festival out of the starting blocks.

Wayne Morse. Morse, like the two choices who follow, probably had greater impact beyond Lane County than in it. And yet his spirit to fight — nay, scratch and claw — for his political ideals has inspired many. At 31, he became the dean of the UO Law School — the youngest law school dean in the country — and immediately took on the State Board of Higher Education and its attempt to combine UO and Oregon State into one institution in Corvallis. He went on to serve 24 years in the U.S. Senate and battled everyone and everything from Joseph McCarthy to those who favored war in Vietnam.

Cool: By next fall, the 100th anniversary of his birth, organizers are hoping to place a memorial at the main entrance plaza of the Lane County Courthouse.

Roy Hicks Jr. You might not have heard of the guy, but after his plane crashed in February 1994, his memorial service outdrew Prefontaine's. More than 5,000 people crowded into the Exhibition Hall at the Lane County Fairgrounds to memorialize the 50-year-old Hicks, pastor emeritus at Eugene Faith Center.

In 1969, Hicks launched a congregation of 75 — infused by the "Jesus Movement" — that turned into one of Lane County's largest churches. It now has more than 4,000 members, a quarter of them coming since Hicks left the church in 1988.

Under Hicks, Faith Center spawned a handful of other Foursquare churches in Lane County, and his ministry is credited with founding some 50 others across the country. "It's not like a candle passing," said one speaker at his service. "It's like a strobe light."

Cool: After hearing Hicks had died, a woman called *The Register-Guard* and said he had talked her out of committing suicide as she stood on the Ferry Street Bridge.

Ken Kesey. The Pied Piper of '60s psychedelia lives on in Pleasant Hill — and in the hearts of free spirits everywhere. Immortalized in Tom Wolfe's *Electric Kool-Aid Acid Test* (1968) for his and his Merry Pranksters' wild bus ride across America, Kesey has seemingly done it all: played football for Springfield High, chummed with the Grateful Dead and written *One Flew Over the Cuckoo's Nest* and that essential Oregon novel, *Sometimes a Great Notion.*

He's pushed the limits of nearly everything — remember his "Bend in the River" experiment in participatory democracy back in the '70s? — and somehow lived to tell about it.

Bertha Holt. If a place is enriched by those who give to others, then Lane County has been enriched by this roll-up-the-sleeves woman.

Moved by orphaned children in the wake of the Korean War, she and husband, Harry, literally got an act of Congress to adopt eight children and were moved to begin Eugene-based Holt International Children's Services.

Harry died in 1964, but Bertha, now 95 and living in Creswell, is still at the helm of an organization that operates in 11 countries and has found homes for more than 100,000 children.

Cool: Still jogging while in her early 90s, she holds the world Masters 400-meter record in the 90-plus division.

Cynthia Wooten. A three-term Democratic state legislator, Wooten lobbied for women's rights, gay rights and environmental concerns during the '90s. But her more visible legacies are the Oregon Country Fair and the Eugene Celebration. In 1969, she was among those who launched the fair, and was coordinator of it during its infancy. And in the '80s, as a Eugene city councilor, she spearheaded the first Eugene Celebration — a "last-minute thing" that drew thousands and has been hopping ever since.

Carolyn Chambers. Since 1957, Chambers has been plying the business waters and, in recent decades, making significant splashes. She is CEO and board chairwoman of Chambers Communication Corp., whose holdings include KEZI-TV and cable systems in four states — though AT&T is in the process of buying the latter. Another branch of the family business, Chambers Construction, is among the county's largest builders.

Cool: Chambers has also done tons for the community. Among her deeds: spearheading an effort that raised $9 million in private support for the construction of the Hult Center.

Royce Saltzman. While a young UO music professor traveling in Germany, he met a young choral director named Helmuth Rilling. It was the seed that grew into the Saltzman-inspired — and Rilling-conducted — Oregon Bach Festival, which is now regarded as one of the world's finest music festivals.

Now in its 31st year, the Eugene event attracted 31,000 people last year from 35 states and seven foreign countries. In 1998, its first syndicated concert series was picked up by 240 radio stations. And executive director Saltzman has been its chief nurturer, even returning after a short retirement to continue leading this blend of music, education and celebration of life.

December 26, 1999

Our defining moments

NOW THAT Bill Bowerman is gone, I wonder: What was it like when he first cooked up his experimental rubber track-shoe sole on his wife Barbara's waffle iron?

After all, it was one of those defining moments in Lane County's 20th Century history, one of those incremental events that ultimately led to the creation of Nike, which helped revolutionize sports shoes and apparel — and, because of growing concern that the company exploits foreign laborers, is now at the center of a world trade debate.

I wish I could have been there that day — to witness history in the baking. And I wish I could have experienced some other Lane County events — not because they had worldwide consequences but just because they were noteworthy.

Here are four such events I'd like to have seen:

Wiley Griffon's funeral, 1913. At the turn of the century, Griffon was perhaps the lone black man in Eugene, the driver of the town's first streetcar service — a single mule-powered car. His funeral, as described in the enlightening *Full of Life: The History and Character of Eugene's Masonic Cemetery*, cost $64.15.

Opal Whitely, the talented and eccentric Cottage Grove woman, trying to convince *Atlantic Monthly* editor Ellery Sedgwick to publish her fanciful manuscript, The Fairyland Around Us, 1919. Sedgwick said no, but later became so intrigued with the 22-year-old Whitely that his magazine published her childhood journal.

Wayne Morse's verbal attack on Oregon State College President William Kerr in opposition to Kerr's plan to merge the University of Oregon with Oregon State College, 1932. By then, voters had already rejected the idea by a 6-to-1 margin but Morse's speech transformed his image from that of a young academic — at 31, he was dean of the UO Law School — to a political maverick.

President Herbert Hoover fly-fishing on the McKenzie River, 1932. He showed up at Holiday Farm Resort two or three times a year with a suitcase and fly rod in hand. "I come to the McKenzie River for a brainwashing to refresh my soul," he once said.

Now, four Lane County-related events I'm glad I did experience:

Steve Prefontaine's first race that brought him national attention, a high school record 8:41.5 two-mile in Corvallis (1969), and the last race before his death, a 5,000-meter event he won at Hayward Field (1975).

Weather's "Triple Crown" of the '60s — the Columbus Day Storm (1962), Christmas Flood of '64 and Big Snow of '69. OK, so I was in Corvallis, but it got blown, soaked and buried, respectively, by the same three storms.

Kenny Wheaton's interception that sealed UO's win over the Huskies win and helped the Ducks get to the Rose Bowl (1994-95). Still get shivers seeing the replay.

Grateful Dead concert, 1994. Not my musical cup of tea but a fascinating experience — and, with Jerry Garcia's death the next year, the Dead's last weekend in Eugene.

OK, four events I'm glad I missed:

Two white-robed Klansmen riding down Willamette Street on Jan. 7, 1922, as part of a Ku Klux Klan recruiting mission.

The opening of the 18-story Ya-Po-Ah Terrace, 1968. Who was asleep at the wheel when this was allowed to block an otherwise awesome view of Skinner Butte?

The 0-0 tie between Oregon and Oregon State's football teams, 1983. This is the kind of travesty that George Santayanna had in mind when he wrote, "Those who cannot remember the past are condemned to repeat it."

The gypsy moth attack, 1985. The largest infestation in the West, it triggered an $11 million aerial spray attack.

Finally, four events I experienced but wished I hadn't:

Gas lines, 1973-74. To get a fill-up, I had to leave my car overnight in a quarter-mile-long line.

UO basketball Coach Dick Harter tripping a male OSU cheerleader who was flaunting a trophy that the Beavers, not the Ducks, were about to win, 1974.

Duck footballers' 14-game losing streak in 1974-75. As an *Oregon Daily Emerald* sportswriter, I saw every home loss. Autzen attendance when the Ducks finally beat Utah after the 391-day drought: 10,500.

A phone call from a panicked young Thurston High student I received as I walked into *The Register-Guard* office just after 8 a.m. on May 21, 1998. Shots had been fired at the school, he said, and rumors were flying that some students had been injured.

December 28, 2000

Lane history: a quiz

TO CLOSE OUT the century, I offer the first — and last — Lane County 20th Century History Quiz. It's your chance to find out what you remember, what you've forgotten and what you never knew about this place from 1900 to 1999.

Answers to the 33 questions — and a "How You Rate" break-down — appear at the bottom. Pencils ready? Begin:

1. Name the Eugene hardware store, operating from 1903 to 1980, where change was made by a central cashier on the second floor who received and sent customers' money on wires.

2. Benjamin Franklin Finn, for whom Finn Rock on the McKenzie River is named, claimed to have been what well-known character from literature?

3. What University of Oregon graduate was credited with helping mainstream America better understand the AIDS epidemic with his book *And the Band Played On*?

4. In the pre-pepper spray days of 1910, what triggered one of the first NIMBY environmental protests in Eugene?

5. What Lane County state legislator — and later a UO administrator — was a driving force behind the nation's first returnable-bottle bill, which passed in 1971?

6. Name the respective leads in the following filmed-in-Lane-County movies: *The General* (1926), *Animal House* (1978) and *Personal Best* (1982).

7. What well-known Oregon politician wrote a column for the *Oregon Daily Emerald* in the '30s called "Sports Quacks?"

8. In 1924, 8,000 people showed up in Eugene to see what?

9. What head UO basketball coach — here for more than one season — has the best winning percentage in school history?

10. Speaking of hoops, what was the nickname of the Oregon men's basketball team that won the first-ever NCAA basketball tournament in 1939?

11. Who benefited most from Eugene's 1911 "local option" law prohibiting alcohol?

12. What Hollywood film star once worked in the Mohawk Valley?

13. Bob Kintigh served as a Republican state legislator for 12 years, but he made national news in 1992 for something else. What?

14. What event commanded the first seven pages of the *Eugene Register-Guard* on Jan. 26, 1969?

15. The first three pages of the *Guard* on Sept. 25, 1982?

16. Name the auto mechanic credited with helping guide Eugene through the treacherous Depression years — and whose garage is now a music venue.

17. In 1918, the *Daily Guard* reported that 15,000 people — the most people in Lane County to ever assemble in one place to look at a single object — had shown up to see what?

18. Name the Eugene hippie co-op that was launched in October 1972.

19. In the '90s, Eugene welcomed its first female mayor, first female chief administrator and first black police chief, none of whom, incidentally, still have those positions. Name them.

20. In the first nine years of the 20th Century, how many different head football coaches did Oregon have?

21. In 1920, why was the 19th Amendment, which gave women the right to vote, somewhat anticlimactic in Lane County?

22. In 1971, what did the *Eugene Register-Guard* salute with a special section dedicated to an "adventure in innovation"?

23. What former television star got his start in Eugene's Very Little Theatre?

24. As the '70s arrived, what did EWEB want to build north of Florence that voters ultimately shot down?

25. Who was Tugman Park in Eugene named for?

26. What singer-composer made the splashiest entrance to the debut of the Hult Center for the Performing Arts in 1982?

27. What technological advance made its debut in Eugene in 1904?

28. In 1950, what City Hall in Lane County had to be shut down because recalls and resignations left too few people to carry out routine duties?

29. What reached 86 mph on Oct. 12, 1962?

30. What smooth R&B star got his start in Eugene in the late '70s?

31. When it began in 1969, what was the price of admission at the Oregon Country Fair — then called the Renaissance Faire?

32. Who was J. Fenwick Insider?

33. What UCLA halfback, who would go on to make history, was held to 14 yards on 15 carries in a Bruin-Duck football game at Hayward Field in 1940?

Answers:

1. Quackenbush's.
2. Huckleberry Finn of Mark Twain fame.
3. Randy Shilts, who died of AIDS in 1994.

4. A plan to deepen and widen the millrace, in which workers were confronted by shotgun-toting landowners who suggested this was not a good idea at all.

5. Nancie Fadeley.

6. Buster Keaton, John Belushi and Mariel Hemingway.

7. Former Gov. Tom McCall, who, besides being a sportswriter, ran a successful impromptu write-in campaign for senior class president — until Wayne Morse, the dean of the law school, deemed the write-in election invalid.

8. The crew of the first round-the-world flight land before its last stop in Seattle.

9. Jody Runge, who is 128-54 (.703) in her six-plus years.

10. The Tall Firs.

11. Springfield, which remained "wet" and welcomed a double streetcar full of thirsty, eager-to-spend folks from Eugene every Saturday night.

12. Clint Eastwood.

13. After a nationwide search, a Christmas tree from Kintigh's ranch in Cedar Flats was chosen to adorn the White House.

14. A surprise storm that buried Lane County under 2 feet of snow.

15. The opening of the Hult Center for the Performing Arts.

16. Samuel Bond, a 12-year City Council member whose other legacy is Sam Bond's Garage.

17. The Liberty Bell, which was en route from Philadelphia to San Francisco for the Pan-American Exposition.

18. The Growers' Market.

19. Ruth Bascom, Vicki Elmer and Leonard Cooke.

20. Nine.

21. Oregon had granted women suffrage in 1912, and Lane County voters had approved such a measure in 1900.

22. The new Eugene downtown mall.

23. David Ogden Stiers, who went on to star in television's "M*A*S*H" and later become a music conductor.

24. A nuclear power plant.

25. William Tugman, bulldog newspaper editor for the *Eugene Guard* and later the *Eugene Register-Guard*, and one of the founders of Very Little Theatre.

26. Mason Williams, who, in a tuxedo with red vest and red high-top sneakers, paddled his way down the Willamette River

from Springfield to Skinner Butte Park, then walked his canoe to the Eugene Hilton, where he asked an attendant to "park" it.

27. The automobile. By 1910 there would be more than 10,000 across the state.

28. Springfield's.

29. Winds in Eugene during the Columbus Day storm, which killed five, left 45 injured and caused more than $2 million in property damage in Lane County.

30. Robert Cray.

31. Fifty cents.

32. Head janitor at the state Capitol — and a fictional character of former *Register-Guard* columnist Don Bishoff.

33. Jackie Robinson, who would later break major league baseball's color barrier.

How You Rate

20-33 correct: Historically speaking, you rule.

10-19 correct: When the barbecue chat turns to local history, you'll be the life of the party.

0-9 correct: New in town, huh?

December 30, 1999

Biggest story of '61

IT WAS VINTAGE Eugene: a controversy that embroiled the left, right, students, farmers, politicians and seemingly everyone else.

Loudspeakers blared at a protest. Bumper stickers urged people to patronize only merchants who were voting the "right way." "Police Order Quiets Rally," read one *Register-Guard* headline.

Parents of schoolchildren banded together to stem a change they detested. Some threatened lawsuits. A Eugene mother went on strike.

The issue wasn't limited to the local level. State legislators pushed for a special session to deal with the dispute. Democrats fired verbal vollies at Republican Gov. Mark Hatfield, saying he was skirting the problem. Three coastal towns announced they were seceding from the state.

The issue? Daylight-saving time.

As we ready for the semi-annual changing of the clocks at 2 a.m. Sunday, we do so with the ho-humness of breaking out the barbecue grill or planting pansies — just a part of the yearly routine.

'Twasn't always so. In the '50s and '60s, some viewed DST as time's evil side, a sinister hour that threatened to send civilization spinning toward disaster.

Think I'm kidding? In 1961, the University of Oregon hired a new president, voters turned down the Spencer Butte Expressway, citizens nearly recalled Springfield's mayor and Duck miler Dyrol Burleson broke the American record for the mile.

The Register-Guard's No. 1 local story that year? Daylight-saving time.

Some believed DST, in Dickensian terms, was the best of times, others that it was the worst of times.

"No other issue, not even fluoridation, seems to arouse such antagonism and to make such bitter partisans of citizens who usually are quite relaxed," *The Register-Guard* opined.

Not that the issue was particularly new. The practice of setting the clock ahead an hour before summer dates back to 1914, when Cleveland, Ohio started it. Congress approved nationwide daylight time in 1917 and the squabbling began, even though the mandate ended in 1919.

States — and in some cases, cities and towns within those states — had the freedom to decide whether to spring ahead or not. A number did. Oregon remained a staunchly standard time state, but as the idea of more evening light during the good-weather months gained steam across the nation, Oregonians went to the polls to decide the issue.

Four times from 1950 to 1960, standard time prevailed, but by smaller margins each time. Then, when Portland went daylight in May 1961, the state's clocks — and citizens — went wacky for more than a year. Other towns made the switch, too. Some businesses and schools — the UO, for example — chose to go with what became known as "fast time" or "summer time," staying with standard but moving up their hours of operation one hour.

In Eugene, you might drop your kids off at school that was on daylight time, stop by a state government office that was on standard time and go to work at a city office that was on "fast time."

Things got so confusing in 1961 that *The Register-Guard* began printing both times, standard and daylight, for meeting notices and news stories.

At the Bend newspaper, the advertising department went daylight to coincide with the merchants, but the news departments stayed standard to coincide with the county.

Gov. Hatfield began wearing two watches. Gearhart, Seaside and Cannon Beach served notice that they were seceding from the state over the issue.

Amid such levity, Eugene, of course, remained its grim-faced, world-is-coming-to-an-end self. When the Eugene City Council voted to keep city clocks on standard time but move its hours of operation up one hour to 7 a.m. to 4 p.m., the protests began.

"We Don't Want a Police State," said signs at a rally, whose backers handed out bumper stickers saying "Patronize Only Standard Time Merchants."

Lawsuits were threatened. Parents complained that their kids couldn't sleep when put down at 8 o'clock — and it was still light out. A Eugene mother essentially went on strike, saying she was banning regular meals and just fixing a pot of stew so her family could eat whenever. Farmers in daylight areas howled that DST threw off their cows' morning milking schedules. "The dang rooster crows an hour later every day," said one farmer.

In November 1962, the state's voters approved the yearly shift to daylight, finally standardizing the state. Slowly, the controversy died.

A lot of time has passed since then, but perhaps none as strangely controversial as the hour we'll lose Sunday morning.

April 4, 2002

'The greatest student rally'

IT'S DISGRACEFUL — this war within a Civil War over which television broadcast crew will handle Saturday's Oregon-Oregon State football game from Corvallis.

The annual rivalry was never meant to be contested in wood-paneled offices with athletic directors and TV execs firing smart-bomb e-mails at each other or hitting "Send" to launch fax attacks.

It was meant to be contested on the turf, which is exactly what Beaver fans had in mind in 1937 when they burned the initials "OSC" on Hayward Field's 50-yard-line. Or in the Eugene Mill-race, which is where a good number of Beaver Believers wound up that same year. Or in Seymour's Restaurant in downtown Eugene, which is where the Beavers huddled after escaping a counterattack from UO students, led by the law school's 51st Battalion, which showered the intruders with a fire hose. Or atop Skinner Butte later that day, where Duck students turned the visitors into human paint brushes to paint the "O" yellow again — but only after a fe-male OSC student, in defense of her boyfriend, "scored with a lusty right to the jaw," according to the *Oregon Daily Emerald.*

Ah, '37. What a year for Civil War aficionados.

To this day, Civil War strategists look to 1937 as the high-water mark for rivalry spirit. To set the scene: The Beaver-Duck rivalry had lapsed into decades of apathy after the suspension of the game in 1911 and it being moved to a neutral site, Albany, in 1912 be-cause of riots between fans.

There was nothing to suggest 1937 would go beyond the usual pranks. The Thursday before the Oct. 23 game, OSC students burned the school's initials — 3-foot-high letters — into the field. And after the Beavers won the game 14-0, OSC students naturally ripped down the goal posts, paraded through campus and painted the "O" on Skinner Butte orange.

But the winds of war didn't blow until Monday morning. After a night of celebration in Corvallis, word spread: A car caravan was forming. Destination: Duckville.

A Junction City resident saw the caravan and called *The Reg-ister-Guard.* Word passed like wildfire: "The Beavers are comin'!" Their motive? Simple: Drive-by gloating.

Police met the throng, estimated at more than 100 cars and 1,000 students, with a stiff warning that there be no trouble. At first, there wasn't. The caravan rolled down 13th Avenue and onto campus. Word spread of the intruders and suddenly hundreds of UO students "mobilized against the battalion of corn-waving Staters," reported the *Emerald.*

OSC students were pelted with "everything from wet mud to water bags, rotten eggs and all manner of well-aged fruits and veg-etables," said the *Barometer,* OSC's student paper. A few eyes were blackened, a few lips bloodied.

In Fenton Hall, home of the School of Law, Dean of Men Virgil Earl decided desperate times called for desperate measures. Never mind that he was in his 50s; Earl, a former UO football player, unwrapped a fire hose and law students began spraying the Corvallis contingent from upper-level windows.

The Beavers were driven back. A number huddled at Seymour's. Ducks demanded the Beavers be ousted. In true UO style, students whipped together picket signs that said "Unfair to Oregon" and proclaimed they would boycott the restaurant if the rivals weren't ousted.

To avoid a riot, police brokered a deal: The Beavers agreed to come out and be subjected to a dip in the millrace.

UO students did more than a little to facilitate the "dip," including tossing in the intruders, all men, after they'd stripped to their shorts. Meanwhile, other Beaver fans were taken atop Skinner Butte where they were forced to return the orange "O" to its original yellow. "They began painting with brushes," reported the *Emerald*, "but at the suggestion of a blood-thirsty Oregon girl, the UO men began to slide the Staters down the 50-foot letter."

The riot made national news. *The Emerald* wallowed in it for a week. "The events should have satisfied the most rabid of the 'old grads' who have annually protested the lack of spirit on campus," it opined.

The paper congratulated OSC students. The attack was "conceived and executed in a sportsmanlike manner." And, "No one seemed particularly angry, and everyone seemed to have enjoyed the day, on the whole."

Though the *Barometer* said that UO students overreacted, one OSC student who'd been "millraced" wrote to the *Emerald* and said, "We bear no resentment as we would probably have done the same thing."

The *Gazette-Times* called it "the greatest student rally in Oregon history."

"Dean Earl Commends Action of UO men in Refraining from Violence," read one *Emerald* headline. "Wet Beavers Heard to Remark on 'Swell Time.'"

Ah, for the good ol' days.

November 19, 2002

Waldo's 'still woods'

One hundred years ago today, Judge John Breckenridge Waldo was camping at Pamelia Lake near Mount Jefferson.

As Oregonians make their final summer forays into the woods, it's good to remember the man for whom Waldo Lake on the Willamette Pass was named.

With justification, our view of that generation's relationship to the land isn't the stuff of John Muir posters. The demand for timber around the turn of the century was so high that mills couldn't always keep pace. In short, nobody was hugging trees.

But here's what Waldo wrote from Pamelia Lake on Aug. 15, 1905: "The still woods; surely they are not all made merely to be cut down. Let wide stretches still grow for the spiritual welfare of men. How good they seem here today — the untrammeled, the unhanseled wilderness, untouched by men.... Cannot wide expanses still be preserved?"

Waldo, whose parents had arrived on the Oregon Trail with the Applegate party, was elected to the state Supreme Court in 1880. That summer, he began what would be a seasonal ritual for 27 years: He headed for the hills.

From July to September, he, a few friends and their pack horses made their home from Mount Hood to California's Mount Shasta. They cleared trails ("one way of paying my share of the moral tax for the privilege of coming to the mountains"), stocked trout, fished, hunted and hiked.

"This," he wrote in August 1905 from Pamelia, "is written with boiled huckleberry juice."

And two years later: "Here I am at Pamelia Lake, breathing the pine scented air and already feeling much stronger, both in body and spirit. Blessed be the mountains and the free and untenanted wilderness."

For those fascinated by local history — to think I've camped at the same Pamelia Lake as the judge! — Waldo's entries intrigue.

They include the surprising: At Pamelia, in 1881, he reports seeing "a huge monster of a bear" that "could be nothing else but a grizzly." In the same entry, he mentions having "learned of (President) Garfield's assassination, or attempted assassination."

They include the lighthearted: Mosquitoes were no less a menace then than now. In an 1882 entry from Davis Lake: "Mosquitos annoyed us so much that we struck into a trot."

They include mentions of places familiar to many today: "No miniature pond is O'Dell Lake, but one of the fairest of the Cascade's liquid eyes (1890)."

On Crater Lake: "This is the most interesting spot I have yet met with in my mountain travels (1882)."

And on the lake named for him: "It is a noble lake — water almost as blue as Crater Lake — deep, and the wooded mountains about it wild and untrodden (1889)."

Occasionally, Waldo quoted Thoreau, Emerson, Shakespeare and others. And as summer waned, his journals often took on a touch of wistfulness. In 1887, from Diamond Lake, he wrote: "The chill airs of Autumn will soon be felt, and then that necessity which compelled men to build houses over them, will hie me down to the house where mortal angels live."

"Tomorrow," he wrote in 1905 from Pamelia, "we leave the lake to kingfishers, the blue cranes and to solitude."

Finally, in 1907, he wrote from Pamelia: "The high wild hills about here, totally unfenced and uncultivated, are good for eyes that would not have the world altogether cut up into cabbage patches."

They were his journal's final words. He died three weeks later at 62. But his legacy — he was instrumental in the formation of Oregon's national forests — is alive.

You feel it each time you find yourself alone in the Cascades, in Waldo's "still woods."

August 14, 2005

6.

Cultural tides

A Bach Festival rookie

AT THE START of Sunday's Oregon Bach Festival concert, the Brandenburg Concertos, a gentleman on the Silva Concert Hall stage informed us that *Concerto No. 6 in B-Flat Major* would not be performed.

A viola soloist had cut her finger fixing dinner and so, just like that, one-fifth of the concert — $7.80 of my $39 ticket — was scrubbed.

Hey, whatever happened to playing hurt? You'll never hear Oregon football announcer Don Essig explain that, say, wide receiver Samie Parker sprained an ankle so the Ducks won't be throwing any passes today.

Had Sunday's concert been a football game, the concerto doctor would have taped up the violist, shot her full of Novocain and she'd have played. Or her backup would have been sent onto the stage.

Despite the letdown, this Bach Festival rookie — and avowed sports nut — found much to like in his debut concert, not the least of which was that the stylish 136-page programs were free. (I'm still paying installments on my last football program.)

I found the dress Sunday surprisingly unstuffy, though it's not as if four guys were shirtless in row one, with "B," "A," "C," "H" painted on their respective chests. Dark suits. Berets. Typical Eugene.

I liked the politeness of the crowd, which, if you're keeping score, was, by my count, 62 percent women. The average age was 50. (I always assumed a Bach Festival crowd would be really old, but now that I'm nearly 50, I no longer think that.)

There were no drunken loudmouths behind me offering play-by-play of the action. ("Now, listen up, the harpsichord is going to — hic! — become increasingly dominant and burst into an extended cadenza!")

Nobody swearing at a flutist whom they thought was dogging it.

Nobody wanting to fight because you went to the "wrong" school.

Instead, just a lot of quiet, polite people, all of them sitting there maybe thinking the same thing I was thinking: May my stomach not be the one that gurgles during this long, quiet stretch of music.

Sure, I would like to have seen some spontaneous applause for concertmaster Kathleen Lenski, a sort of player-coach who plays the violin with an infectious enthusiasm.

I was ready to yell "You duh man!" when Owen Burdick finished a riveting harpsichord solo.

And I thought trumpet player Guy Few deserved some hoots and fist pumps after he tooted about a bazillion notes in eight seconds, all of them seemingly in perfect pitch.

He plays trumpet with the same frenetic grace that a hummingbird flaps its wings. And accented his performance with a pair of black, burgundy-trimmed, knee-high boots — outside his pants.

(Note to Duck fans who think that sounds really bizarre: Your team next fall, with its new "lightning" uniforms, is going to look like an 11-pack of yellow Hi-Liters.)

But give this Bach crowd credit: At the end of each of the four concertos, the audience clapped with the endurance of marathoners.

At intermission — halftime to me — people talked quietly and sipped wine, draft beer, juice and water. I saw no flasks, nor guys in suits with beer cans strapped to their heads and tubes leading to their mouths.

In the men's bathroom, nobody waiting in line said, "Hey, speed it up, guys, there's another half to play." Nobody grumbled about the concertmaster, as in: "What's Lenski thinking, opening with *Concerto No. 3 in G Major?*"

At the concert's close — this was really cool — the musicians segued into the finest rendition of "Happy Birthday" I've ever heard to honor 70-year-old Helmuth Rilling, the Oregon Bach Festival's founding artistic director and conductor.

Amid the celebration, an item was held up on stage that reminded me of the best of both worlds: the whimsy of sports and the beauty of music, tied together as a token of a community's appreciation for a man who has greatly enriched our summers for the past 34 years.

It was the bobblehead Helmuth Rilling doll, of course.

July 1, 2003

The fine art of s'mores

THIS WEEKEND, according to my seasonal senses, marks the unofficial start of summer. Therefore I plan to try out the birthday present I got from friends last February, a glorious gift like none other I've received:

My own personal s'mores kit.

Everything for making my own s'mores: a box filled with kindling, logs, newspaper, matches, marshmallows, graham crackers and milk chocolate candy bars.

What more could a man ask for? (I know exactly what you're thinking, but don't go there. True, a personalized roasting stick would have been nice, but I dare say this was a thoughtful gift nevertheless.)

To me, s'mores, if not unique to Oregon, are at least one of our state's culinary delights, ranking in the lofty environs of barbecued salmon, strawberry shortcake and the cheeseburger basket at Vickie's Big Wheel in Waldport.

And yet in the otherwise wonderful book, *Northwest Basic Training: Essential Skills for Visitors, Newcomers & Native Northwesterners*, there is nary a mention of the art of s'mores-making. I can only surmise that the authors, to cater to our region's ever-increasing upscale crowd, felt it necessary to explain how to brew the perfect latte, but considered the act of s'mores-making as somehow gauche.

But to ignore the art of s'mores-making is to ignore regional history itself. While it may be true that the Girl Scouts introduced s'mores as popular culture in 1927, there is growing solidarity among Northwest academics that the three-part concoction has been around far longer.

When University of Oregon archaeologist Luther Cressman discovered the 9,000-year-old sandals at Fort Rock in 1938, for example, the soles tested positive for microscopic bits of all three s'mores ingredients. This led researchers to surmise that the wearer of the sandals may well have been history's first person to experience what's become known as "s'mores remorse" — the accidental dropping of a s'more and later stepping on it in the dark.

As with many good things, the growing popularity of s'mores has led to their exploitation. In the '80s, S'Mores cereal — like Golden Grahams though with bits of marshmallow and chocolate — hit the shelves. Now, stores sell instant s'mores in palm-sized packets.

The "S'mores Tart" is catching on at the Sundance Resort in Utah. And in San Francisco, the Buckeye Roadhouse restaurant encourages its guests to enjoy their post-dinner s'mores with a glass of port.

Must we tarnish every blessed tradition? Drink your port with some $7.95 Martha Stewart dessert, but please don't taint such a sacred aftertaste as that of the s'more. (A word, by the way, that Webster's dictionary has finally recognized.)

Why must we complicate the simple? Why must we change the very nature of this outdoorsy delight with such sickly variations? (Never mind that the palm-sized packets are actually extraordinarily tasty and will do quite nicely in a mid-winter pinch.)

I have read all the books and heard all the back-kitchen banter about what makes the perfect s'more. Homemade graham crackers, insist some. Use double chocolate. Don't let your marshmallows become Olympic torches; toast them to a golden brown.

To which I say: poppycock.

The keys to a good s'more are threefold and have little to do with marshmallows, graham crackers and chocolate. (Though, I confess, I plan on upgrading my birthday-present ingredients that were bought more than three months ago.)

First, be outside. The main reason s'mores taste good is the same reason nearly everything tastes good outdoors: Because it just does. It's one of nature's secrets, that all food, including mush, tastes better while camping or sitting around a beach fire or at a tailgater than inside. I've tried indoor s'mores. It's like watching a football game from a sky box, which I've also tried: just not the same.

Second, however you make your s'more, make it the same way each time. There is woefully little tradition in our lives these days and if it takes a gooey campfire treat to preserve the remnants of ritual, so be it. Repetition seals the experience. It's what unleashes all the memories of s'mores gone by. It's what makes grown-ups feel like children again. (Honestly, would there be wars if world leaders shared an occasional campfire and s'mores? I don't think so.)

Finally, ring your campfire with people you care about — the s'more the merrier. People who know you well enough to give you kindling for your birthday. And, most importantly, people who will happily hold the two pieces of graham cracker as you make a culinary delight — and a summer memory.

May 26, 2002

Hot chocolate travesty

ON A SUNDAY MORNING, June 8, 1930, University of Oregon professor Luther Cressman stopped at the lone cafe in Gold Hill near Medford. He was meeting a party of archaeologists planning to excavate a buried tomb near the Rogue River.

For the man who would, two decades later, discover a number of the century's most noteworthy archaeological finds, this day would represent Cressman's first dig.

"The owner-cook-waiter put a mug of hot coffee before me without waiting for my order," he writes in his memoir, *A Golden Journey*. Whereupon Cressman drank that coffee, ate his soon-ready breakfast and headed off to dig up bones.

Now, don't you see the travesty in all this? The presumptuous owner-cook-waiter assumed professor Cressman wanted coffee

— without even asking!

If, like the archaeologist, you contrast this seven-decade-old incident with the stone-flint artifacts of our current culture, you discover the obvious: We have been, and still are, a coffee-centric culture that deifies java at the expense of its brown-sheep cousin: hot chocolate.

More than 70 years after Cressman's discovery, we still percolate pathetically in the primordial ooze of "mono-drink think." In short, we still worship at the foot of a hill of beans, overlooking the many alternatives, including, ahem, cocoa.

"The government of a nation," the Duc de Richelieu observed centuries ago, "is often decided over a cup of coffee."

Sure, and Michelangelo painted the Sistine Chapel over a vanilla latte.

On this, the first day of winter, I come not as Old Man Bitter, here to blast coffee drinkers from Florence to Foley Ridge. (As Voltaire once said, "I may not agree with your choice of drinks, but I will fight for your right to drink it.") I seek only to awaken those who live with blinders on, unaware that there are hot chocolate drinkers in our midst. And, frankly, we're steamed.

We're tired of concession-stand workers who lavish their coffee customers with piping hot brews — "Cream? Sugar? Carrying tray?" — and, when asked for a hot chocolate, shove us a cup of lukewarm water, a Carnation packet and a wooden stir-stick the size of an anorexic Popsicle stick.

We're tired of seeing the name of our drink of choice tacked to the bottom of the cafe wall menu like a footnote, right next to "Children's Specials." So it doesn't have a sophisticated name such as "espresso macchiato" or "decaf sumatra" or "tazoberry frappuccino." We drink for substance, not style. (Plus, it's easier to pronounce and spell.)

We're tired of being looked down on because we order our drinks like this — "two medium hot chocolates, please" — instead of "ahem, I'll have a grande Ethiopia sidamo and a Tazo chai creme — easy on the froth."

On the other end of the social scale, at an elk-hunting camp, I recently found myself the only one of eight guys drinking hot chocolate. I sensed the held-back snickers when I asked to stow my packets in the chef's portable kitchen. You'd have thought I just rolled up to a bikers' bar on a fat-tire Schwinn, ringing my handlebar bell.

(Never mind the ugly truth that these hunters don't want revealed: This band of rough-tough cowboys brought along two — count 'em, two — espresso makers.)

But who was mentally scoffed at? Me.

Hot chocolate drinkers are looked upon as weaklings, wimps, the kind of folks who wear those Santa hats for most of December. No famous authors work deep into the night, fueled only by a pot of hot Swiss Miss. No power deal has ever been brokered by people with whipped cream on their upper lips.

After a while, you accept your second-class status. You accept that songs and books and movies glorify coffee, not cocoa. That the book *Northwest Basic Training* has two pages on "How to Be an Amateur Barista" but no mention of, say, "How to Make Your Own Mint Hot Chocolate."

We live in a coffee-crazed world. We live in a world of coffee tables, coffee cake and coffee klatsches.

Still, with all due respect to Mrs. Olsen and Juan Valdez, the world needs to realize that coffee isn't everyone's cup of tea.

All I ask is for a little respect. To those who scoff at those of us who are different from you, I offer warm winter greetings. And one small, chilly admonishment: Don't make the same mistake that owner-cook-waiter made 72 years ago in that Gold Hill cafe.

Instead, wake up and smell the hot chocolate.

December 22, 2002

Running from the truth

WASHINGTON — The FBI is warning police nationwide to be alert for people carrying almanacs, cautioning that the popular reference books ... could be used for terrorist planning.
— From a story in the Dec. 30, 2003, *Register-Guard*

This isn't easy for me to write, but when you've been running as long as I have, there comes a point where you simply say "Enough."

You're tired of living a lie. Tired of playing the game. And so, like

Leonardo DiCaprio in *Catch Me If You Can*, you finally stop, raise your hands and say: "OK, you win."

You see, I not only carry almanacs, I read them. I collect them. I'm trying to get every *World Almanac* since the year I was born (1954) and an *Oregon Blue Book* from every year it's been printed (1904-on).

That's not all. I've transported almanacs across state lines. Twice. I've bookmarked almanacs. Highlighted them. Asked for, and received, them for Christmas — as if, wrapped in festive paper, I could rationalize that they're actually virtuous "gifts of information" instead of the more sinister reality. As if I believed I had a constitutional right to keep and bear almanacs.

Like DiCaprio, I convinced myself — and others — that I was someone I was not. That I was a journalist, say, checking the spelling of Russian writer Aleksandr Solzhenitsyn's name or, in less tawdry pursuits, a trivia-lover fascinated with the idea that somewhere you can find what is the Westernmost Town in the 48 Contiguous States (La Push, Wash.).

Carrying an almanac from, say, the Book Mark to my house, I was so intent in avoiding the darker truth that I willed myself to believe my intentions were honorable. As if, were I questioned about carrying that almanac — in some warehouse with a lone light bulb swaying ever so slightly — I might say: "Honest, I needed to know what day of the week June 10 was in 1944" (Saturday).

If you live a lie long enough, you forget what truth really is. I found myself carrying almanacs often, sometimes in broad daylight. Yachats. Newport. Lincoln City. My trail of deceit knew no end as I poked around in used-book stores while "vacationing" at the coast.

I would walk into some shop, ever mindful of an ambush, and say something like: "Do you have any, uh, books published annually, containing information, usually statistical, on many subjects?"

The clerk, often a middle-aged woman wearing a "Life's a Beach" button, would act decidedly nonplussed. "Depends on who's looking," she'd reply with a slight bat of the eyes.

Quickly, I would check the store's seagull woodcarvings and glass floats for bugs. "Let's just say I'm an ordinary Joe looking for a list of some Notable U.S. Tornadoes Since 1925 — if you know what I mean."

It was always a nervous moment, like when you blindly press

your remote without knowing whether you're going to get "Last Channel" or "Volume Up." Was this clerk on to me, perhaps a government plant? Or did she have ties to al-Qaeda and suspect I was some CIA mole with an inordinate amount of interest in 5-point facts about poker odds and Opera Singers of the Past?

To be honest, I liked the risk involved. In a way, I suppose, I was the klepto wanting to get caught, knowing deep down that I was wrong and needed help. And knowing that this little story would always have an unhappy ending — me, sitting in jail somewhere, wondering if I'd ever again have the chance to look up Tokyo Disneyland's yearly attendance (17.7 million in 2001).

But in my dreams, I'm more heroic in the end. A couple of fresh-from-Quantico FBI suits are chasing me around the lobby of Mac Court during a game when I see them head into the vacant press room.

I walk in. Their backs are to me. It's just me and them.

"Freeze, suckers!" I say. "I have an almanac and I'm not afraid to use it."

January 8, 2004

The hidden life of authors

A NUMBER OF YOU have asked me what it was like on my "book tour" this summer, so I'll tell you.

First, I've been on a "book tour" in the same way a man canoeing the millrace has been on an "exotic cruise." Mostly, I've spoken to lots of service clubs — the *Pledge of Allegiance* is now almost the daily experience it was in grade school — and done lots of "book signings," a sometimes inaccurate phrase in that it suggests — "signings," plural — that you sold more than one book.

People like ex-Baywatch star Pamela Anderson, another of my editor's authors, go on book tours. People like me do not, the authenticity of our bodies apparently doing nothing to score us points with our publishers.

A lot of people imagine a certain romance to "book touring" that is hard to see when you're speaking to a dozen members of a Lions Club at the Pearl Street Ice Cream Parlour and a siren suddenly starts blaring in the other room and someone begins beating a bass drum. Someone, you realize, is getting a free birthday sundae — right during your speech.

And you think: Does John Grisham have to go through this?

Two minutes before a scheduled interview at a small-town radio station, is Maya Angelou told by the person interviewing her that "I'm sorry, but I don't know who you are or why you're here."

Does Mitch Albom show up to give a speech and find himself, and those who have showed up to hear him, locked out of the auditorium?

In New Orleans, I was speaking and showing a DVD to 100 nurse practitioners. Five minutes before I was to take the hotel stage, the Barnes & Noble representative who was supposed to be selling books hadn't arrived — and the sound system wasn't working.

In Boston, I showed up at a B&N, only to find that it had canceled my signing weeks ago but hadn't bothered to inform me or my publisher. I told the man, as pleasantly as possible, that a deal is a deal. I didn't care if only four people showed up, we're going to have a signing. We did. Four people showed up.

That's four times as many people as came to a signing in Portland for a previous book of mine years ago. And the lone person who did thought I'd written a book on goat cheese. (After two hours of doing nothing, you're tempted to pretend you are the author of the book on goat cheese.)

In June, I got up at 3 a.m. to drive to Portland for a national TV interview. In a studio, I sat in front of a picture of Mount Hood while a man in New York interviewed me through a little earpiece for six minutes. The piece never ran.

On one of the hottest nights of the summer, I spoke in a Bellingham, Wash., bookstore. Eighteen people showed up, which was encouraging given that I have no Bellingham ties and the room was a book-lined sauna. But only two bought books.

Like gone-ballistic Michael Douglas in the Whammy Burger scene in *Falling Down,* I wanted to block the exit with a kung-fu stance and say: "OK, folks, nobody gets outta here without buying at least one book — understood?"

What makes it all worthwhile are the signings with good hosts, speeches with great audiences and interviews by media types who have actually looked beyond the back cover. Then there's the occasional reversal-of-fortune moments: In New Orleans, just as you step to the podium, the DVD sound gets fixed and the B&N woman magically appears with 80 books, all but seven of which will be sold an hour later.

Ah, but as an obscure author, you must never get cocky. You're signing books in the Smithsonian Institution when a young man spots you and strides purposefully your way. He picks up a copy of the book like Indiana Jones having finally found the Lost Ark of the Covenant.

"Did you write this?" he asks.

"I did."

"So," he said, "is there a bathroom around here?"

July 31, 2004

My evening with Andy

TUCSON, Ariz. — On the roof of the Sonoran Ballroom at a cactus-ringed resort, columnists from around the country sipped drinks and shared small talk. The same warm, evening winds that were whipping the Aspen Fire 40 miles east fluttered ties and dresses.

Suddenly, I saw him, the man whose favor I coveted: Andy Rooney.

The "60 Minutes" commentator and 24/7 curmudgeon was surrounded by people. This was a hopeful sign; I was thinking he might slip in, accept the Ernie Pyle Lifetime Achievement Award from the National Society of Newspaper Columnists, then split. And I'd never get my big chance.

Frankly, I was surprised he'd agreed to come; after all, this was the same guy who'd recently chided journalists for giving out too many awards. But, drink in hand, he seemed to be enjoying himself.

From a distance, I clutched my copy of *My War*, his book about reporting for the army's *Stars and Stripes* newspaper while in France during World War II.

The autograph, I confess, wasn't my ultimate goal. Though nice, I hoped it might stall him so I could make my pitch: Would he consider endorsing a book I've written — and due out next spring — about the first World War II nurse to die after the landings at Normandy? Twice I'd written him. No response.

I joined the ring around Rooney and realized just getting to him was going to be hard enough, much less getting time to chat. But suddenly, a group left, and it was just one man telling a Charles Kuralt story to Rooney. And me.

I tried to pretend I was the third part of this conversation — you know, nodding and looking interested even though I wasn't. Once, Rooney, dressed in a dark suit, nodded at me, which I took as a subtle sign that he'd somehow welcomed me around his campfire.

But I knew I didn't belong. This was, after all, one of the most recognizable faces on the planet, a man who tells stories about sharing a tent with Ernie Pyle. Author. Columnist. Commentator. And all-around equal-opportunity offender, a guy who's honked off presidents, gays, blacks, Republicans, Democrats, the French and a truck driver in New York whom he yelled at for littering.

And who was I? Some nobody from Are-Uh-Gawn wearing khakis and a poorly tied basketball tie.

Suddenly, it was just Andy Rooney and me. It was as if the wind stopped blowing.

We shook hands. His eyebrows, I noticed, look even larger in person than on TV, like those cotton ball eyebrows kids glue on their construction-paper Santa Clauses.

He's a small man, around 5 feet. His cheeks aren't as rosy without makeup. He walks with a stoop. (Heck, he's 84; he has a right to.)

I'd considered leading with a quick "ice-breaker" — something like, "You're right, naps are underrated" — but instead began stammering about my book. About this nurse who wrote a touching letter about the American GI to the same *Stars & Stripes* newspaper for which he had written in 1944 — and then was killed in a field hospital tent the next night.

I showed him a copy of the nurse's letter as it appeared in *Stars & Stripes*. He looked at it. His brow furrowed. "Yes, yes, I remember this," he said. "Sure."

My heart quickened. I'd survived the preliminary heat; now for the finals. "So would you consider reading the galleys and perhaps — "

"No," he said, about as subtly as a belly flop. "I never do endorsements. I get three offers a week, and I turn them all down. Don't have time."

He looked at the name on my badge — "want to spell it right" — and wrote in the book: "To Bob Welch. Tucson. Andy Rooney."

After dinner, I found myself next to him in the dessert line. "Don't suppose you've reconsidered," I said.

"No," he assured me.

Later, he gave a light yet crusty acceptance speech. Then, during a transition in the program, he got up and shuffled toward the door. "No offense," he said to anyone within earshot. And, just like that, he walked into the warm Arizona night.

I smiled to myself. None taken.

June 24, 2003

Peace with the past

H E HEARD the commercial for the play on a Eugene radio station, but tried to ignore it.

For nearly five years, roughly since he had moved to Eugene, he had been trying to ignore *Les Misérables*. That's what you must do when, if not running from the past, you're at least trying to put off the pain of making peace with it.

After all, that's what the play's lead character, the thief Jean Valjean, did, didn't he? Tried to run from his past?

Ah, but then, out of nowhere, comes a touch of grace and, depending on what you do with that grace, you're blessed. And equally blessed are those who have offered it.

Kurk Davidson remembered the times he had turned down friends who wanted to drag him to the play, set in 19th-Century France. "I can't," he'd say. "It's like surgery. The wounds are too fresh."

But something — serendipity, he would later surmise — drew him in this time. And so last Friday night he spent $5 on a play at North Eugene High for which people on Broadway once paid $90 — in part, to see him as the lead, Jean Valjean.

From 1993 to 1998, Davidson, 43, performed the National Tour show about 2,000 times — eight shows a week, across the country, including at Eugene's Hult Center. And during that time, he spent more than a year on Broadway.

Davidson had made a six-figure salary. And had fallen in love with Eugene when he performed here in the mid-'90s, thinking sometime he might settle here when he "semiretired." He did, in 1998, taking a job in sales.

Now, in his North Eugene theater seat, he fidgeted slightly. "It's like having a dog you really love for a long time and then having to take him to the pound," he would later say. "You don't want to see him again."

Meanwhile backstage, the cast of 70 prepped for a show that, though simplified and shortened for high schoolers, was still a huge leap; every line, for example, is sung, not spoken. Director Al Villanueva had put on 26 shows in the past 13 years. None was the challenge of *Les Misérables*.

Through a cast member's mother who knew Davidson, word filtered to the director about the actor's presence. "Listen up, folks," announced Villanueva shortly before curtain. "A man who's played Jean Valjean on Broadway is in the audience tonight."

Some thought "Mr. V" was joking. Then a buzz rose from the cast and crew. A huge smile creased the face of Greg Mathans, who plays Javert, the inspector who dogs Valjean.

Steve Fargher gulped; he plays Jean Valjean. "I was freaked out," he says.

Once on stage, Fargher couldn't forget who was out in that audience. It was like a Kidsports quarterback playing a game with Joey Harrington in the stands.

In the audience, Davidson's apprehensions began melting like spring snow. "I was really, really impressed," he says. "These kids exceeded all my expectations. They had obviously made a serious commitment to a very difficult piece. It wasn't flawless, but it worked."

After the play, when Villanueva asked Davidson if he would come backstage, something happened: It turned out that these kids needed him as much as he needed them.

He figured he'd stay for 10 or 15 minutes. He wound up staying for three hours.

With Villanueva's blessing, Davidson offered vocal tips. He answered question after question.

"Like an onion, we tried to peel away the layers to see who these characters really were," he says.

"He showed me how my character, Marius, goes through all these maturation stages," Justin Diller says.

"He'd ask you questions so you'd think more about your part," Fargher says. "He said: 'How do you think a father would act if he were saying goodbye to his child for the last time?'"

"You would take in every strand of her hair and the way it falls across her face," Davidson told him, "and how her fingers feel in your hand. Because that would be your snapshot for eternity."

Co-director Maida Belove watched in awe. "It was as if he just got the bug again," she says. "You could just feel it oozing out of him."

Someone asked if Davidson would sing for them. No, thanks, he said; anyway, there's no piano player.

"Javier!" people started shouting. Javier Hernandez, the orchestra's pianist, went to the piano and began playing *God on High*, one of the show's more moving pieces. Davidson broke into song, his voice strong and pure.

"He wasn't doing this for himself," says Chelsea Mortenson, who plays Madame Thenardier. "He was doing it for our benefit."

Finally, about 1 o'clock in the morning, Villanueva intervened. "Hey, folks we have another show tomorrow," he said. "Let's get some sleep."

The next afternoon, Davidson showed up before the play with a dress. He'd made it — yes, made it — for Molly McCarthy, who plays Fantine. "She looked too frumpy," he says. So he'd prowled thrift stores until he found old drapes that he dyed from yellow to blue and turned into more appropriate attire. The dress imbued McCarthy with new confidence.

"He's helped Fantine more than any other character," Belove says. "He told Molly: 'Fantine is the diva of *Les Miz*.'"

The next day, for Sunday's matinee, Davidson brought a coat that he thought would be more appropriate for Eponine (played by Logan Loomer). And helped with hair and makeup.

On Wednesday, he was back on stage, coaching actors. The lines flowed from him as if he were still singing the part nightly.

In the same situation, some directors might have worried about Davidson "stealing the show." Davidson worried himself about overstepping his bounds. "But one thing about Al," Belove says: "He doesn't have a huge ego."

"Kurk raised the level of the show," Villanueva says. "He's been an amazing gift to us."

Ah, but, again, touches of grace work both ways.

"Al's been awesome about this whole thing," Davidson says. "I mean, when *Les Miz* was first put on, it had eight directors — eight. But with few resources, Al found a way to make this play work.

"The cool thing for me is how these kids 'get it.' It's not, like, 'Dude, whatever.' You can see the light come on. It's been a very healing experience for me. Cathartic. A sort of closure."

Saturday night, when the curtain comes down on the end of the three-weekend run, Davidson will return to his life. And the North kids he's touched will return to theirs.

But for now — "it's almost as if the stars were lined up just for this," Davidson says — North Eugene thespians have a "remember-the-time" story for the future. And one of Broadway's Jean Valjeans has made peace with the past.

February 27, 2003

The Bard and I

ASHLAND — I'd make a pathetic Renaissance Man, not that I'd ever be invited to join the club.

There I was Saturday afternoon, sitting in a 1905 Victorian cottage, trying to understand Shakespeare's *Richard III* by reading Cliffs Notes. (What, you expected me to be doing something as gauche as, say, watching the NCAA basketball tournament?)

I might be a cultural neophyte, but when that curtain went up at 8 o'clock Saturday for this Oregon Shakespeare Festival production, I was going to be ready for my first experience with Live Bard.

This weekend, given to us as a gift, was not to be frittered away, but embraced. Thus had my wife and I already taken in the Friday night production of *The Philanderer* and were transitioning into the Shakespearean spirit by staying in a cottage well-splashed with Bardian themes. Soon came the inevitable "Shake-speak."

"Parting is such sweet sorrow," I said when leaving to fetch hot chocolates for breakfast. And later: "My wallet, my wallet! My kingdom for my wallet!"

And yet three paragraphs into the *Cliffs Notes'* "Historical Background" my new-found bravado wilted like a Love Canal daisy. "Head of the White Rose party was Richard Plantagenet, third Duke of York, whose claim to the throne was an impressive one. On his mother's side of the family, he was descended from Lionel, Duke of Clarence, elder brother of John of Gaunt, from whom the Lancastrians were descended."

Say what? I was so confused that, in an attempt to block outside distractions, I nearly resorted to turning off Gonzaga-Texas Tech. Undaunted, I multitasked my way onward, trying to figure out who this Richard dude was and where he was headed.

Just before show time, we stopped by a gift shop where, flipping through a book on Shakespeare, I learned something that only increased my mounting fear: *Richard III* has 3,619 lines, making it among the longest of Shakespeare's plays.

Gulp.

Out of the darkness came Richard, Duke of Gloucester, part monster, part George Carlin.

Barely had he spoken the first of his 1,117 lines — "Now is the winter of our discontent ..." — when I was mesmerized. As were many of the nearly 600 people in the Angus Bowmer Theatre, I believe.

This was drama like I had never seen it. Drama where you needn't worry about some sophomore with braces flubbing a line or falling into the orchestra pit. Where gestures and nuances explained what the *Cliffs Notes* could not. Where you became so absorbed in the story that you completely forgot about what might be happening with, say, Wake Forest-West Virginia.

Like some rule-defiant 16th seed, cocky enough to believe it could win the NCAA tournament, Richard worms his way deep into the bracket. He lies, cheats and beheads his way into the Final Four. (Motto: "We will, we will rock you.") And soon wears the crown.

At intermission I headed for the bathroom with shouts of "Long Live King Richard III!" still ringing in my ears. Unlike in the bathroom at a high school play, where you might overhear someone say something like, "Richard is rushing his lines because he wants to catch the dance in the cafeteria before it gets over," people keep to themselves during Shakespeare breaks.

After the break, ominous signs suggest his reign will end. His victims haunt him in a dream, a sort of ghostly "wait till next year." Finally, on Bosworth Field, Richmond, apparently some Atlantic-10 upstart, challenges Richard III.

He doesn't have the horses to pull it off — "my kingdom for a horse!" — and his reign endeth, though Richmond & Co. are classy winners and don't resort to chants of "It's all over! ... It's all over!"

But it was all over.

And I was the richer for having experienced it, this intriguing new March madness to which I must hasten back.

March 22, 2005

Ward & the Country Fair

IT IS SATURDAY morning and we are getting ready to go to the Oregon Country Fair. "We" meaning my alter ego, Ward Cleaver, and I.

"Honey, have you seen our loincloth?" we ask June.

We are just kidding, of course. We don't actually own a loincloth. We rent one from The Loin Shop, complete with cummerbund.

No, actually, not being hippily hip, we do the best we can: throw on an old growth forest green T-shirt. ("Save a writer. Buy a book") Beige shorts, whose mainstream look, we hope, will be mitigated by their being splashed with housepaint. And sandals.

(We hope nobody will see the little Nike swoosh on the sandals. If they do, we fear being boiled in patchouli oil or, worse, forced to eat a falafel.)

To give us that social-revolutionary look, we have not shaved our face in three days, which instead gives us that "this-guy-is-try-ing-too-hard-to-make-a-statement" look — unlike, say, the guy with what appears to be a blue goiter the size of a watermelon on his head or the 10-foot-tall, all-silver woman with the traffic-cones bra.

Somewhere between seeing a CPA-ish sort of guy wearing deer antlers and a woman in a giant high-chair put 10-foot long "nir-vana tubes" into each ear — like a jet being refueled — I realize something: We're not in Mayfield anymore.

Not, of course, that this is the first Country Fair for us. It is our second.

Some things are a rerun. Like last time, we see a guy with a small spear through his nose, like in *National Geographic*. And, like last time, we want to ask him how he blows his nose but, of course, wouldn't want him to feel self-conscious.

But some things have changed. Our first clue is when we see a young man wearing a sarong. Nothing new about that, of course. But, we confess, it's the first time we've seen a young man wearing a sarong and holding a cell phone in his hand at the same time.

Cell phones are sprinkled throughout the forested paths, like an outbreak of measles. But if it's odd to hear one ring amid, say, a pulsating ancient drum ritual, it's not like we don't see and hear a few other odd juxtapositions on this sunny Saturday.

We hear a young woman dressed like Cleopatra address a friend with that common 35 B.C. greeting, "Wassup?"

We see people meditating in a temple of idols; nearby, blues-singer Eagle Park Slim rasps, "come back baby — please don't go."

We see a fairy princess — wings and all — lying on the grass near the Long Tom River, as if straight from some children's picture book, then taking a deep drag on a Marlboro.

We see people who have forgotten clothing items they need, including a heavy-set reveler whose breasts jiggle like Jell-O. And we think: He's going to get a killer sunburn if he doesn't get a shirt on fast.

This is the only place in the world where, relatively speaking, Frog the jokebook salesman comes off looking like the president of a Rotary club.

We conclude that the Oregon Country Fair is part Halloween, part Woodstock, part Renaissance Fair and part Costco, though the latter doesn't sell hemp jewelry, tie-dye tepees and bedspreads made of recycled clothes.

We journey on. We see The Mud Woman. We see a woman with so many facial piercings that her head looks like a giant pin cushion. We see a guy in a robe so bright and flowing he looks like a human spinnaker.

We smell food, incense, cigarette smoke and, occasionally, burning leaves. We taste the former — stir-fried chicken and loganberry punch from the Bi-Coastal Cafe. Excellent.

So, too, is much of the music, especially some of the "ambiance" folks such as Jonny Hahn on the piano and Eagle Park Slim.

We hear a laptop-connected astrologer trying to cut a deal with a prospective customer by saying he's not in this for the money.

"Cool," says the client, "because that's not an energy force I'm hip to."

Everywhere we go, people want to do something for us: They want to give us a massage or read our palms or blow into our ears ("sound therapy") or sell us something from Dr. Vortex's Traveling Medicine Show.

But all we really want is a bathroom, in that we're not wearing diapers like another 40-something guy we saw.

With the heat intensifying and the crowds clogging the pathways, we decide to go home. We head back to Mayfield on an LTD bus. Back to 211 Pine St., where we kick back in our easy chair.

"Did you have fun, dad?" asks our youngest son.

"Well, Beaver," we say, "sometimes in life we — well, we encounter energy forces that we're not hip to. But other than that, yeah, we had a swell time."

July 5, 2001

Cowboy Dinner Tree

EDITOR'S NOTE: The following column contains graphic descriptions of beef. Reader discretion advised.

SILVER LAKE — The great thing about Oregon is that just when you're feeling it's becoming like every other state in the union — neutered into PC-injected, strip-mall-reflected sameness — you find yourself sitting in a restaurant from whose ceiling hangs an "emasculator," a pliers-like implement used to castrate bulls.

Welcome to the Cowboy Dinner Tree Restaurant, which, even as it thrills your taste buds and clogs your arteries, warms your soul with the assurance that the Wild West still lives.

After chowing down at the restaurant Saturday night, I've concluded that what it doesn't have is as significant as what it does.

It has no menu. It has no electricity. And, as you might have gathered by the pliers, it has no pretense whatsoever when it comes to decor.

What it has, instead, is a following that seems totally incongruous with its location: 80 miles southeast of Bend, surrounded by nothing but sagebrush, juniper trees and howling coyotes. There've been lunar landings in less remote spots. Some waitresses commute 2 1/2 hours — one way.

But when our party of four arrived, about 50 people were already packed into the restaurant and another half-dozen waited outside. Owners Marcie and Al Prom have served up to 299 people in a single night.

The Proms — he's 63, she's "in her 50s" — opened the restaurant in 1993 with a hunch and a $27.50 ad in the Lake County *Examiner*. Now, thanks to word of mouth and a few newspaper and magazine articles, the Dinner Tree attracts an average of 200 people per summer night.

The restaurant is named for a massive juniper out back where cowboys once congregated for chow.

Regular customers drive — and sometimes fly, there being a Forest Service airstrip nearby — from Alaska, California, even New York. The couple sitting next to me were from Connecticut. Folks from Eugene have been known to make the 3 1/2 -hour drive — one way — just for dinner.

"We figure we have to give people a reason to drive out here," says Marcie.

And that reason, basically, is steaks roughly the size of catcher's mitts, which is why nearly everyone goes home with a plastic bag of meat.

The front-door frame of the Dinner Tree — indeed, its entire roof — sags like a telephone line. You open the door by pulling on a deer antler. You pour salt and pepper from jars that have nail-punched holes in the top.

The floors are wood-planked, the ceiling held up by pine poles, the seating tight. The place has fewer matching chairs than Eugene has matching opinions.

Smoke wafts through from the propane-fueled, half-barrel grills out back; otherwise, it's a nonsmoking restaurant. A handful of bare light bulbs hang from the ceiling, available for generator-driven use after sunset.

But enough bragging about the atmosphere; on to the food, which is the real reason that more than just hunters frequent this place.

The choices are simple: beef or chicken. And you must make your pick when making your reservations.

"We have no menu," says Marcie. "I'm the menu."

If you order the chicken, that's what you get: a chicken.

Either way, the meal costs $18.50.

Ours began with salad, soup and yeast rolls, the latter made from Al's grandmother's recipe, and concluded with apple crisp; excellent, all.

But beef was the star of the show.

The restaurant is just a day's cattle drive south of Fort Rock, where those 9,000-year-old sandals were found. That seems appropriate because there's something almost cavemanlike about this experience.

When the waitress brings your steak, you imagine that Flintstonian scene where the carhop places Fred's dinosaur ribs on the window tray and his foot-mobile flips.

"Today, 8- to 10-ounce steaks are the norm and it's highly unusual to find 16-plus," says Marcie. "Ours are 26 to 30. Everyone has a gimmick; this is ours."

After the steaks arrived, our table looked like an egg carton stuffed with bowling balls. Tasty bowling balls, though: tender, juicy and spiced with a 14-ingredient dry marinade.

We finished about a quarter of our main courses, paid our bill — no credit cards accepted — and stopped by the gift shop. There we all resisted buying the rattlesnake skins that had been mounted by an 82-year-old woman down the road who, of course, had shot and skinned them herself.

Outside, Marcie's grill sizzled. And diners headed off into the sunset, nearly all of them clutching a plastic bag.

And a little piece of the West.

July 5, 2001

Feeding the lake

PORTLAND — For every student who, far from your youth, decided to pursue something new, this story is for you. For every teacher who, flailing in inexperience, wondered if you put even a small piece in a student's puzzle, this story is for you, too.

It reached its zenith Saturday night when Willamette Writers, the state's largest literary organization, presented Jane Kirkpatrick with its Distinguished Northwest Writer Award. Among recipients of the past: Ken Kesey and Ursula Le Guin.

In accepting the award, Kirkpatrick, 59, quoted author Jean Rhys to 400 people at the Airport Embassy Suites Hotel: "All of life is like a lake made up of many stories, fed by many streams. Some of the streams are long and mighty, like Tolstoy and Dostoevsky, and some are small, like me. The size of the stream doesn't matter. All that matters is the lake. Feed the lake."

Kirkpatrick, who lives on the John Day River in north-central Oregon, told how, at age 36, she first tested the literary waters. Head of Deschutes County Mental Health in Bend, she took a writing class through Central Oregon Community College's adult education program. "I was terrified," she said Saturday in a post-event interview. "I thought: I don't belong here."

The teacher, she later learned, felt the same way about himself. But, neophyte that he was, he still recognized good writing, once choosing a piece by Kirkpatrick to read aloud. "My heart was pounding so hard I could hardly hear the reading," she said. When he handed back her paper, it said at the bottom: "You have a gift."

At the time, she and husband Jerry were still reeling from the loss of Jerry's son, murdered at 21. She was suffering from a serious gluten intolerance. They needed a change.

The two decided to sell everything, leave secure jobs and homestead on the John Day River, where Jane would write.

At a place called Starvation Point, the home would be known as their "Rural 7-Eleven" — seven miles from their mailbox, 11 from pavement. They built it. Dug a well. Battled rattlesnakes. And ran seven miles of underground phone wire.

Once semi-settled, Jane began writing and sending stories to magazines. Rejection. Rejection. Rejection. Then it happened: One sold. *Sports Afield*, for $75, bought a piece she wrote on repairing fishing poles with pine tar. Then *Northwest* magazine bought the story her teacher had read aloud in the class.

She began wondering: Could I?

Jane began working as a mental health counselor at Warm Springs Indian Reservation. On Tuesdays, she would make the nearly three-hour drive — longer during snow and ice — and on

Thursdays, return.

Then she would start writing, disciplining herself to get up at 4 a.m. Her first book, *Homestead* (1991), was about her experience on the John Day. Thirteen followed — fictional stories of the human heart, based on real events, and often involving women and Native Americans.

The latest release is *A Land of Sheltered Promise*, about the area near Antelope that the Rajneesh cult developed in the '80s and is now home to a Young Life youth camp.

At least some of her empathy for those overcoming odds comes from her own experiences. She and Jerry were badly hurt when their small airplane crashed. They took in a granddaughter whose drug-hampered parents weren't able to raise her. She lost a sister to disease in 1997. Now, Jerry, 75, is battling bladder cancer.

"It's the obstacles in life that carve out our character," says Kirkpatrick. "Character comes from the Greek word 'to chisel.' It's what's left after you've been 'gouged out.'"

What some of her colleagues were applauding Saturday night — none perhaps more enthusiastically than I — was the never-quit spirit that she writes of. And lives.

While working on a book of my own, for instance, I would often hear the alarm at 5 a.m. and think: no, no, no. But then I would get up, remembering that, at Starvation Point, my ex-student Jane had already been up for an hour.

Feeding the lake.

August 9, 2005

7.

Games
of life

Desperately seeking Jerry

YACHATS — I thought I'd gotten beyond all this. Thought I'd grown up. Thought I could spend a weekend at the coast without watching an Oregon football game that promised to be a lopsided yawner anyway.

In a 70-year-old cabin with no television, I had made peace with the idea of listening to the Oregon-Arizona game on the radio. In fact, the idea had a certain nostalgia to it. As a kid, I'd spent many a Saturday night listening to my then-beloved Beavers on the cabin's radio. It would be fun. Alas, sometimes we forget how sick we really are.

When I first found the game on the dial, KUGN sportscaster Jerry Allen sounded as if he were broadcasting from 20,000 leagues beneath the sea — "Fife ... glub, glub ... Parker wide open ... glub, glub ... back after this glub, glub ... "

Never mind that the Washington State-USC game from Pullman was crystal clear. Never mind that Cal Davis-Sacramento State came in as if it were being played just down the beach. Never mind that I could get hockey from Canada, road reports from Seattle, talk radio from San Francisco and channels in Spanish and

German.

The Ducks faded in and out as if the AM frequency gods were fiendishly twisting the volume dial just to spite me. Allen was losing the broadcasting war to oldie goldies, some guy talking about "getting inside the transient mind" and the president of a long-shoremen's union in San Francisco.

I heard a scratchy "48-12." Had the Ducks' offense gone berserk? No, lotto numbers from Washington. Then, later, "85 to 90." Sunday's predicted high for San Jose.

After experimenting with three radios for 20 minutes, I determined that Oregon was down 14-7. The Ducks were in trouble, all because I was unable to connect with them.

You see, I'm one of those fans who believes the more "connected" I am to a game, the better Oregon will play. Is it any coincidence that, in 1988, I left for Haiti with the Ducks 6-1 and bound for the Rose Bowl, and returned to find them 6-4 and bound for 6-6? Is it any coincidence that my moving to Eugene in 1989 coincided with the Ducks' rise to national prominence?

I don't think so. But now, if I didn't connect soon, Oregon was looking at an upset loss — and Bellotti would be pointing the finger my way. I madly twisted the dials. Allen was fading and returning like Eugene's cross-on-the-butte controversy.

Once, he came back with a voice reverberating like Tommy James and the Shondells singing *Crimson and Clover*. Then he'd be broadcasting live from inside the engine of a turn-of-the-century locomotive. And, finally, from beside a giant maraca keeping beat to *The Girl From Ipanema*.

I started getting worried when Fife threw a long pass to Lucy in the sky with diamonds.

Enough of this. I raced outside and flicked on the truck radio. But Allen's voice was no stronger than that guy who gets transformed from man to insect ("Help me! Help me!") in *The Fly*. I drove down the road trying to find a better spot for reception. ("Help me! Help me!") Nope.

Third and long. Don't panic. Look for a secondary receiver — in this case, the vacant vacation home of a friend. Before leaving town, I'd gotten the OK to watch the game on his cable TV should the unthinkable happen. And, clearly, the unthinkable was happening. Who knows how many touchdowns Arizona had scored with me out of touch.

I couldn't read the numbers on the house's lock-box so I drove my truck onto the cement porch for light. Once inside, I was faced with two remotes, a defense I hadn't expected.

Too late to call a timeout. I started madly punching buttons on both. I surfed high and low. Baseball. Talking heads. "Cops." But no Ducks. Whatever cable company my ex-friend had, it wasn't carrying the Oregon game.

Fourth and long. I drove through the fog-shrouded night toward my only hope. I'm not, by nature, a "lounge guy" but desperate times call for desperate measures; suddenly, I found myself standing next to a two-man band whose lead singer was pretending he was Rod Stewart singing *Tonight's the Night*.

Indeed, I knew it was gonna be all right — when I found a TV in the loft tuned to the game. No sound. But an image — and a score that showed the Ducks up 24-14 — not surprising, now that I was reconnected.

I watched for about half an hour, long enough to hear the singer sound like Elton John, America and a host of other oldies. And long enough to watch a bride and groom saunter in, she in a floor-length wedding dress, he in a tux.

I'd never experienced Duck football quite like I did on this night. I left with Oregon up 31-14, feeling a bit sheepish that I hadn't stayed until the end.

But, hey, it's only a game, right?

October 8, 2002

Return of the tailgater

IT WAS SATURDAY morning before the Oregon-Arizona football game. "I'm scared," I told my friend Ann.

A professional caterer, she tried to be empathetic, but how could she know the fears coursing through the veins of a guy who was only hours away from hosting his first tailgate party in six years?

A guy still haunted by '94 — the ghostly faces of the weary guests who, when they finally found my pickup, looked like the Donner Party in Duckwear?

A guy still stung from the computer-made map that one such

guest had later sent out, mocking the map I'd made, his sardonic "replica" showing the Earth with a giant arrow pointing toward North America above the label: "Welch's tailgater. See you there!"

So I'd become like Ted Striker, the guilt-ridden former military pilot in *Airplane!* — a man whose failures prevented him from ever again taking control of his two-burner Sunbeam.

But as the years passed, a lone briquette burned deep in my soul. Life is short, I've realized; you must make burgers while there's propane in your tank.

Thus did the maps go out last week, only this time imploring my guests to look for the high-flying American flag/UO flag combination. I would not be humiliated again. I would be distinctive. I would be found.

I bought the food: burgers, dogs, chips and — the coup de grace — green and yellow cupcakes that contained a bunch of those ingredients you've never heard of, like pyrophosphate, which sounds like it could catch your intestines on fire. Perfect.

I confess, though, I put more attention into the flagpole than the food. I'd devised a 30-foot, three-section pole consisting of 1 1/4-inch PVC pipe, the lower splice fortified by a 5-foot-long wooden dowel.

Along with thousands of others, I arrived at Autzen Stadium as the gates opened, found a spot and began duct-taping together the pole — just as I'd done in my mind so many times before. I wedged a barbell bar vertically between the pickup cab and bed, securing it sideways with rubber tie-down straps from my tire chains and at ground level with a 60-pound concrete block left over from a landscape project.

The PVC pipe would slide neatly over the barbell. But as I picked up the flag pole, fear gripped my gut: This baby was far heavier, and flimsier, than I'd imagined. I'm an arts guy, not a science guy, and in my zest to have the best I'd forgotten something important: physics.

Alas, I am my father's son and believe that with enough duct tape, anything is possible. So I stood in that pickup bed and, with an Iwo Jima pose, tried desperately to plant the flag. By now, a cold wind had picked up; the flags whipped this way and that. People were stopping to watch. The butt of the pole gyrated wildly in my hands.

This was not at all how I'd imagined the moment. I was sweating. Exhausted. Embarrassed. From the eyes of my fellow tailgaters, I must have looked like a madman trying to stuff a crazed cat in a box. But finally I slid the PVC over the barbell bar and stood back with relief and pride.

One slight problem: My flagpole was bent like a pole-vault pole at full flex. I'd imagined it going straight up, the two flags waving proudly as guests instantaneously flocked to my tailgater: "More cupcakes with sodium silico aluminate anyone?"

Instead, the pole was bent like an upside-down fish hook, swaying back and forth, threatening to snap. I wrestled it down, ripped off the duct tape, took out a 10-foot section and replanted it. Still too whippy.

I was doomed: Take off another entire section and I'm lost in RV Canyon, destined to repeat the miserable failure of '94. Don't and I'm facing a wrongful death suit.

Suddenly, I remembered it: the miniature hacksaw in my emergency tool chest. I sawed off a portion of a 10-foot section — were other tailgaters using their hacksaws, too? — and planted it. Perfecto!

I set up the rest of the party: An old closet door stretched from the tailgate to a contractor's roller-stand tripod as my main serving table. My grill was ready to go. So where was everybody?

I waited and waited. Finally, I walked a few rows over and another one of those uh-oh feelings hit: I realized I wasn't the only one to have the American/UO flag combo. In fact, many others had stolen my idea.

Alas, all I could do was wait some more. Finally, nearly an hour after the event was to begin — I was doing my best to act like I enjoyed partying solo — a former college roommate showed up. Two-thirds of the guest list eventually trickled in.

Most said the same thing: That, gee, I sure seemed glad to see them. And that mine was about the 9 millionth American/UO flag setup they'd seen. Ah, but I was having too much fun to feel the barbs, the highlight being a visit from a guy down the way.

"Cool setup," he said, nodding his head.

What can I say? I'm back.

October 24, 2000

Huskies' turnaround

L AST YEAR, before the Oregon-Washington football game, Seattle Times columnist Ron Judd wrote that "two things stand
out about our friendly neighbors to the south .... 1. They ain't like
us. 2. Thank God."

"Oregon fans ... emerge from the bogs each fall to gather in large
groups, consume mass quantities of fish-label beer and verbally
whiz all over people from Seattle."

He made four references to bodily waste in describing us. He
likened us to the measles. He claimed our tailgate party ingredients
include "one 12-pound bag Cheez Doodles. One box of Gallo, 17
straws."

Just when I thought U-Dub fans could get no more self-righ-
teous, no more obnoxious, no more nose-in-the-air arrogant, this
guy goes out and ... and ... totally redeems the Huskies in my
eyes!

Don't you see? Judd's column is written proof that the Huskies
have lowered themselves to the rest of the world. It's Richie Rich
coming out to skateboard with the tenant kids, Donald Trump at
a drive-up window, the honor student in your fourth-grade class
firing her first spitwad.

All along we've thought Husky fans were these purple-and-gold
sophisticates, tailgating on Lake Washington aboard their 50-
foot cabin cruisers. "Pardon me, Nordstrom, would you have any
Grey Poupon? I say, Jim, do you read me? This is an emergency
— over!"

We thought they were giving jobs to UW players at the golf
courses they owned, which, of course, led to those ugly sanctions
and the resignation of St. James.

We thought they were the Microsoft couple — Todd and Muffy
— coming out of a swanky Seattle mall, pushing a stroller that has
nicer shocks than my truck's.

Suddenly: "My goodness, Todd, this isn't our baby!"

"Shhhhh. It's a better stroller."

But, no, they've become pathetic, blue-collar whiners like the
rest of us — fans so devoid of real lives that they're forced to write
about Duck droppings.

Seven years ago, no Seattle columnist would have written that column for the same reason Bill Gates wouldn't bend over to pick up a $100 bill: Why waste the effort?

Then it happened: The Pick. On Oct. 22, 1994, UO's Kenny Wheaton intercepted a U-Dub pass to snuff what looked to be a certain game-winning touchdown drive. Before that day, Oregon had won only four of the previous 21 games; since that day, it's won four of six.

In that moment, everything changed. Now, the Lilliputians have Gulliver tied down and, for the first time, he's mad; his sweater-vest is wrinkled. It's been so long since the Huskies made the Rose Bowl — '93 — they need MapQuest.com to find Pasadena.

"We're insufferable snobs," Doug Margeson, a former colleague and current Husky fan, told me back in the '80s, when we worked in Seattle's high-brow cousin, Bellevue, where women think natural childbirth is giving birth without makeup.

And now? "We still have an understated sense of superiority," he says, "but we're no longer insufferable snobs. More like borderline boors. At halftime of a recent home game, I walked out to have a cigar and our fans were booing Miami."

Husky fans exerting the energy to boo? What's next from the purple and gold? Fish-label beer?

Ah, but I confess a concern in this shift of pigskin power: If the Huskies are becoming the whiners we used to be — remember Lambright trying to get the Duck-beaten Dawgs into the Cotton Bowl using his fax machine? — I also see some UO fans becoming the pompous bullies the Huskies used to be.

Two years ago, before the Oregon-Washington fray in Eugene, I was sitting in the Moshofsky Center with my son and his Husky-fan college friend when a well-Galloed Duck got in our guest's face. The grown man wanted to fight the 18-year-old because, well, the kid had on a Husky sweatshirt.

We can't go there, my fine-feathered friends. We need to mark our territory in a classier way, respecting our rivals in the process.

No fighting. No trash-talking. No throwing dog biscuits out your tailgate while on I-5.

No more chiding the Huskies about building that new grandstand that promptly fell down in '87. Let them all die believing they actually did start The Wave. And isn't it time we gave Neuheisel a full pardon for running that silly fake punt with that huge lead in the Cotton Bowl?

To set the tone for such classy fandom and underscore my sincerity, I'm going to honor my Seattle counterpart, Mr. Judd, by addressing his flagship statement that, "They ain't like us. Thank God." Ron, I couldn't agree more.

September 28, 2000

Beavers' misery is over

SCENES I NEVER thought I'd see in my lifetime: my 73-year-old mother and a classmate from her mid-'40s Oregon State days wheeling their luggage to baggage check-in, en route to the Fiesta Bowl.

That same mother returning to the Eugene Airport three days later wearing a Fiesta Bowl shirt with this score emblazoned on it: "Oregon State 41, Notre Dame 9."

"Mom," I say as we head for the parking lot, "remember how you used to say you felt sorry for players on the losing team because 'They have moms, too?' "

"Yes."

"Do you feel sorry for those Notre Dame players because, well, they have moms, too?"

She ponders the question for a few seconds — or about the time it took OSU to score its 29 third-quarter points and rattle the bones of Knute Rockne.

"No, not really."

Ah, the power of winning. It changes everything. Changes everybody.

Reminds me of a joke I heard about Mother Teresa moving to L.A. but vowing to remain steadfastly focused on the spiritual essence of life. Months later, a friend calls her, but gets only a recorded message: "Hi, this is Teri. I'm at the mall, but if you'll leave a message ... "

Raised a Beaver in Corvallis but now a born-again Duck, I admit some of the orange and black revelry has bugged me — the literal dead ducks being swung around at the Civil War game, the TV news Friday night from Tempe showing bar-beached Beavers rooting hard against Oregon in the Holiday Bowl and the strut-and-jut OSU players during the Fiesta Bowl win.

"Erickson Turns Oregon State Into Pac-10 Bully," read a headline in Tuesday's *Los Angeles Times.* Wrote one columnist: "The hot-dogging was ridiculous, and it will not win the Beavers any friends."

But then I remind myself: We all might break a few lamps if we were just learning to dance. I don't recall Duck fans being exactly subtle while quacking their way around Pasadena in 1995 — their first trip to the Rose Bowl since about the time Plato was an undergrad.

What's more, I'm not letting a few Beaver Aggrievers sour what's an amazing story: a football program rising — if not phoenix-like, then Tempe-like — out of the ashes of despair.

It didn't take much imagination picturing OSU playing Wednesday in the Orange Bowl for the No. 1 spot in the nation; heck, in the early '70s the joke at Corvallis High was that the Beavers were No. 2 — in the city, that is, behind us.

We had a quarterback, Mike Riley, who led CHS to the state Class AAA championship in 1970 and returned to Corvallis nearly three decades later to help turn around the OSU program.

In between, though, the Beavers set an NCAA record for futility. They slogged through 28 straight losing seasons. They won fewer games in the seven seasons from 1979 through 1985 (10) than OSU won this season alone (11). Only four years ago, they were losing to Division I-AA Montana by three touchdowns, at home, and drawing 17,215 fans — or about what they got at their pep rally Sunday in Tempe.

So you can understand why your Beaver neighbors have had those orange-and-black flags on their cars since October.

You can understand the post-touchdown theatrics by OSU receivers; it was only a few years ago that Jerry Pettibone had to literally rehearse with his players how to carry him off the field should hell freeze over and they actually win.

You can understand why my formerly sensitive mother — the same mother who once ironed the "Winning Isn't Everything" motto on my City League basketball uniform — would morph into Vince Lombardi. (I keep imagining her and her 76-year-old sorority sister sitting in the stands after the game, smoking orange and black victory cigars.)

What's happening to Beaver fans is no different from what happened to Duck fans a decade ago: rebirth, only in time-lapse photography. New life, seemingly overnight. Rejuvenation, like the senior citizens in the movie *Cocoon* who discover their very own fountain of youth.

I'm standing at the airport, a Duck adrift on a sea of orange, and can't help but smile at what I see: tired but happy people.

I see my wife's uncle, a 73-year-old man who's witnessed the dark years of Beaver football and the really dark years. I see my own aunt and uncle, Beavers who live in Duckdom and have endured the local feather-strutting for decades. I see my mother and her friend, widows both, who look like a couple of kids just home from summer camp.

Oregon State's dream season was for folks like these. And for all who find themselves in the midst of 1-10 seasons and wonder if life will ever get better.

January 4, 2001

Ducks' darkest day

SEATTLE — Somewhere, amid a too-long weekend of rain and Wake Forest touchdowns and Husky fans reveling in every single ounce of Duck misery, I pulled my car up to an intersection and saw a sign that said it all:

"Hell."

Never mind that it was just a Shell station whose initial letter was obscured by a telephone pole. This beacon in nearby Bothell was nothing less than a reminder of where the darkest journeys end; all that was missing was the "Now entering" preface.

What could be worse for a Duck fan than being humiliated in a bottom-rung bowl game by a 6-6 team in front of Husky fans who are literally parading through the stands screaming anti-Duck epithets?

It was like Bush inviting Gore back to the White House, then giving him and Tipper a bedroom wallpapered in hanging chads.

The Seattle Bowl trip hadn't been my idea; I would have been happy to stay home, save money, watch the first quarter on TV and then go do something more fun, like clean out gutter sludge by hand while eating cold spinach. But youth spoke.

"If we're going to be fans, we've got to be fans in the good times and in the bad," reminded my 23-year-old son, Ryan.

By now, one would hope he would have discarded such Cleaverisms — where did they come from anyway? — but I soon found myself in Seattle with Ry and his 20-year-old brother, Jason. The "bowl spirit" wasn't exactly thick. Kurt Cobain was making bigger headlines — and he's been dead for eight years.

"So, who's gonna win the big game?" I asked the cashier at the Hell station.

"You wanna car wash with your fill-up?" she asked.

OK, so this wasn't Pasadena or Tempe or even Shreveport, La., where the throng of Duck fans at the 1989 Independence Bowl all but saved the city's economic bacon. This was Seattle, where Duck fans are about as popular as, well, Husky fans would be in Eugene; the UO team was introduced at a Sonics basketball game — and was roundly booed.

A year ago, UO fans were sitting at poolside in Tempe and eating $49 resort brunches. Sunday night, we ate at a Renton Burger King.

Later that night, heavy rains returned. And we hadn't seen a single Duck flag, though ours — torn and tattered — fluttered away.

The next morning, we headed from the car to the stadium, the three of us laden in cold-weather gear and carrying binoculars that had seen too much this season. But when we started seeing the gathering of the green-and-yellow flock, our hopes soared. And when we heard our first-ever street musician rendition of the *Oregon Fight Song* — on an accordion no less! — we were ready to smite the Demon Deacons and find some smidgen of salvation in this riches-to-rags season.

Alas, that meant playing football, which hasn't been our team's forte.

Nobody wants the favorite part of his bowl experience to be a lack of rain. Or a stadium whose enclosed concourse is swankier than most Hyatts. Or a nice conversation with one of the few Husky fans who wasn't cheering feverishly for Wake Forest.

But all three were better than the game, in whose aftermath we quietly walked to the car. I'd taken off the flag, fearing that during the game it might lead to anti-Duck vandalism.

"You gotta put it back up for the drive home," Ry said.

I did, just to be a good sport, but my heart wasn't in it.

Driving home — I-5 was like a 300-mile-long car wash — I thought of where I was a year ago at this time, in Tempe, where palm trees swayed and the victorious Ducks enjoyed what may have been their finest football moment ever. Now, I'd just experienced the lowest moment for UO football since the 1996 Cotton Bowl when Colorado thumped the Ducks 38-6 in the Rick Neuheisel Fake Punt Cotton Bowl.

It got me thinking about that movie, *Trading Places,* in which a tycoon played by Dan Aykroyd winds up losing everything, standing in the rain on a street corner dressed in a tattered Santa Claus outfit as a dog uses his leg for a fire hydrant.

That image only depressed me more, so we stopped in Kelso to take the sting off. I walked into the joint and bellied up to the counter, eager to fall off the wagon.

"Fish sandwich, fries and a large Coke," I said. "And make that extra sauce on the fish."

By the time we arrived home, just before midnight, I had slumped into Aykroydian depths. The rain pounded on the carport roof. I tossed the Duck seat cushions in the shed and was just going to turn off the light when I saw it lying on the cement floor: one of those giant foam UO "No. 1" fingers that someone had given me years ago.

I wanted to toss it, but I couldn't. I remembered that "good times, bad times" line from Ry. Maybe I'd need that No. 1 finger in seasons to come. And, besides, how can you give up on a team for which you've just been to Hell and back?

January 2, 2003

UO's gridiron grinches

Every Duck down in Duckville liked football a lot
But the Grinches who taught on campus did NOT.
The ivy-twined Profs hated football, the whole football season!
Now, please don't ask why, no one quite knows the reason.

Some said they chafed at the gridiron grandeur
Feeling lost in the shadows of Bellotti's mergansers.

But I think that the most likely reason of all
Was the gone-nuts nature of college football.

But whatever the reason, they clucked and they clucked
They stood there on Sun Bowl Eve hating the Ducks.
Staring down from their towers, and across the Willamette
"We must stop this flood of excess. We must, we must dam it!"

They believed Sir Frohnny was half off his rocker
For approving billboards and X-Box-stocked lockers.
"And those players are watching a 60-inch Zenith TV,
While alums at nearby Cas sip vintage Chablis."

Such venom they spouted with snarls and with sneers:
"Football is supplanting square roots and Shakespeare!
The university exists not for such sophomoric 'fun'
As face-painted students shouting 'We're No. 1!' "

Then they growled, with their Grinchy minds fixed on a pox:
"We must get this duck-lipped Pandora back in her box."
For the Sun Bowl was coming and seasons beyond
And they sarcastically spoke of more muck in the pond:

"Why stop at locker rooms straight from 'Star Trek'?
Let's put in a theme park at what once was WISTEC.
'Duckyland' — for players and donors blue chip
To lure more recruits into Duck membership."

The Profs imagined a billboard — "Uh, woah!"
A 10-story Clemens hanging from tower Ya-Po-Ah.
And players in golf carts being chauffeured to classes
To keep them from having to mix with the masses.

They imagined neon "O's" atop Skinner and Spencer
And Autzen fans separated by donation-smart sensors.
The $10,000-and-ups will get "express lanes" to use
When headed for bathrooms and refills of booze!

When Reser is raised the Ducks will, of course, answer
With 12,000 more seats and theirs, naturally, fancier.

So the Profs stroked their beards, like dozens of Tolstoys
And thought of 70,000 fans — oh the noise, noise, noise, noise!

Then they got an idea! An awful idea!
The Grinches got a wonderful, awful idea.
"We know just what we'll do," they said, suddenly perky
And they put on their tweed coats and re-fastened their Birkies.

In the darkness of night, they ringed Autzen in Hummers
With the quiet commitment of Watergate plumbers.
Their faces were darkened, this band of brothers
Each of their laptops linked to the others.

"Hasta la vista," one Grinchy Prof hissed
As he rappelled down the very first stop on his list.
In a locker room plush as a Royce of the Rolls
He took out the batteries from all the remote controls.

"Hey, hey," he smirked. "We'll see how long they can last
Having to manually program their TV sportscasts."
He plugged in his laptop and tapped in some codes
And the players' Internet ports all were TKO'd.

He had just made his way toward the slide-up door
Behind which intelligence said X-Boxes were stored.
When he heard a small sound like the hoof of a buck
He turned around fast, and he saw MegaDuck.

Not Baron von Moos, but a heart-stopping sight
For there in lightning yellow stood Sir Nike of Knight
Who stared at the intruder and said, "Sir, why?
Why are you taking the whistles and bells, why?"

But, you know, that old Prof was so smart and so slick
He thought up a lie, and he thought it up quick!
"Why, Sir Nike of Knight," said the Prof, while evading
"The software running this stuff needs some upgrading."

But Sir Nike wasn't fooled; said he, "Sir, you blew it.
But for rightness, I'll grant you one chance to Just Do It."

Huddle your Grinches for a game of two-handed touch
To the winner goes the spoils, if that's not asking too much.

"You win and the Swoosh God will turn back time
To the days we were 'Poor, Uncool and Two-and-Nine.'
When our offense played like 11 men sauced
And we held San Jose State to five points and still lost.

"Agreed," said the Prof, "and if your team should prevail
We will embrace with gusto this shift to upscale.
We will play halftime bingo to help Daisy Ducks
And hold Keats-read-athons to raise scholarship bucks."

Later, the two shook hands, the kickoff ensued
And backers of both teams cheered, clapped and booed.
A hard Oregon downpour muddied the campus' green grass
As the two traded touchdowns, a run and a pass.

A Grinch music prof made trash-talking an art
While running pass patterns, she quoted Mozart.
James Earl, as a tailback, ran like Jim Thorpe
And celebrated a score with a spike and some gorp.

But the MegaDucks countered with the Baron von Moos
Who bulled up the middle with the thunder of Zeus.
As Bellotti fired passes and Knight called the plays
The MegaDucks tied the game and fans were all crazed.

Then darkness descended with the surrealness of fog
And fans couldn't tell Frohnny from the court jester, Frog.
Then came eerie calm, like before a mattress-torched riot
With the score in a knot, both teams grew quite quiet.

And as fans edged forward, they saw a small Who
Little Quacky-U. Who, who said "after further review."
Said she: "Tis the season of peace and goodwill,
So allow me to assess this culture, a la Tocqueville.

"MegaDucks, are your heads screwed on all right?
Or could it be that your Nikes might be a wee bit too tight?

Maybe, just maybe, your hearts are two sizes too small
And your next donation should go to St. Vincent de Paul.

"And, Profs, don't forget that this Knight seen as scary
Has given much green for the law school and library.
Despite this duck-adent spending you'd now like aborted
What other department is self-supported?"

And Sir Nike of Knight stepped out of the huddle
All covered with mud, swooshes submerged in a puddle.
"I've hung with Tiger and built a shoe kingdom vast
But football with you profs — well, I've never had such a blast!

"It came without custom, self-ventilating lockers
And sky suites and field houses and rich donors in Dockers."
"Maybe football," he said, "doesn't come from a store.
Maybe football — perhaps — means a little bit more."

And a Prof stepped forward with a lump in his throat
And finally spewed forth with a Bardian quote:
" 'Though this be madness, yet there is method in't.'
And, frankly, we Profs wanted badly to win't.

"But today's great game set free a truth that I've harbored:
I still rub in the Michigan win to my friends in Ann Arbor.
Theoretically, maybe academia could loosen up more
Maybe academia — perhaps — needs fewer stuffed-shirted bores."

And what happened then? Well in Duckville they say
That the Profs and MegaDucks traded high fives that fine day.
They chanted "Go Ducks!" and even "sis-boom-bah!"
And sang "Mighty Oregon!" to the tune of "Kumbaya."

A biochem Prof, with Bellotti, shared thoughts
On enzymes, hormones and his views on sunspots
He then asked the coach for some Sun Bowl tips
As the Duck mascot whipped by, doing 18 back flips

Suddenly, the field became a giant tailgating bash
The teams ate Ritta's Burritos and organic Duck hash.

Drank valley wines and, with an Oregon Coast cleaver,
They — the MegaDucks and Profs — carved the roast beaver!
                                                    December 21, 2003

Mac Court's upper deck

IF I TOLD YOU my two reserved seats at McArthur Court came complete with cable vision, you would think I was lying. And you would be right.

Technically, they aren't my reserved seats; I'm only a part-owner with a friend. But they do come with cable vision — three horizontal strands of tightly wound wire to keep people from falling out of the upper deck. And to keep me thinking that I'm watching a basketball game from behind a giant bar chart.

You see, I'm one of the few. One of the proud. One of the people who sit in the 1,359 seats that hang, like roof gutters, from the rustic rafters of the 77-year-old building.

The upper deck is all about unpainted plywood, unpretentious fans and unseen portions of the basketball court. Indeed, the upper level of Mac Court — the second-oldest on-campus arena in the country — is a world all its own.

At Autzen Stadium, the upper reaches are filled by people of means who might take an escalator to the top; at Mac Court, by people pitted-out by the 72-step climb. We bring a whole new meaning to that "friends-in-high-places" phrase.

"The upper level is like being in steerage on the Titanic," says Sandy Silverthorne, a third-level regular from Eugene. "Every time I open the door, I expect to see Leonardo DiCaprio leading the other passengers in an Irish folk dance. It's like we have our own culture up there. We're having a ball."

The upper level is five rows of wooden seats, like something built by a high school shop class, ringing the court from the hoop heavens. It is fans in the back rows sitting a few feet below a 50-year-old air duct. It is a visual jungle of two-by-fours and plywood and catwalks and pipes and faucets and, in Section 317, a piece of duct tape slapped on a vent.

Mac Court's upper deck is the Jerry's Home Improvement of basketball perspectives, though with hardware whose replacement parts were last available about the time Elvis was here, singing the venue-appropriate *Whole Lotta Shakin' Goin' On.*

It takes five flights of stairs to get from floor level to third level, part of the cold journey through a winding, metal staircase that makes you feel like a gerbil. But once you've summitted this time-worn Everest — passing by the skeletal remains of those whose dreams fell short — what a view: Watching a game from the upper deck is like peering into a table-top aquarium.

And the ambiance: Here is a cardboard patch on a ceiling wound. There is a brace that looks like it belongs on the Ferry Street Bridge. Everywhere is a sense of the past and the future, the latter so eloquently expressed in the words of my partner in climb: "In case of a fire, would you head for the door or just jump?"

Beyond the level's bare-bones nature, the fans give the upper deck its blue-collar charm. In the walkway behind the seats — "concourse" would be a bit of a stretch — a couple is huddled against the wall in a curious game of one-on-one. And down the way, Terry Holo affixes a bottomless popcorn container to the wall with electrical tape and a paper clip: a hoop for his nephew and niece, 7-year-old Ty and 5-year-old Savannah Boespflug.

"They love it up here," Holo says.

What's not to love? A whiff of cigarette smoke from fans outside seeps through a stylishly painted-over window that's propped open with an old towel, joining the alluring blend of sweat, popcorn and the time-seared mustiness of thousands of games since Mac Court opened in 1927.

Of course, we upper deckers aren't here only for the ambiance and the view, sometimes obscured by beams, flags or cables. In Section 321, Row 1, Seat 1, you have a wooden beam 8 inches from your face. In Section 316, you can't see the score on the scoreboard. In Section 307, you can't even see the far basket.

No, we're here for deeper reasons. Some of us are cheap. Some of us like a challenge. And some of us, of course, are secretly waiting for Leonardo and the Irish folk dancers.

January 31, 2004

Track's enduring appeal

ONE WINTRY MORNING in the early '90s, I dressed for a run in a tackier-than-usual ensemble: Long johns, a Taco Bell stocking cap and up-to-my-elbow socks instead of mittens.

"What if someone sees you?" my wife said.

"Who am I going to see on the path between here and Island Park?" I said.

Ten minutes later, I got my answer. She was boring toward me in a sleek running outfit — at the time, the reigning American 3,000- and 1,500-meter champion: Annette Peters.

Gulp. It was like meeting the pope dressed as a hooker. But as she passed me, Peters nodded, smiled and said hi, as if I were an actual runner — a fellow member of the club — instead of some midlife geek in sock mittens.

I remembered that moment Saturday night as Peters ran her final race at Hayward Field — a sixth-place finish in the 10,000 meters in the USA Outdoor Track & Field Championships.

The incident — and much of what I saw at yesterday's meet — reminds me of how track and field athletes still have a refreshing realness to them.

How, in a time when America's big-time athletes are becoming increasingly inaccessible to fans, you can, at Hayward Field, still look your hero in the eye.

How, in a time when *Sports Illustrated* rarely runs a cover anymore that doesn't have a millionaire on it, some amazing athletic efforts are being performed by humble, happy-to-be-here sort of people.

The best example of that on Saturday may well have been Lisa Nye of Bend, whose American record-setting win in the steeplechase was lost in the shadows of teenage mile/1,500-meter sensation Alan Webb.

What impressed me about Nye — Lisa Karnopp when she ran for the University of Oregon a decade ago — wasn't only that she won, but how she won: after having a major family crisis Saturday morning in Bend before leaving for the meet.

"We lost the tail to my son's Godzilla," she said. "I'm trying to make him breakfast and the dog's under foot. It was a stressful morning."

Nye isn't one of those athletes with a two-comma income. She works for a water conservation company, coaches Mountain View High's cross-country team and trains across the street from her house in Drake Park.

Between Thursday's prelims and Saturday's finals, she drove back to Bend and, along with husband Brad, painted their house.

"Hey, I'm just a mom out for an afternoon run," she says.

A fairly impressive afternoon run, as it turned out. After the last water jump, Nye, 32, kicked into first place and held off Elizabeth Jackson by half a second to win in 9:49.41.

When asked what triggered her win, she said it was the fans. "I don't think I would have won without the crowd," she says.

"It's impressive, this intimacy and respect between track athletes and fans," says her husband Brad, who came late to the sport of track. "They feed off each other. And after a race, there's intermingling in a way that isn't going to happen at a Blazer game."

Afterward, in taking a victory lap, Lisa Nye didn't call attention to herself with look-at-me gestures. (Is anyone else tired of football players who make a tackle and strut as if this has never been done before?)

Instead, Nye invited Jackson and third-place finisher Kelly MacDonald to join her for a lap, then continually thanked individual crowd members for wishing her well. When autograph-seeking kids sought her signature, she knelt and looked them in the eye.

"This is what it's all about," she says. "I feel lucky I can do this kind of stuff."

In a time when some NFL players won't even sign, much less look someone in the eye, how refreshing.

In a time when some PGA golfers look as if they're on a death march with caddies, how cool to see someone enjoying the moment.

I watched as Gail Devers, the American record holder in the 100-meter hurdles, started to make a cell-phone call but kept getting interrupted by autograph seekers. Her patience blew me away: You could tell she wanted to make the call, but she kept signing autographs, posing for photos, making some kid's day.

"Track stars are good about autographs," says 17-year-old Stephanie Burdick, here from North Dakota. "Like if it were Michael Jordan, you wouldn't even get close."

For whatever reason, track and field — at least in Eugene —

seems willing to let its heroes be amazingly ordinary, which makes them all the more extraordinary.

After her final race, a teary Annette Peters jogged down home-stretch as her 3-year-old daughter, Emma, ran beside her. And the last I saw of the Nye family, Lisa was hugging someone and Brad was holding a plastic Godzilla.

Tail and all.

June 24, 2001

Stay, Rid, stay

Dear Rid: Everybody says it's a done deal, you skipping your senior year to go to the NBA and all. And, hey, it's not as if you asked for my opinion. But as one small tree in your forest of fans, allow me the 11th-hour privilege of falling across your trail.

Here are the top 10 reasons why you, Mr. Luke Ridnour, might consider staying another year at Oregon:

1. Money can't buy you love. Yes, with a single signature, you're set for life. But will anybody stick with you like Duck folks?

When you're 38 and hinting retirement, will the people in Los Angeles (lock your car), Minnesota (button up your overcoat) or Cleveland (what, you've never seen a river on fire?) be chanting "One more year, one more year"? Naw, these are pro fans; they'll be heckling you because you — "the bum" — blew that game-winning layup against Sacramento back in '09.

2. The Other Luke. I loved that photo Sunday of you and your pal Luke Jackson celebrating the Pac-10 Tournament champion-ship. Arms around each other. Hats askew. You looked like a couple of kids from "The Little Rascals." So why break up the Luke-and-Luke act now? Did Lewis leave Clark at Fort Clatsop just because he got an offer to hang with some fur barons back East?

3. The Pit. You're going to be playing in a bunch of cavernous, half-empty, corporate-named arenas whose scoreboards not only won't shake, but whose stands won't rattle and roll. At the last NBA game I went to, the fans were so lethargic that the Blazers piped in cash-register sounds each time Portland scored. Is that what you really want instead of a Mac Court roar? Plus, you won't find another mascot like The Duck in the NBA. (Most are being sued for exploiting fans.)

4. Playing time. Last we heard, ex-Duck Fred Jones, a rookie with Indiana, was averaging six minutes per game. You dribble longer than that while eating breakfast. If you stay another year, you'll get your 35 minutes, help pass the point torch to Aaron Brooks and be that much better prepared for the pros.

5. You're not a big-city guy. Goodness, you're from Blaine, Washington. Your idea of a good time is a spirited Bible study or sneaking into Mac Court for a summer rat ball game. You turned down *Playboy*. Are you really ready for this jet-setting world, Rid?

6. Heaven can wait. OK, what's the worst thing that could happen if you wait a year? A career-ending injury? There's a better chance of lint on Ernie's suit. You go a notch lower in the draft and make a million less? Maybe you know what it says in — hey, what are the chances? — Luke 12:15: "A man's life does not consist in the abundance of his possessions."

7. You'll get one last shot at the Huskies. We saw you helpless in Seattle — standing there while the seconds ticked away toward the U-Dub victory. Do you really want to live with that the rest of your life?

8. You can earn a college degree. Leaving now would be like twisting your way through all those defenders for that game-winning shot against Arizona State, then not taking it. You're almost there, man. Fire that rock.

9. In college, basketball is still a game. A year from now, if you go pro, you won't be what you are now — Peter Pan with a basketball. You'll be a millionaire businessman in really long shorts.

Your teammates won't be guys like Jackson, guys you can discuss the meaning of life with over, say, a broken-lamp game of Nerf basketball in your apartment. They'll be walking corporations, gold-chain guys with entourages. And your coach won't be someone like Ernie, telling the post-game radio audience how a team is like a "family." Instead, he'll be some greased-back guy who lost his passion for the game long before three-pointers were allowed.

10. Finally, you can never be a kid again, Mr. Pan. So why grow up when you could fly as a Duck for one more year?

March 18, 2003

The greatest athlete

AS THE GREATEST athletes in the world bid farewell to the Athens Olympics today, I find myself thinking about the greatest athlete I've ever known.

I met him on the sidelines of a church turkey bowl football game on Thanksgiving 2002. I wasn't playing because I'd torn ligaments in my knee. He wasn't playing because he didn't have a right leg.

Bryant King, then 11, looked longingly out at the field, wearing a Green Bay Packers jersey that hung on him like a parachute. "Wanna play catch?" I said.

He said sure. I stepped toward him and tossed the ball underhanded as you might to a 3-year-old. He caught it with ease — ever try catching a pass hopping on one leg while letting go of your two metal canes? — and gave me a "have-a-clue" look.

"Go out for a pass," he instructed. In slow motion, I started "running" away from him. "Faster!" he yelled. I picked up speed. Bryant cocked his arm and zipped a spiral to me as if he were a pint-sized Brett Favre.

Mia Hamm kicks a great soccer ball, Michael Phelps swims like a fish, Roman Sebrle sets decathlon records. But when it comes to the world's greatest athlete, I'm sticking with Bryant King, the only human being I've seen kick dead-straight field goals while balancing on a cane, the football teed up in a cut-off toilet-paper tube.

If there's a way, Bryant will find it. Soccer. Baseball. Basketball. Badminton. Air hockey. Ping-pong. He's played them all. His room is sprinkled with Kidsports trophies. "It's pretty amazing to see him get up and down the basketball court," says Andy Hill, a friend and fellow Monroe Middle School eighth-grader. "He scores points. And if he can't do something, he motivates others."

He skateboards, drives ATVs and rides a bike. Last year, he wanted to try knee boarding behind the Kings' boat. His parents, Steve and Lisa, were skeptical. But soon Bryant was doing so well that his grandfather, Emile Mortier, bought him a board of his own.

In rare moments of inaction, he dreams and schemes in one of 12 spiral notebooks. "What I need for a go kart" is one heading. Other topics include "What I would wear snowboarding," "How to make money" — including "Be on 'Fear Factor' " — and "What to be when older" (pro paintballer, video game inventor, singer, host of a sports quiz show and 17 others).

Bryant, 13, has brown eyes and shaggy brown hair. Once, I told him he looked a lot like — "I know, Luke Jackson. Everybody says that." Only Luke Jackson is 6-foot-7 and 215 pounds. Bryant King is 4-foot-1 1/2 and 68 pounds.

Luke is Bryant's hero. His room and wardrobe pay homage to the ex-University of Oregon basketball star. But would Jackson still be great if he'd had more than 20 surgeries? Were on his second kidney transplant? Had been tube-fed for the first 11 years of his life?

Such has been life for Bryant King, who was born with caudal regression syndrome, a disorder affecting the legs and lower intestines. "He just won't be stopped," Steve King says.

He's suffered four broken legs. Spent a year traveling to Corvallis and Portland for kidney dialysis. And recently had a spinal fusion, two rods being placed in his back.

"I just do what I can," he says. Once, kids at school were reluctant to let him play hoops. "I don't get bitter," he says. "I just try to prove it. Then they're like, 'Whoa.' "

Another "whoa" came in the spring of 2003 when he was playing in a wheelchair basketball game at Mac Court against UO players. At one point, Bryant found himself guarding a guy whose picture hangs on his bedroom wall: Luke Jackson.

Bryant rolled up and began applying defensive pressure. Jackson got flustered. He lost control. His wheelchair tipped over, spilling him out.

"It was pretty funny," says Bryant, who wound up with the ball. "Basically, I schooled him."

New category for my spiral notebook: "What to add to my office: autographed picture of Bryant King, my hero."

August 29, 2004

Just glad to be here

BLUE RIVER — Lately, I've found myself so disgruntled by the sports world — NBA players brawling with fans, the Rose Bowl selling out to BCS bucks, the NFL prostituting itself with sleazy TV ads — that I needed a breath of fresh air.

I found it here, at McKenzie High, nestled in snow-dusted mountains and alive with a certain something that's fading fast in our me-first sports world.

On Friday at 5 p.m., McKenzie High — enrollment 90 — will play for the state Class 1A football championship at Autzen Stadium. And the school's happy-to-be-here attitude reminds you of what sports should be all about.

I wish every college football coach whose annual bonus pays him more than the college president's salary could have heard senior running back Dillon Bellmore talking about practicing at Autzen Stadium last week.

"It takes your breath away," says Bellmore, who may be going to diesel mechanics school next fall. "I mean, I've never been on a field that has stands all the away around it instead of on just one side."

I wish every NFL player who plays in a climate-controlled dome could have seen the Eagles practicing in the snow Monday afternoon. "Most of our guys also play basketball and knew they could have been in a nice, warm gym," says Rick Gardner, football coach, baseball coach, athletic director and science teacher. "But they said they wouldn't trade the chance to be practicing for state."

I wish the NBA's Latrell Sprewell, who makes $14.6 million a year and recently complained, during a contract dispute, about having a "family to feed," could talk "perks" with Gardner, who makes $2,600 a year as coach and, like other staff members in the district, has taken pay cuts the past two years to help keep the district afloat.

"I get the same perks the volunteer assistants do," he says. "A cap, a whistle and a pair of shorts."

I wish every college athletic director who thinks it's all about skyboxes and million-dollar locker rooms could hear Gardner talk about the Eagles' six-row bleachers — "we're one of the few 1A schools that has covered stands" — and see the team's locker room. It's about the size of a kitchen, but doesn't smell quite as good, and features a portable stereo loaned to the team by one of the players.

"We're pretty fortunate here," says Gardner, who spruced up the locker room with paint he bought himself. "When we go on the road, we use some locker rooms that aren't nearly this nice."

I wish the same NFL marketing exec who thought it'd be a cool commercial to use a locker room liaison between a player and a nude actress could see the hand-painted signs at McKenzie High — "Eagles soar at Autzen!" — and hear Gardner talk about worrying about his wife, Mandy, driving to night road games. "I never relax on the sidelines until I see her in the stands."

I wish that steroid-fueled Goliath, Barry Bonds, could listen to a David — Steve Harbick, the Eagles' defensive coordinator and McKenzie Bridge General Store owner — talk about how a team with only 15 players still has a shot at a Perrydale team that has 35. Maybe he'd remember the pride of accomplishing something — on your own.

"We tell our players: 'They put out eight guys and we put out eight guys — and whoever wants it more, wins.' "

I wish all of these people — and college team "boosters" who, in letters to the editor, call for coaches' heads on a plate and youth sports parents who embarrass their children with childish tirades against officials — could see this tiny school along the McKenzie River.

I wish they could hear the wisdom in folks who'll never make "SportsCenter."

"You just can't take the good things you've been given for granted," Gardner says.

I wish they could remember the way games are supposed to be played.

December 9, 2004

A Titan for all times

Jeff Gerot, coach of the Sheldon Titans, first heard about Tyson Mageo-White from Tyson's brother, Curtis, who plays on Gerot's Pop Warner football team.

"My little brother really loves football," Curtis, 12, told his coach.

'He'd love to be out here, but he's kinda sick.'

More than "kinda sick," Gerot discovered. At age 11, Tyson has an aggressive form of leukemia. And hasn't responded to treatment.

Gerot started making calls. Soon, players on the Titans were telling their parents that Coach wanted all their uniforms back. Why? Because he was having ribbons sewn on that said "In honor of Tyson."

His cancer is too far gone for a transplant. But Gerot had something else planned for the 5-foot "little brother," the kid who, while watching games, would sometimes say something like: "Hey, I coulda broken that tackle."

Last week, Curtis came home from a practice. "Coach wants you to run a play for us in Sunday's game," he told Tyson.

Tyson was psyched, then "scared senseless." Psyched until he tried on the blue Titans uniform — No. "1," with his name stitched on back. If his gear made him look this big, he figured, how much bigger would the North Eugene players look? As big as Curtis, who at almost 6 feet was nearly a foot taller than his little brother.

On the way to the game, Tyson wasn't sure he could go through with this. But then he thought of his big brother — how much it meant to him. How pumped he was knowing Tyson was going to play for the Titans.

"I was still scared," Tyson says, "but I said to myself: 'I gotta do this for my brother.'"

The Titans were trailing just before halftime when they drove to North's 7-yardline. Time-out was called. Coach Gerot turned to Tyson, a sapling among tall firs. "Get in there," he said.

"I was just hoping he'd have the stamina to cross that goal line," says his grandmother, Judy Saling Field.

"I was terrified," Tyson says.

The play was a quarterback keeper over right guard. Tyson ran onto the field. "I was just thinking 'hike, run, hike, run!'" He crouched behind center. North's players lined up in their defensive formation.

"Hike!" Tyson said. He grabbed the football, tucked it and charged for the goal, guided by his Titan teammates. The North players didn't move. Their coach, Scott Mills, had agreed with Gerot that Tyson's well-being was worth far more than six points on a scoreboard.

Touchdown, Titans! Tyson's teammates slapped him on the helmet and gave him high-fives. "Even the North guys were, like, giving me skin, saying 'Way to go,'" Tyson says.

"It was unbelievable," says Stacey Conlon, whose son Christian plays for the Titans. "The North players, coaches and fans were so classy. Everybody was just clapping and cheering for this one kid."

"Tyson was beaming," Gerot says. "Coaches were wiping back tears."

Curtis put his arm around his little brother on the sidelines. "Love you, man," he said. "Good job."

After the game — North had won easily — the Titans hoisted Tyson on their shoulders. He was presented the game ball, signed by players on both teams.

Nobody I talked to could remember the score — or seemed to care. On this day, the only thing that mattered was that Tyson Mageo-White's touchdown was etched in history, never to be forgotten.

October 14, 2004

8.

Going places

Elk hunter
Part one

SUMPTER — Deep in Northeast Oregon's Blue Mountains, as the late afternoon cold tightens its clutch, it hits me: I'm going on a weeklong elk hunting trip, complete with horses and mules.

Me — the guy who recently wrote "I don't 'get' hunting." Me — the guy who, until a recent trip to a range, had never shot a gun. Me — the guy whose horse experience doesn't go much beyond the coin-in-the-slot type.

At the trailhead, the Eugene friend who invited me, Jason Schar, cinches down the gear on his mule, Molly Brown. The horse I'm ticketed to ride, Rusty, whinnies. I tug on my stocking cap, my runaway mind already having established its Five Worst Fears:

No. 1: I'll get shot. No. 2: I'll freeze to death. No. 3: The guys will laugh at my orange safety vest. No. 4: I'll get bucked off Rusty. And No. 5: My radio won't pick up the Oregon-Stanford game.

I hear the sound of horses headed my way. Mounted on those horses are two of the six other men in our hunting party. They've come with mules to help us carry our gear four miles into camp.

It's the first of numerous *Meet the Parents* moments to come

— me, the outsider, trying to somehow fit into a group of men who have nearly two decades of shared history.

They are guys from places such as Joseph, La Grande and Pendleton, guys who've gathered for the past 19 years at what's now sacred ground to them. They are dry-side cowboys, guys who say "crick," not "creek." Black coffee guys. One has a dried antelope scrotum on his truck's gearshift knob and NRA and Bush-Cheney stickers on the rear window.

Me? I am a wet-side journalist, a columnist from the Land of 10,000 Animal-Rights Activists. Until recently, I used a golf ball as a gearshift knob. I say "creek." I drink hot chocolate. And I've written a column that, while pointing out I'm not opposed to hunting, says, "I don't understand the allure of pulling a trigger and killing an animal."

I've chosen to go on this elk hunting trip not to prove to the angry letter writers that I was right. Nor, actually, to see if I can somehow be "converted." I've come simply to try to better understand hunters.

Wearing chaps, cowboy hats and neckerchiefs, the two men on horses look like something from *Legends of the Fall*. They look at my royal blue duffel bags and my backpack, whose net pouch is full of pens, "sticky notes" and an emergency flasher my wife bought me at Wal-Mart.

"This your stuff?" says John Groupe, a veterinarian from Pendleton.

"Uh, yep," I say, the bags suddenly standing out like Flintstone pajamas at a men's retreat. Groupe just nods ever so slightly. We load them on the mules. "Anything else before we head out?" he says.

"Guess not," I say, "other than notifying Life Flight to be prepared for me."

I laugh a little. John doesn't. "Guy up the crick got helicoptered out just last week," he says. "Fool pulled his gun out of his scabbard and had a bullet in the chamber. Shot himself in the leg. Died."

Okaaaay. Groupe and Larry "Hawkeye" Snook, who owns a sporting goods store in Joseph, head toward camp. Schar hops on his horse. I'm next. I've had about 12 minutes of training on this half ton of uncertainty.

Encumbered by sagging longjohns, I can't even get my foot in the stirrup. I try again. Schar, my Cowboy Mentor, watches.

He hides his smirk. Finally, grabbing the saddle horn, I clamber aboard.

We head along the mostly frozen creek, Rusty and I bringing up the rear. After a quarter-mile, I relax. I remind myself of actor Bill Murray in that scene from — appropriately enough — *What About Bob?* It's the scene where he's been lashed to the mast of a sailboat, wearing a bulky life jacket. "I'm sailing!" he cries. "I'm sailing!"

Only I'm thinking: "I'm hunting! I'm hunting!"

A few hundred yards later, a cold chill scares away such levity. The trail has risen some 100 feet above the creek and, chiseled into a steep ridge, appears to be roughly the width of a skateboard. I look down. I feel like I'm on Disneyland's Thunder Mountain ride — only at the moment this doesn't feel like the Happiest Place on Earth, but the Scariest Place on Earth.

"Good boy, Rusty, good boy," I say.

Gradually, the trail drops to creek level. Up ahead, the other horses and mules cross on a narrow bridge. Rusty suddenly stops, then goes into reverse.

I try to get him to go forward. He backs up faster. I get that helpless, something-bad-is-going-to-happen feeling, like right before you throw up.

"Whoa," I say. Rusty responds by bucking me off. I land facedown on a log.

November 10, 2002

Part two

I AWAKE to bruised thighs, bruised ribs and frozen contact lenses encased in their soaking solution. It's 4:30 a.m., normal wakeup time in elk camp. One thermometer says zero, the other minus-5. It's so cold that when the horses sneeze the mist crystallizes into "snot flakes."

"How you feeling, Cowboy Bob?" says John Groupe, one of my three tent mates.

He's referring to me having been bucked off a horse, Rusty, en route to the elk hunters' camp where I'm spending a week in Northeast Oregon. (I can't be more specific about our location, under penalty of death.)

Physically, I'm fine. Emotionally, I'm The Pathetic Little Engine

Who Couldn't. It's hard enough earning respect from a bunch of leather-skinned elk hunters who think you've arrived from Pluto. ("Seriously, you've never shot a gun?") It's all the harder when you come limping into camp behind a riderless horse that has a dude-ranch name. (Why couldn't I have been thrown by a horse named Devil Boy?)

The hunting season begins the next day, Saturday, so we make final preparations. One group leaves to get more hay for the horses and mules — we have 15 in camp. I join the five-man firewood crew.

These guys, ranging in age from 27 to 60 and in occupation from jewelers to plumbers, work amazingly hard. No grumbling. No leader. They just know what to do and do it. Me? I don't know what to do and try to do it anyway.

The white canvas tents look like something from the Civil War. Each of the two tents used for sleeping has a bare-bones stove, as does the mess tent.

Among elk hunters, this is as rough an experience as you'll find. Just off the main roads, guys hunt out of six-figure motor homes. You find trailers, campers and all-terrain vehicles. You find hunters cruising the roads in pickups, using field glasses fixed to their half-down windows like drive-in movie speakers.

But the seven guys in our elk camp will have none of that. They're purists who love the bare-bones experience.

"There's something about the simple life," Groupe says. "Life at home is complicated and noisy." And he lives in Pendleton.

On opening day, we chow down on pancakes and eggs; with La Grande pharmacist Bob Coulter — the "drugstore cowboy" — behind the propane stove, the food is tasty, filling and a cholesterol-counter's nightmare.

Stars and a sliver moon hang above. I follow my Eugene friend, Jason Schar, up a ridge trail. He has a gun strapped to his shoulder. I do not.

I shot a 7 mm rifle at a range before we left. It was louder and more powerful than I imagined. (Also, extremely inaccurate; I couldn't hit a thing.) I've heard of first-time gun shooters who feel a certain "rush" and are hooked. I didn't and I'm not.

Before leaving on the trip, I'd read a story about a hunter who was carrying an elk head and was shot and killed. (Note to myself: No carrying elk heads.) Someone else sent me a story about a pheasant hunter who got shot by his dog. (Note to myself: Keep an eye on Rusty. True, he's a horse and less likely to shoot than a dog, but he's already tried to kill me once.)

Though some people encouraged me to get an elk tag and shoot — "How else can you understand hunting?" — I have chosen not to. If I were another hunter, I wouldn't want a guy in the woods with half an hour's experience and no safety training. And I have no desire to shoot an animal.

Most guys in our party dress in "camo," hunter-speak for camouflage. I dress in "fluoro," nonhunter-speak for a fluorescent orange vest. I look like I should be directing game-day traffic. I take some ribbing from the others, but I've decided I'd rather be a live nerd than a dead hunting-fashion icon.

The forest, extremely dry, is quiet except for our steps; we sound like we're walking on cornflakes. And there's not enough snow to make the elk stand out: terrible conditions if you're a hunter, great if you're the hunted.

We glimpse three elk about midmorning, then work our way down a ridge to a rock outcropping. We "glass" — look through our field glasses — the ridges around us. We eat, whisper and nap.

I wake up. Schar is still snoozing. Suddenly an ethical dilemma confronts me: What if I see, say, a dozen elk? Do I wake up Schar so he can kill one of them? Or do I quietly wave my arms and try to scare them toward safety?

The decision is lost amid a more serious concern: It's 12:30 p.m. and I can't get the Duck game on my radio. Three of my Top Five Fears have now come true: bucked off a horse, laughed at for my vest and no radio reception.

The two other fears have this in common: death.

November 12, 2002

Part three

AT THE END of the day, the bone-weary hunters return to camp. They "water" their horses after busting holes in the creek ice, then gather in the mess tent to compare notes and to engage in that well-known hunters' ritual: eating garden salads — after saying grace.

"Salad is long tradition," says Jason Schar, the Eugene man who invited me on this elk hunting trip in northeastern Oregon.

Three kinds of dressings are offered, plus a stunning homemade mix brought by Leroy Carlson, a jeweler from Puyallup, Wash.: an oil-based herb variety spiced with garlic and basil. Bob Coulter's 27-year-old son, Rob, wows us with chicken cutlets in a marinara sauce.

Like a drainage basin that funnels into a single river, all elk-camp talk eventually flows into a single subject: hunting. Like, "Great dinner, Rob. Say, where ya huntin' tomorrow?"

The hunting stinks. With one day left, only one guy, Carlson, has even gotten off a shot — and he missed. But the mood stays lively. There's more to this hunt than elk.

For starters, these guys clearly enjoy each other — and are more than just "huntin' buddies." One night, Pendleton veterinarian John Groupe, eyes glistening, talks of his 16-year-old son, Ole, dying in a fall near Mount Hood in 1994. And how John's friendship with Brad Wheeler, another member of our party, was galvanized because Brad was the one who broke the news to him.

Beyond the camaraderie, these guys like lassoing the last vestiges of a cowboy life that's elusive back home where you're paying mortgages or nail-gunning roofs or watching TV. When, in the middle of the night, a handful of horses break free and rumble through camp, the guys revel in the excitement with a sort of boyish "snow day" delight.

Another reason they hunt the "cowboy way," I think, is because it involves a certain risk. While they pooh-pooh my city-slicker caution, they tell endless stories of injuries and near-misses. They are careful with their guns. And, in bed by 7, they hardly spend nights shooting beer cans off stumps.

But mention cougars and Groupe is telling about a mountain lion jumping a guy. Mention hunters who might be a few points shy of an antler rack and Larry "Hawkeye" Snook is telling about not only being "scoped" — looked at by another hunter through a gun's scope — but being shot at. Mention me — "Cowboy Bob" — being bucked off Rusty and someone is telling about Schar's horse, after Jason had dismounted, cartwheeling 300 feet down a ridge — and living to neigh about it. (After my accident, I heeded the advice, "If you get bucked off a horse, walk. It's safer.")

Finally, these guys are here for the challenge alone. On the last day, I roam the ridges with Carlson, the Jeremiah Johnson of jewelers. He tracks elk with the diligence of a forensic pathologist. He explains the difference between cow and bull scat. (I'll never eat a black olive again.) He drags me up ridges steeper than an IHOP roof. He's thinking: Elk. I'm thinking: I wonder if I'm being scoped?

By midafternoon, the sub-freezing temperature drops. Carlson is a man on a mission. I am a man wishing I'd bought those battery-operated socks at GI Joes. "Check this out," Carlson whispers. "Cougar tracks!"

Oh boy! If I don't get shot or die of exposure, I can get mauled to death! I've read in *Outdoor Life* that if you come across a grizzly bear, you're supposed to pretend you're dead. "Make no eye contact and, if you can, talk softly to the bear. The bear is likely to maul you for a few moments, but then lose interest."

We've been tracking for eight hours. Carlson is thinking: Elk. I'm thinking: When you talk softly to a bear — or, in this case, a cougar — what do you talk about? The weather? What do you say: "How 'bout them Ducks?" And why does being mauled "for a few moments" still sound like no fun?

We find no elk. We return to camp, going past a sign that says "Ole's Basin," presented to John by the guys in honor of his son.

Our group has been skunked. I've missed the essence of the true hunting experience: the shots, the hit, the blood, the skinning, the guts, the packing out of the meat. I've missed everything. Or maybe nothing at all.

When I explain how foreign that hunting can be to someone who hasn't grown up with it, "Hawkeye" Snook, who owns the Sports Corral in Joseph, says, "I never stopped to think that there are people out there who don't hunt."

It has been, to say the least, an enlightening week.

To honor my having survived, the guys autograph my fluorescent orange vest. Then Groupe, who's involved in the Pendleton Roundup, turns to me. "Say, Cowboy Bob, for a story next year why don't you be in our parade?" he says. "You could ride Rusty!" The tent erupts in laughter, mine loudest of all.

I still don't "get" hunting, but I do get its best parts, of which there are plenty.

November 14, 2002

Fish herding

LEABURG — The water in this particular rearing pond at the Leaburg Fish Hatchery is only knee deep, but as the process begins, I fear I'm in over my head.

A member of the Northwest Steelheaders' Emerald Empire chapter has invited me on a "fish recycling" venture. "You'll have a day like no other," Jane Kammerzelt promises.

It sounded wonderfully Oregon — fish recycling — and I quickly said yes. But now, as I watch her 14-year-old son, John, netting 7-pound summer steelhead that thrash like Santiago's "great fish" in Hemingway's *The Old Man and the Sea*, the memories come back.

"Get the net!" my father yells from 1968. I, too, am 14. We're in a boat on Diamond Lake and, as usual, he is reeling in a beautiful rainbow. I ready the net in the water. Suddenly, the trout gyrates wildly in a last-gasp quest for freedom. I lunge. All goes still. The fish has flopped free — as would others in my youth.

"Wanna try this?" Another Kammerzelt boy, Paul, 17, snaps me back to the present with the question. Net in hand, he is standing on a truck into whose tank we're loading the fish that will be returned to the river.

Immediately, I imagine failure. I see the volunteer below handing me the net with a 30-inch steelhead in it and me dropping it — splat — onto the ground. Or me falling into the tank, being bludgeoned to death by revenge-seeking steelhead who haven't warmed to this "recycle" idea, knowing it means they could become some fisher's dinner.

"Sure," I say unsurely.

I get the first two fish stuck in my net, but the others come easily. I gain confidence. Somebody asks if I'm ready for the pond. I look down. It is the size of a single-wide trailer. About 160 steelhead have been herded to one end by these hatchery cowboys, some of whom are Oregon Department of Fish & Wildlife employees, others volunteers.

One person nets two or three fish at a time. Another grabs one and places it on a rubber-padded cradle where two others tag it. It's then transferred, net to net, up and into the truck's tank. It's just another adventure for fish that were released into this river three years ago and have, incredibly, returned to their home after sometimes thousand-mile forays into the Pacific Ocean.

I cinch up my chest waders, then head down the ladder into the pond. It's time to exorcise the demons of Diamond Lake.

First, I try the transfer job. Slippery business, this — like getting a fussy year-old kid into his pajamas after you've overdone the baby lotion. But after a few attempts, I clamp my gloved left hand around the tails and lift from the underside with my right. Bingo!

Later, I do the net-dipping job, bringing up 15 to 30 pounds of fish at a time. The steelhead thrash and splash. Surrounded by scores of fish, you feel as if you've been plopped into some *Indiana Jones* scene, only without the snakes.

Finally, I try being a cowpoke going after strays — fish that have broken through the netting and are loose in a pond 10 times larger than the temporary pen. They dodge. They dart. They generally make a fool of me — as the vets topside watch my vain attempts.

Suddenly, it happens. "Tagged-fish loose!" someone shouts. We can't let these escape. Two guys next to me dip their nets and lunge for the streak of gray with the flash of pink tag.

"Get the net!" my father yells from 1968. Naw, forget the net. I see the fish. I reach into the water, barehanded, and, like a Kodiak bear, start groping. Amazingly, I feel the fish's tail. I clamp my hand on it, squeeze the belly with the other hand and lift.

The fish wriggles. Water splashes. But in one smooth motion, I lay it on the cradle, Santiago bringing home his marlin. The crowd goes wild. (OK, a few fellow fish wranglers whoop it up.) Adrenaline pumps. I thrust my arms into the air.

It is just a fish. But the Old Man — my old man — would have been proud.

July 1, 2004

Walking across a lake

FERN RIDGE LAKE — Figuring it was a rare opportunity, I walked across this muddy abyss Wednesday — and I'm a bigger man for it.

By that I mean I was 5-foot-9 and 182 pounds when I left Highway 126 just after sunrise and, thanks to mud-caked boots, arrived at the lake's north edge nearly five hours later at an estimated 6-

foot-5 and 290.

Fern Ridge, north to south, is 4 1/2 miles, though for reasons I'll explain later, I walked 7. The journey was, at times, fascinating (if you're missing an 8-horsepower Johnson outboard, I can help) and at times scary (mud sucks, literally). But, then, how many chances do you get to walk across a lake?

Normally, the reservoir is full in the spring. Because the dam is undergoing repairs soon, however, the water level is being kept near its minimum; thus, the lake bed is now only 15 percent water and 85 percent mud/stumps/beer cans.

"This is probably the lowest the lake's been this time of year since it was formed in 1941," says Jim Beal, the U.S. Army Corps of Engineers' park ranger for Fern Ridge.

As the sun burned through the fog, I began the trek north from the Perkins Peninsula boat ramp at 6:46 a.m. I was carrying a backpack stuffed with two water bottles, binoculars, candy bars, a digital camera, a cell phone, a pair of tennis shoes and a poncho.

As I walked the west edge of Coyote Creek, the trip was, at first, surreal. I soon lost the noise of Highway 126 and was alone in a fog-shrouded landscape that reminded me of post-eruption Mount St. Helens: ghostly stumps silhouetted against gray. A hardened mud floor that, with squiggly cracks, looked like a suburban street grid from the window of a Boeing 707. Desert-esque nothingness.

Then came the discoveries: tattered pilings of what was once a bridge over Coyote Creek on what was then Elmira Road (now Royal Avenue). Heron, ducks, geese, killdeer, crawdads and fresh-water clams and muscles. Three rusted "jato packs," used to help launch aircraft at takeoff, then dropped.

The walking was easy; my boots were barely leaving imprints. Earlier, I'd mentally gulped when realizing I'd left my map and Beal's phone number in my truck. But just short of the pool that still remains, I was making great time, great memories and great discoveries.

Then my boots started sinking deeper in what I realized was a diabolical blend of Willamette Valley clay and Silly Putty. Visibility was a quarter-mile, max. I was about three miles from Highway 126 and nearly two miles from the lake's north end. Suddenly, I sank nearly to my knees.

At 8:48 a.m. my notebook entry was simple: "First fear."

Each step was the mud-'n'-muck version of walking in hip-high snow. I was breathing hard, sweat moistening my turtleneck. I tried to keep a sense of humor (" ... Rick Dancer reporting live from Fern Ridge.") but also felt that stomach churn like when you're doing minor-league rock climbing and suddenly realize you can't go up — or down.

Seeing the skeletal head of a carp didn't help. But then came a blessed, out-of-the-blue warble: a cell phone call from Beal, with whom I'd left my number. I told him, best I could tell, where I was. He routed me back south, then west, then headed out himself to try to find me.

The fog began lifting. With two more phone calls and a mile of muck-walking, I met Beal at the north end of Perkins Peninsula in an hour. By truck, he drove me to the drier west side of the lake, where I walked three miles to finish at Richardson Point at 11:22 a.m.

I had found 89 bottles and cans, three golf balls, a pair of sunglasses, a boat ladder, a waterski binding — and adventure! Despite boots that ended up the size of a deep-sea diver's and hamstrings that will recover, I suspect, sometime near Thanksgiving, the walk was a hoot.

But if you try it, stay out of the deep stuff. Trust me. It's no fun being a stick-in-the-mud.

April 28, 2005

Climbing Autzen's crane

Part one

MAYBE IT'S because ever since I saw that huge crane erected at the Autzen Stadium construction site, I harbored a haunting vision of going to the top of it.

Maybe it's because, deep inside, I'm still jealous of Everest-conquering Jon (*Into Thin Air*) Krakauer, a Corvallis High classmate of mine who ran off with my ex-girlfriend in the winter of 1972.

Maybe it's because, in the words of Eleanor Roosevelt, "you must do the thing you cannot do."

Whatever, on Friday, as ominous clouds shrouded the sacred

shrine of Autzen, I attempted to become the first human being to climb the hammerhead tower crane and play the Oregon fight fong on a set of plastic duck lips.

The truth is, I'm not fond of heights, but I've learned that if I'm in a gondola or an elevator car I can manage.

I sought permission for the Autzen adventure months ago. When Wildish Construction's John Norton, the project administrator, gave me the thumbs up, I was thrilled. I was less thrilled when I discovered that there's no elevator to the operator's cab up top. There is, instead, a steel-runged ladder. And no hook-on safety device.

Gulp.

But something kept telling me to do it — and friends encouraged me.

"Hey, I hear there's a chance of lightning later in the week," one said. "Wouldn't that be a rush?"

I explained to another friend that because the tower was divided into nine sections, each with a grated landing, the farthest I could probably fall — unless going over the edge — would be 20 feet. "But if you bounced and rolled you could fall farther, right?" he said.

Seeking further assurance, I spoke with Ray McArthur, the "tower hand" who placed much of the structural steel beams for the new grandstands. "Eat light," he said. "You can get a little queasy up there."

He then proceeded to tell me what it was like being up top for the November windstorm that snapped some Willamette Valley trees as if they were Popsicle sticks.

"Now that was a ride," he said. "The ol' cab was really buckin' and snortin' that day. But the good thing was that my rigging was going with the wind, like a weather vane. If I'd of had it crossways to the wind, well, that'd be different."

Before he started climbing down that day, McArthur glanced at the wind gauge in his cab: It said 67 mph.

Double gulp.

The hammerhead tower crane at Autzen Stadium is 180 feet high "at the hook" — construction talk for the top, where the giant hook comes down from that horizontal arm and trucks stuff around. The elevation at the base of the tower is 448.1 feet above sea level. Exactly.

What this means, I realized the night before the climb, was that if I made it to the top I would be at 628.1 feet, only 28,226.9 feet lower than Krakauer and his trifling Mount Everest conquest. (So it's not like he has a lock on thin air, OK.)

By the morning of the climb, though, I was wondering if most of that thin air was between my ears. In all honesty I worried about freezing up. Vomiting. Falling.

I stuffed a backpack with gear: water bottle, camera, cell phone (so I could pre-dial 91 and punch the final "1" on my way down) and, most importantly, the plastic duck lips.

For sentimental value, I also packed a family photo and pictures from my 2001 Civil War tailgate party, to honor those Duck fans who would be with me in spirit as I climbed.

I arrived at the site and met my hard-hatted sherpa, Matt Huffman. I wanted to believe that he was a trained crane guide, certified by the National Association for the Ascension of Crazed Columnists. I wanted to believe that he had been up and down 1,200 times and had taken hundreds of neophytes like me safely to the top.

"Nope, only been up once myself," he said. "But it's a hoot."

The good news was that Huffman, 27, was built like those gigantic construction workers who trudge over the oil pipes in that Chevy pickup commercial; the bad news was that I was built like a middle-aged man whose doctor had told him to lay off the Big Macs.

"It sways pretty good up there when he picks up a load," said Huffman. "When it gets a little windy it's like a teeter-totter."

Yippee, I said to myself, mentally eating my fist.

I looked up at the yellow tower above me. The wind was light, a weak sun just starting to burn through thick overcast.

"Ready?" asked Huffman.

"Re — re — ready," I said with an air of resignation.

I put my gloved hand on a rung and stepped up. It was 12:22 p.m. Show time.

June 16, 2002

Part two

CLIMBING A 180-foot crane tower is like being Jack on the beanstalk — only you're thinking more about nightmares than fairy tales. And every nightmare ends in the same place: an emergency room.

For those of you who find my Oregon fight song goal a bit on the trivial side, consider my more profound motive for climbing the crane: to prove to myself that Jon Krakauer, the Everest-climbing ex-high school classmate of mine in whose arms my ex-girlfriend wound up, had nothing on me.

Unlike Krakauer's team-oriented trip up Everest, mine was a lonely journey. (I had tried to secure sponsors for my climb, but the only nibble I got was from Life Flight.) It was just me and 27-year-old Matt Huffman, a Wildish construction worker built like a strong safety.

I wrapped my gloved hands around a straight-up steel ladder and began climbing. Huffman led, I followed.

The tower was divided into nine sections, each separated by a 10-by-10-foot platform. Once you reached another platform — a grate that you could, yikes, see through — you carefully crossed to the opposite diagonal corner where the next section of ladder began.

While going up the ladder, you did have a metal rim every few feet behind you. And when you reached a platform, horizontal bars guarded the edges every few feet. But this wasn't exactly the Space Needle elevator.

I was fixating on each yellow rung, one after another, right in front of my face. But when I'd reach another platform, it was impossible to not notice the construction workers below. They looked like picnic ants.

I was surprisingly calm until, making a platform shift, I found myself staring down at the sky boxes on Autzen's north side. I felt that what-am-I-doing-here? tingle in my feet.

Onward I climbed, 20 rungs per section. The wind was light, but I was sweating profusely in a long-sleeve shirt as a weak sun burned through heavy overcast. Suddenly, I heard a conversation and looked up: It was Huffman talking to crane operator Dave Cox, who was on his lunch break in the cab.

It was that joyous moment of completion — the immigrants seeing the Statue of Liberty. After 11 minutes and 186 rungs, I pulled myself into the cab like John Glenn climbing into a space capsule.

Whoa, baby! With windows on three sides of the cab, the view was as if you'd been suspended above Autzen Stadium by a hook on the back belt loop of your jeans.

Below, the Autzen Stadium project unfolded with the dramatic feel of that scene in *Close Encounters of the Third Kind* when you first see the mother ship's landing port beneath Devils Tower, hundreds of workers scurrying here and there.

Beyond: Eugene like I've never seen it. The Coburg Hills. And, as Cox executed a slow yet sufficiently frightening 360-degree turn of the cab, Springfield, Spencer Butte and the Willamette River.

The moment was so magical that there was only one thing I could do in response: I pulled out my plastic Duck lips and began a rendition of *Mighty Oregon*. I then took some photos, made a few cell phone calls and was generally reveling in the moment when Huffman said, "Well, on to the top, huh?"

Say what? "Only 20 more feet," he said. He opened a hatch at the top of the cab and started climbing through. Wa — wa — wait a minute. I thought we'd already arrived at The Promised Land.

"Come on up, Bob," said Huffman. "Great view." I poked my head up and momentarily felt like puking. In front of me stretched the horizontal arm of the crane, balanced by 30,000 pounds of counterweights. The wind had picked up.

Huffman was standing 20 feet up above me at the top of a pinnacle that looked no more substantial than the hardened chocolate on the top of a Dairy Queen dipped cone.

He scooted down. "Your turn," he said. Thinking of three decades of chiding from hiking pals who goaded me for not signing the registry atop the South Sister — "at least *we* went to the top" — I stretched, crablike, across a platform to the base of the ladder. Unlike the others, this ladder had no surrounding tower, nothing but occasional 4-inch curved metal bands between me and the earth beyond.

I clutched that ladder like a preschool swimmer clinging to the rail in the 10-foot area, then slowly worked myself up. Suddenly, I was there. I'd reached the ultimate Autzen high.

I turned toward Huffman and his camera, then did it: flashed the absolute fastest smile you've ever seen.

June 18, 2002

The 7-mile golf hole

YACHATS — In the cool of the August morning, two golfers blow on their cupped hands to ward off the chill. They stand on the tee and look ahead toward their target, lost somewhere in the darkness of 6 a.m. It's an arrow-straight hole until a slight dogleg right at the end. Water — actually, lots and lots of water — left. Trees and beach grass right.

And lots of sand. Lots and lots of sand.

You see, this golf hole stretches seven miles long. It was created by me and my 16-year-old son, Ryan, by sticking a soup can in the sand about 12,320 yards north of my grandfather's cabin on the Oregon Coast, then driving back to play our one-hole course.

Essentially it's Yachats to Waldport. Par 72, we figure.

The sea monster makes the 948-yard sixth at Australia's Kool-and Island Golf Course — the world's longest, according to Guinness — look smelt-esque by comparison. But this challenge is more than man versus monster. It's also father versus son, as it's been since the knee football games began nearly 16 years ago.

Ryan steps to the first — and only — tee. Like a young gymnast, he fears nothing. *Thwack.* He hits one straight down the middle.

When did he get so strong?

I step to the tee, like a 41-year-old man who fears nearly everything, particularly a water trap on my left — the Pacific Ocean — that spans 70 million square miles and covers one-third of the earth's surface. I don't like the odds.

But I, too, hit straight and long. I may be aging, but I refuse to go gently into the good night.

We're off into the morning mist. The gullery is decidedly uninterested, most of the feathery fans too busy ripping the guts from washed-ashore crabs to pay much attention to us.

That's fine; we're not here for glory. On the low side of the split-level green of life, we're here for the same reason one man in an office will shoot a crumpled memo into a wastebasket and another man will slap it away as if he were David Robinson: We're competitive freaks who do crazy things involving sports.

But on the high side of the split-level green, we're here because the father part of this twosome is increasingly aware that time and tide wait for no man.

He sees a son who, Lord and admissions directors willing, will be off to college in a couple of years and will probably be doing more mature things, like painting his entire upper body with school colors for home football games.

This father-son stuff won't go on forever, this dad has realized lately. Plus, he's read the late golf guru Harvey Penick's book that encourages golfer to "take dead aim." The axiom, the father has come to understand, goes beyond the golf course to life itself.

What's more, the same father determined months ago that a minus-tide on this particular morning would stretch the fairway to its optimum width. Three hundred yards is a gloriously wide margin of error for someone who once shattered a car windshield with a wild hook.

And because of the early-morning tee time, the father reasoned, few people would be soulfully walking the beach, thinking deep thoughts about moving to the Oregon Coast to write novels when, just as they are mentally accepting the Pulitzer Prize for fiction, reality hits them right between the eyes — in the form of a Titleist 2.

Down the windless beach we head, two waves at different points in our journeys to shore. I see Ryan as a silhouette against the eastern sky and think, *When did he get to be so tall?*

We each carry but one club: a driver, for maximum distance. I hit the ball farther in the air, but Ryan takes better advantage of the hard sand with line drives that hit and roll like marbles on ice. At Big Creek, three miles after teeing off, he has a stroke on me, 26 to 27.

We each wear a fanny pack filled with extra golf balls that unmask my spoken bravado. Ryan has packed three. Me? Twelve.

As the charcoal sky turns to light blue, then salmon pink, the match remains tight. The sun bursts through the trees at the four-mile mark, turning the surf to a frothy white. The smoke from a state campground flavors the cool air.

We play Rules of Golf with Beach Alterations: Every shot may be placed on a wooden tee, of which we've brought many. But anything in the water — be it ocean, tide pool, creek or lagoon — cannot be removed without a one-stroke penalty. Seaweed, logs and dead gulls are not considered loose impediments and, thus, cannot be moved.

Hit, walk. Hit, walk. The journey continues. Past motels. Past cabins. Past deep-thinking walkers who stroll the fairway as if they were on a beach.

We make small talk. In the months to come, as Ryan grows more independent, there will be time for deeper things; for now, both of us still yawning, it is enough that we comment on flocks of sandpipers, rib each other relentlessly about who will win and compare hunger pains, which our Big Hunk candy bars soon fix.

Then, suddenly, it happens: near Yaquina John Point, with a mile to go, disaster strikes Ryan: His last tee snaps in half. It is the long-distance golfer's equivalent of a sailor's mast breaking. He must now hit off the hard-pan sand with a driver — a difficult task.

Half of me wants to console him and loan him a tee; half of me wants to exploit this advantage for all it's worth. Being the sensitive mid-life father I am, I smile like the Grinch who stole Christmas and push the thrusters to Full Exploit.

I must cling to my dignity any way I can get it. Ryan doesn't grouse; he simply buckles down and does his best.

When did he get so mature?

A hundred yards out, with the seaweed flag now in sight, we are dead even. Father and son. Sixty-two shots each.

After we each hit four more, Ryan is 12 feet and I am 3 feet from the hole. The pressure mounts.

Ryan lines up his putt, steps over the ball, strokes and — misses. He looks into the sky in agony before tapping in for a 4-under-par 68.

So it comes to this: After seven miles and 16 years, I make this simple three-foot putt to remain the family's beach golf king.

I stand over the ball that I teed off with four hours earlier. All is quiet. A few crabbers watch curiously from their boats in nearby Alsea Bay. The air is still.

I stoke the putt. As if pulled by a soup-can magnet, the ball rolls straight for the cup, for the jaws of victory, for the gentle reminder to my worthy young foe that, in the sea of life, I'm more than just some 40-something flounder; that I'm not just an over-the-hill dad; that I'm — suddenly, the putt inexplicably veers left like a sickly crab and dies two feet from the hole.

Huh?

We tie. but after a handshake and a maple bar, I realize that we have come a long way, father and son — much farther than seven miles. We have shared a sunrise, something we've rarely done. We have made a memory that may be told around beach fires for years to come: "You *know* I purposely missed that last putt."

"No way, dad."

"Sure. You didn't think I actually wanted to beat you, did you?"

Above all, we have taken dead aim and hit life's real target, which has nothing to do with swinging a golf club and everything to do with seizing a moment.

No, I realize as the incoming tide erases our footsteps on the beach, we don't tie.

We win.

Sept. 10, 1995

9.

Heroes

The trail less traveled

MCKENZIE BRIDGE — We met last August, just beneath Little Belknap Crater. I was heading south on part of the Pacific Crest Trail. She was heading north.

After a summer of too little exercise and adventure, I was feeling a little smug about my six-mile day hike; at 6,000 feet, I wasn't even into sort-of-thin air, but in my midlife mind I'd rationalized that I'd accomplished something.

Then along came Laura.

"Where'd you start?" I asked.

"Mexico," she said.

I mentally gulped, hoping she wouldn't ask where I'd started.

"And, uh, where you headed?" I asked.

"Canada."

OK, so maybe this wasn't the time to boast that I'd just bagged Little Belknap. I soon learned that Laura Buhl was hitting the 2,000-mile mark on this day. A 26-year-old University of Oregon graduate student, she planned to arrive at the Canadian border Sept. 25, return to Eugene the next day and start school the next morning.

She said it matter-of-factly, as if notifying a roommate that she was headed out to get bagels and would be back at 5. But I later learned she did exactly what she'd hoped to: walk 2,658 miles in 148 days and arrive on the day she predicted, a feat that seems as amazing to me as the Eagle landing in the Moon's Sea of Tranquility after a 238,000-mile journey from Earth.

The world is full of Laura Buhls, people who accomplish amazing things with no thirst for fame or fortune. The problem is, the media cater to the rich and famous; thus, while Buhl was quietly averaging 21 miles per day through the Mojave Desert, over 13,200-foot Forester Pass in California and across remnants of one of the heaviest snowfalls in Northwest history, the press was keeping track of such deadbeats as Latrell Sprewell.

Sprewell, a 29-year-old NBA star, is the guy who nearly choked his former coach to death during a practice session. But that didn't preclude him from nailing a $9.1 million-a-year contract with the New York Knicks after Golden State traded him — understandably, because who wants to coach a guy who might firebomb your house if you ask him to, say, hustle more on defense.

It's ironic that in September, as Buhl was trudging through obscurity to arrive on time, Sprewell was making headlines for not only failing to arrive at training camp on time — he was a week late — but for failing to tell his employers where he was. When he finally arrived — in a Mercedes-Benz that he'd recently driven onto a freeway from an exit ramp and broadsided another car — he was asked why he hadn't checked in.

"That's what agents are for," he said.

Sprewell's approach to life is why I find Buhl's so inspiring; while he would seemingly have it all and appreciate so little, she has learned the secret of simplicity. The value of discipline. The satisfaction of doing something just to know you've done it.

"I've always been intrigued by the romance of the border-to-border trip," Buhl says. "Two borders. One trail. It's perfect."

This year, 270 attempted the same journey, according to the Pacific Crest Trail Association. Fewer than 60 made it.

Buhl, carrying a 30- to 35-pound pack, walked much of the trip alone, beginning May 2. A typical day involved hiking from about 6 a.m. to 7 p.m., her record being 31 miles.

"I don't consider myself hard-core," she says. "Some hikers walk 40 miles a day."

She had food mailed to pickup points along the way, such as Elk

Lake Lodge. She encountered two bears, seven rattlesnakes, about 7 trillion mosquitoes, 30- and 95-degree temperatures, 35 miles with no available water, rain, snow and a desert windstorm that left her sunscreened face "feeling like sandpaper."

No animals hassled her, nor people for that matter; the most dangerous point was a stream crossing when she lost her footing and was nearly swept over a waterfall ("Dear Folks, having a great time; no need to worry ... ").

Spring became summer. Summer became fall. And suddenly Buhl saw a 10-yard swath in the forest — the border between the United States and Canada — and knew she'd done what she set out to do. It was Sept. 25.

Her father met her and drove her home. She arrived in Eugene at 10:30 the night before school started, caught some sleep and made her 9 a.m. class: Jog-Run.

"What I learned was that if I decide to do something, I can do it," she says.

To honor her, some friends bought Buhl breakfast. A few weeks later, the Knicks gave Latrell Sprewell a new contract: $61.9 million over five years.

But to hear Buhl talk about reaching that border or watching a Sierra sunset or being invited to join the Saltmarsh Family Reunion just past the California-Oregon line begs a question: Who, really, is the richer of the two?

November 9, 1999

Footprints at Normandy

NORMANDY, France —It looked like a lot of beaches I've seen on the Oregon Coast, only this one was part of the greatest amphibious assault in history: D-Day. June 6, 1944.

A light surf broke onto the sands of France's Normandy coast this past September as I stood and tried to imagine what it had been like.

Not far from the remains of a German concrete pillbox, where machine guns once tried to mow down those who had come to liberate France, I heard laughter. It came, I soon realized, from what appeared to be a mother and her little girl flying a kite.

The sky seemed too blue, the English Channel too smooth, the beach too quiet to have once witnessed the horrors of war.

Nevertheless, such places beckon us to remember. And so on days like today — Veterans Day — we return, sometimes in body, more often in spirit, to honor those who were once here, on the battlefields of the world.

John Bonzer's footprints once creased these sands; so, too, did Sallylou Bonzer's. They're a couple from Eugene, both 83, who were part of the 45th Field Hospital, he as a doctor, she as a nurse. They saved some lives. They patched the wounded. And sometimes they saw the wounded die; 309, to be exact, in the 45th's journey from Normandy to Czechoslovakia.

"I got so tired of seeing young men all shot up," says Dr. John Bonzer from the couple's home near Laurelwood Golf Course. "They were mostly kids, you know."

The thing is, you could be standing next to John and Sallylou Bonzer in the Albertson's line and not know they'd served their country like that. And so it goes for vets.

Oh, a few have those "Korean War Vet" license plates or proudly wear those navy blue hats that feature the names of the ships they were on. But, for the most part, they don't make a big deal about what they did.

"I've never felt like a hero," Sallylou Bonzer says. "Once, one of my daughters saw an article that had been done on me and said, 'You were in the war, mother?' I said, 'So were a lot of people.'"

Places keep calling me back to vets I've written about such as John and Sallylou.

When I drive through Junction City, I sometimes remember the story of a Korean War vet who, upon returning home, was so distraught over two men dying on his watch that he threw himself in front of a car on Highway 99.

When I drive past Springfield Memorial Cemetery, I remember Tim Ownbey. He was 19, the same age as my younger son, when he left for Vietnam. He came home 10 months later for a funeral — his own.

Last September, when the Normandy waves lulled me to sleep each night, I remembered, too. In France, lots of people still remember. The hotel lobby has a pictorial tribute to Allied troops who fought to free France from Nazi rule. The route from Normandy to Belgium is lined with remembrance markers. World War

II museums dot the landscape.

One morning, I walked Omaha Beach at low tide: Beach villas that once hid German guns were nestled into the bluff with a look of vacation bliss. A miniature golf course beckoned near hedgehogs and tetrahedrons, steel obstacles designed to rip the hulls off Allied landing craft.

Later, I walked Utah Beach, which gives way to flat sand dunes and beach grass. (Picture the stretch of beach just north of Florence, where the horses often romp.)

Utah Beach was far less grisly on D-Day than the Omaha debacle featured in the movie *Saving Private Ryan* but "Beachcomber Days" it wasn't. As the 45th Field Hospital Unit — including Sallylou Bonzer and 17 other nurses in combat fatigues — waded ashore, the face-down bodies of soldiers floated by.

"Chaos," Sallylou says, remembering what it was like landing at Utah Beach four days after D-Day. "Total chaos."

On D-Day, 856 vessels had come ashore at Utah. Troops unloaded, fought their way across France, Luxembourg, Belgium and, finally, Germany to stem the Nazi tide.

Then the war was over. Those still alive went home, and the vestiges of war gradually faded from the Normandy beaches.

At the exact swath of beach where the 45th had come ashore, I knelt down and scooped a handful of sand into a plastic bag. Once home, I dried it, funneled it into a couple of pill bottles and gave it to John and Sallylou Bonzer.

I wanted them to know what all vets — and their friends and families — need to know: Though their footprints in the sand are gone, they haven't been forgotten.

November 11, 2001

A 200,000-child legacy

WHEN LEARNING of Bertha Holt's stroke, legacies come to mind.

When she dies — and family members have gathered for that imminent possibility — what legacy will she leave, this 96-year-old dynamo who founded an international adoption agency that has placed more than 200,000 children in homes since 1956?

Honors? She earned tons of them, the latest being a Kiwanis award whose earlier recipients include no less than Mother Teresa.

Energy? She rose daily at 5:30 a.m. to pray, set a 400-meter record at age 92, drove a VW bus and flew so often she was up and down more than the stock market.

But her real legacy lies in people — people who have been given second chances.

People such as Mare-Lee Vance, adopted out of Seoul, South Korea, in 1961 and now, at 43, the director for academic support and advising services at George Mason University in Fairfax, Va.

"Had Harry and Bertha Holt not come along, I'd probably be screwing in light bulbs at some city-sponsored shelter with a bowl of rice as my ration," says Vance, who earned a doctorate from Michigan State in 1994.

She still has the hand-written letter of congratulations from Bertha Holt that arrived after graduation. "Dear Dr. Vance," it begins, and ends with, "... may the Lord bless your work. Grandma Holt."

People such as Brian Hester, adopted out of South Vietnam in 1974 and now, at 27, a house painter in Columbus, Ohio.

"The Holts played a huge part in my life. I got a second chance. Without them, I'd probably be back in Vietnam. Probably dead."

He's now engaged to be married, and he and his fiancee have already decided to not only have children, but to adopt a child.

"There are only a few people you can label as heroes in life, and I'd label Bertha Holt as one," he says. "There are sports heroes and entertainment heroes, but Bertha Holt is what I'd call a silent hero. A lot of people are surviving today because of what she and her husband did behind the scenes long ago."

People such as Asha Gayatri Noah, adopted from an orphanage in Pune, India, and now, at 18, heading to school.

A recent North Eugene High grad, she's twice been to New York as part of the Zap Dancers team, serves as a leader in her youth group at Grace Community Fellowship church and will leave for Capernwray Harbor Bible School in British Columbia come fall.

"I've always known what's going on with Grandma," says Noah, whose parents, Mike and Becky, work for the Holt agency. "She's done a lot of great work."

People such as Marylinn Munson, adopted out of Seoul in 1967 and, now 36, working as a strategic account executive for a biotech company in Oakland, Calif.

"My mom heard Bertha Holt talk at a meeting in Portland (in the '60s) and was absolutely inspired," Munson says.

Not only did the Holts make the adoption possible, she says, but they saw to it that Munson's twin sister was adopted by the same family in West Linn. "What they did was critical," she says.

She graduated from the University of Oregon in 1987 with a degree in biochemistry and now sells high-tech work stations that provide information about genetic diseases.

"You don't get to negotiate $10 million contracts in Korea as a woman," she says. "I have the opportunity to do that here."

People such as Todd Kwapisz, adopted from South Korea and now, at 28, an administrator with Holt International in Eugene.

"I met her in 1993 when I was a counselor and was intimidated — I mean, here's this woman who has done so much for the world — but when she sees you, she smiles and gives you a hug.

"She and Mr. Holt brought the plight of homeless children to another level. And without her, I'd probably be languishing in some orphanage or hanging on the streets."

People such as Russell Lawton, airlifted out of Saigon on the last flight in April 1975 and now, at 25, a second-grade teacher in Omaha, Neb.

"The chances of my still being alive, had I not been adopted, would be about one in a million," Vance says. "I was a sick baby. Malnutrition. I weighed four and a half pounds at five months."

He was adopted by a family in Grand Island, Neb. He graduated from the University of Nebraska, recently met a Korean ballet dancer from New York — also adopted through Holt — and hopes to be married soon.

"We are the new adoptees of our culture," he says. "People who look at us just see us as Asian or Vietnamese or Korean, but they don't know our stories, don't know what we've overcome. When Bertha passes on, we are the ones who will carry on what she and her husband began."

July 30, 2000

Wisdom of children

MAYBE IT was a case of midwinter blues. Maybe it was a growing sense that the world, as this week's headlines suggested, is spinning out of control.

U.S. READY TO GO TO WAR, ALLIES OR NOT ... CRIES OF 'NO BLOOD FOR OIL' RING OUT AROUND THE WORLD ... ENERGY HIGH AT ABORTION RALLIES.

For whatever reason, my mood mirrored the fog that hung low in the fields and forests along Bailey Hill Road as I approached Twin Oaks Elementary School for a speaking gig.

MAN KILLED AFTER STANDOFF ... FATAL FRATERNITY FIGHT ... GRANDPARENTS BEATER KILLED ...

I'd been asked to teach the kids a lesson about writing. Instead, they taught me a lesson about something far more important than writing: life in general.

I came away wondering if the world wouldn't be a better place if, instead of the so-called sophistication of adults — COUPLE SUSPECTED OF CONNING ELDERLY DRIVERS — we'd do better to rediscover the innocence we left behind in the Twin Oaks schools of our lives.

It is Robert Fulghum ("All I really need to know I learned in kindergarten") meets St. Matthew ("Whoever then humbles himself as this child, he is the greatest in the kingdom of heaven").

I learned part of the lesson by simply looking out at a sea of (sometimes nearly toothless) smiles and other intriguing facial expressions, and thinking: *What a wonderful collection of humanity.* And later: *What a shame that they must inherit the flawed world we're handing them.*

On the other side of the planet you'll find the equally irrepressible faces of Iraqi children, perhaps also yet unsullied by the ways of the adult world. If they're the age of Twin Oaks kids, these are children born just after the gulf war was fought in 1991.

They may have lost fathers or siblings in the war; in the first seven months of 1991, 46,900 more Iraqi children died than normally would have been expected to die, according to a study by the *New England Journal of Medicine.* This was due mainly to an outbreak of diarrhea caused by disabled water and sewage systems caused by the war — a nearly full Autzen Stadium worth of dead children.

Which makes you wonder if war is the only alternative for today's Iraqi situation — if this is the absolute best we can offer the next generation.

I also learned this "life lesson" by noticing how trusting these Twin Oaks kids are of adults, be they teachers, volunteers, guest speakers or their much-adored principal.

The kids look up at you as if you're The Hope. The Answer. The Expert. And yet, given that you're part of this adult world that will soon be handed to them, what you really want to tell them is: *Don't grow up. Don't become one of us.*

SCHOOL SEGREGATION ON THE RISE IN SOUTH ... MAN HELD IN ATTACK ON 8-YEAR-OLD. Instead, go create a finger painting. Lie out in that field next to your school — the one with the antique goal posts — and see how many objects you can see in the clouds. Play tag. Dream big. And, as one of the first-graders did Thursday, keep raising your hands and saying, "Geth what? I lotht three teeth."

I learned part of the lesson when I sat down with 10 kids and asked them what they'd do about the state's school-funding fiasco. Of six who ventured an answer, four said they'd help put together fund-raisers, which seems a tad more compassionate and community-minded than some of the over-my-dead-body anti-Measure 28 letters I've read.

But, then, the world of adults is complex.

MAN WILL SERVE 13 YEARS FOR DRUNKEN DRIVING ACCIDENT ...18-MONTH-OLD LEFT IN BUS ... PARENTS CHARGED IN SCAM ...

Finally, I learned part of the lesson from an essay that a Twin Oaks fifth-grader, Amy Poeschl, wrote for the Eugene School District's Martin Luther King Jr. Essay Contest.

"If you want to make peace, do what you tell your children to do," she wrote in what was the district's winning elementary school entry. "Adults, here's an idea that can help both generations: Take your own advice — talk the talk and walk the walk."

She suggested a "National Neighbor's Day, a day where the government and all people — rich, poor, young and old — will shake hands with their neighbors."

"Our country," she later wrote, "needs to demonstrate peace in order to have peace. We can each take a turn in doing that, forgetting our differences and focusing on making this country a just and

ЦΙ.

=ime

true country."

But they are only children. What do they know?

January 26, 2003

Eugene's 'Karate Kid'

HE HAS BLOCKED OUT the memories of humiliation, but mothers don't forget. Even 10 years later.

"He got beat up nearly daily," says Carol Still, whose son, David Olson, was 12 at the time. "He'd cry every morning on the way to school."

At Madison Middle School, Carol says, a P.E. teacher humiliated him in front of the class when he could do only two push-ups. The bullies stuffed him into garbage cans, shoved him into lockers, pantsed him. Once, they ran an extension cord down his jeans.

"In middle school, if you aren't 'cool' and 'normal,' you're considered 'weird,'" says Sandra Stenius, who remembers David from her days as the school's counselor. And in a youth world where labels are tickets to acceptance, "autistic" isn't, say, Abercrombie & Fitch.

People such as Stenius were supportive, Carol says. But others wagged fingers of fatalism at her — never expect your autistic son to graduate from high school, get a job or make much of himself, they said.

Once, after being bullied, David blackened the eye of — in his words — "a tormentor"; he got suspended.

Amid this pain, David watched *The Karate Kid* with his mom.

"I wanna learn that karate stuff," he said out of the blue.

Carol rolled her eyes. "I didn't think that's what he needed. I had visions of more violence."

But she was a single mom with a kid in trouble. Why not?

Alan Best, chief instructor at Eugene's Best Martial Arts Institute, remembers meeting Carol Still. David doesn't like to be touched, she said. He's anti-social. He flips out.

Best welcomed David. No meltdown ever came. Instead, David emerged as a model student.

Someday, David told himself, he would earn a black belt.

After eighth grade, David enrolled at South Eugene to leave the bully gang behind. "At South, he simply got ignored by students," Carol says. "That's all he ever wanted."

It was hard, however, to ignore him at the institute. Respect between students isn't optional. And David was getting good.

"The place became like family for David," Carol says. "It was safe."

As classmates dropped out, David kept training: three times a week, 52 weeks a year, year after year, earning higher-level belts in the process.

He graduated from South in 1999, went to work at Down to Earth's warehouse and hung out with his girlfriend, Dawn, who's also autistic.

Last December, Best came to David, by then 22 years old. "I'm recommending you for a black belt in karate and tae kwon do," he said. David tried to conceal his smile. He couldn't.

Two weeks ago, David took the required two-day test. "He did 4,000 kicks," Best says. "He sparred with a 215-pound teacher who used to worry about hurting him. This time, the teacher worried about getting hurt."

The last item after 15 hours of physical testing was push-ups. Fifty were required. David did them all.

He had passed, becoming only the ninth student in 14 years to earn the black belt. When David walked into the gym the next day, his classmates stopped what they were doing and, as is customary, bowed in respect. It was a magic moment for David — as it was when Best asked him if he would help teach younger students.

But the greatest moment of all came recently when, at the counter of a video store, David realized one of his middle school "tormentors" from 10 years ago was working the cash register. "Hey," the kid said, "didn't you used to go to Madison?"

David nodded yes. "I could have really embarrassed him in front of his co-worker," David says. "I could have said, "Yeah, weren't you one of the guys who used to stuff me in garbage cans?' "

Or he could have returned when the guy got off work and pummeled him in the parking lot; "sure, I knew I could beat him up."

But David had nothing to prove to the kid. He'd already proven it to the one whose opinion, in the end, matters most. His own.

April 13, 2003

'I'm still here'

When she was 4, Desire Fountaine watched her mother's boyfriend put a bullet though her mom's head after the two argued about what to have for breakfast.

In time, Desire would tell her story to the police, to her grandmother and to her therapists. But it wasn't until this summer, at age 16, that the Springfield girl told her story to the world.

The murder happened in Oakland, Calif., in 1992. When police arrived, Desire and her then-2-year-old brother, Jayme, had been alone in the apartment for nearly an hour. "Wake up, Mommy," Desire kept saying, hovering over the body. "Wake up."

But Glynda Hammell, 24, would never wake up.

Her killer was convicted of murder. His friends threatened to kill Desire, her brother and Sherry Neal, Glynda's mother who took in the children. In 1994, the three moved to Springfield.

Desire hated it. She hated being the only black girl in her classes. She hated how her grandmother wouldn't let her wear makeup. She hated her mother for being beautiful and smart and yet throwing her life away on drugs and "loser" men.

For a long time, Desire had been afraid to love anyone, including herself; she blamed herself for her mother's death. But, gradually, it happened: The hate began thawing.

For the first time, she met her father, who'd split with her mom before Desire had been born. That healed some wounds. She came to realize the reason her grandmother often said no to her was because she didn't want Desire to get hurt. She learned what a painful childhood her mother had endured: raped at age 8; an abortion at 16. She forgave her mom — and herself.

Early last year, she heard about ACT-SO, the Afro-Academic, Cultural, Technological and Scientific Olympics. The national contest, for students of African descent, offered competition in 25 categories, from architecture to physics. Someone suggested Desire, then a sophomore at Springfield High, enter the essay division.

She did, though hardly with lofty expectations. Jose Chaves, a Lane Community College English teacher, was appointed as her mentor. "What do you want to write about?" Chaves asked. Desire shrugged.

"Well," he said, "have you had any major events that have drastically changed who you are?"

Her essay, "Still Here," took three months to write. In it, Desire writes of the impact her mother's death had on her, ending with a reference to Langston Hughes' poem "Still Here."

"I been scarred and battered / My hopes the wind done scattered .... / They done tried to make me stop laughin', stop lovin', stop livin'— / But I don't care! / I'm still here!"

She rewrote it dozens of times, then submitted it. In May, winners in the regional ACT-SO contest were announced. Desire's piece had won a gold medal, the best of the bunch.

In July, she and a group of other regional winners went to Miami for the nationals. When Desire walked into the Miami Convention Center for the awards banquet, she was stunned: thousands of people from across the country, big-screen TVs, a huge stage.

Finally, time came to announce the three winning essays from about 100 finalists. "And from Eugene, Oregon ... ," she heard. The announcer mispronounced her name, first and last, but it was her name nevertheless. She had won a bronze medal — third place.

She remembers finding her way to the stage, her picture on the big-screen TV "and just not being able to stop smiling."

"It was an incredible moment," says Marilyn Mays, head of Eugene's NAACP chapter and of the local ACT-SO chapter.

"I've been through some things," Desire says, "but I'm healing. I'm still grieving but I refuse to live in misery."

Desire Fountaine is still here. And the world is better for it.

September 4, 2003

The vision of Mr. Groff

YOU'RE A LITTLE down this morning. So much work, so little time. The youngest son's car is in the shop — again. The ice maker in the fridge is busted. The post-vacation weight you lost has been found.

Then you meet Forrest Groff. He's the blind man a couple of booths over at Rose's Diner in Springfield. Walks here a mile every weekday morning with his yellow lab, Texas.

Invites you home to meet the wife. Forrest is 86, Della 88. Married 64 years.

He rambles. But eventually gets to where he's going, and it's well worth the wait.

"My life's motto is 'I will overcome no matter what comes my way,'" he says with I-have-a-dream fervor.

brother, Orville, was run over by a car. As he lay dying, says Forrest, the boy said two things: that he loved his brothers even though one of them, Everett, had once poked him in the cheek with a pair of scissors, and that he could see Jesus and was going to go be with him.

Never forgot that. Says he "gave my heart to the Lord" and was baptized in a horse tank at "Moe's barnyard." He was 12.

Returned to Oregon. Did yard work when the migrant season was over. Walked six miles into Newberg each day and six miles back.

Grew in his faith at the Church of the Brethren's Camp Myrtlewood near Myrtle Point.

Remembered words of his grandfather: "If something needs doing, do it right; if it needs to be done, do it now; and there's a place for everything."

Decided his place was in Chicago, going to a Church of the Brethren seminary. Hitchhiked there. Met Della on his first Sunday at church; couldn't resist those long braids.

They married in 1936 — Depression days — and later moved to Springfield. The seminary wanted him to be the denomination's national church building director so he attended University of Oregon's School of Architecture.

They had four kids. At one point, he was pastoring a church, building a house, attending school, working in a cabinet shop, leading a Boy Scout troop and serving as director of Camp Myrtlewood, all at once. "I've never lived such an exciting life," he says — and means it.

The flood hit in '45. The Willamette River ruined the family's Glenwood home. Forrest built a new one. "I'm a stubborn man," he says. "Ever since I took care of my mama and our family, I vowed I wouldn't let my family suffer like that."

Designed some 150 churches; built a dozen. Tried to donate half of all he made to the church.

Retired. Moved to California. Started investing in property. Did well.

Prostate cancer, 1975. Surgery, one of 25 he's had in his life.

Moved to Brookings. While building a boat-themed gift shop in 1981 was walking on rafters when he realized he couldn't see out of one eye. Glaucoma. Right eye. That's OK, he figured, still have the left.

Was making a ship's wheel on a lathe a year later when a piece of wood shattered and hit his left eye. That's OK, he figured, still have arms and legs.

Moved to Springfield in 1989. Hit by a car five years ago on his way home from breakfast. Broken leg. Cancer returned three years ago. More surgery.

Then, two years ago, remembered those words of his grandfather. If it needs to be done, do it now. Told Della — "my pretty lady" — they should donate money for a new log lodge at Camp Myrtlewood. And design it, too.

But how? she wondered.

We can do it, he said. Together. He talked. Della drew. And erased. And drew again. Six months of this, on and off. "Blood and sweat," says Forrest.

Then, finished. Sent plans to Lodge Log Homes in Boise, whose president says he had little problem turning them into reality. "A lot of our clients don't understand construction," says Bill White, the company president. "Forrest does. We spoke the same language. He had the mental picture." And Della made it a visual picture.

Originally, the lodge was to be called Forest Cove. Forrest liked that, what with his name and all. But then he got a better idea.

Remember: A place for everything. What about Della, who has been his wife for 64 years and his eyes for nearly 20?

Opening next spring: Forest Dell Lodge, the legacy of a man with great vision.

October 22, 2000

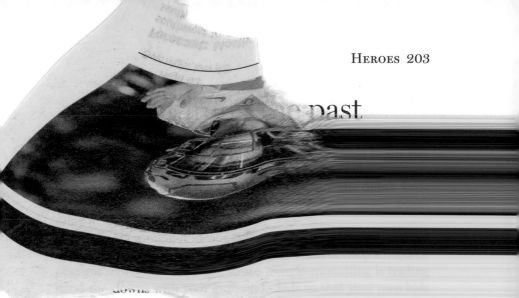

past

don't have to wear their sisters ... on clothes."

Most of my students concentrated on grades. Gries concentrated on learning. She had a seriousness about her, a passion not to waste a moment of this chance to learn — as if making up for lost time.

Last week, after interviewing Gries, I understood why. Katey Gries is like the 1,500-meter runner who gets tangled up at the start and falls flat. In similar situations, some quit. Others get up and run with abandon.

Gries is a high school dropout who was preyed upon by an alcoholic stepfather. She got into drugs and began hooking up with one loser after another. "My self-esteem," she says, "was in the toilet."

Things got worse. After getting her degree through a correspondence course, she moved from the Southwest to Portland. One night, her VW stalled on a rural road. A man in a pickup pulled over, ostensibly to help. Instead, he raped her. Repeatedly.

After he left, Gries knocked on the door of the only house in the area. Nobody came out. There she was: a 22-year-old woman, lip bleeding, hair torn out — the rapist had dragged her — and her body battered and bruised.

Only one thing, she says, is worse than being betrayed by a stranger: being betrayed by someone you love. Later, that happened: A man she married, she found, had been cheating on her repeatedly. The two divorced, one of numerous failed relationships she's had. "I've made some bad choices," she says.

She found herself having horrible nightmares. Sleeping with a .357-Magnum under her bed. Drinking. "I remember thinking: You're never going to amount to anything."

After moving to Eugene in 1994 with her three daughters

— now 18, 17 and 14 — the comeback began slowly.

She enrolled at Lane Community College. Through Womenspace's "Turning Point" program, she rediscovered her value as a person. She learned why she kept clinging to losers — and stopped it.

In 2001, she transferred to the UO, where she landed in the School of Journalism and Communication. She survived two classes that weed out the wannabes, one known affectionately as "Info Hell."

Once afraid of computers, Gries found herself rapping out stories for journalism classes — and liking it. She made the Dean's List, posted a 3.66 GPA and was inducted into the invitation-only Kappa Tau Alpha national honor society.

All while being a single mom, working in the dining room at Ya-Po-Ah Terrace and volunteering for Womenspace.

Earlier this month, she won the journalism school's Gretchen Starr Scholarship. And landed a yearlong internship with *Oregon Quarterly*, the UO's alumni magazine.

But the real celebration comes Wednesday, the 25th anniversary of her rape. Each year, Gries does "something special" on Sept. 29. The idea isn't to dwell on what happened — the rapist, by the way, is still in jail — but to remember that she overcame it.

"I survived," says Gries, now 47. "And I celebrate that. I celebrate that I'm still alive. I buy a book or go see a movie, nothing big."

This year, she'll celebrate by donating $25 to Womenspace. Some of the rest of us will do the same — to honor Katey Gries and others like her, who stumble and fall, but refuse to quit the race.

September 28, 2004

Shadowlands

FOSSIL — When an August evening cools this land of rimrocks and hills, what's most beautiful are the shadows: cool fingers stretched across flutes of parched brown.

The land of sage and juniper where Bill Bowerman grew up and died. The land of time-locked fossils that still surrounds his widow, Barbara, who sits across from me at the Big Timber restaurant on this Saturday as the human embodiment of this gritty and engaging place.

"I always thought of Bill as that surfer who would pick the biggest wave and ride it better than anyone else," she says with Katharine Hepburn zest. "And I got to go along for the ride."

She says so not with a sense of bitterness, but of privilege — as someone who feels blessed to have spent a lifetime with someone most know only from the headlines, but whom she knew as the kid shooting spit wads at Medford High, where they met in 1928. The dreamer doodling track-shoe ideas on napkins. The husband of 63 years she went to kiss goodnight on Dec. 24, 1999 — only to find his lips cold.

"My life is divided into all these segments, and it was almost as if each segment was better than the last," says Bowerman. "At the time I never had time to think about it. Now I do. And I have no regrets. What an adventure!"

At 91, Barbara Bowerman has the verbal endurance of a marathoner, the eloquence of a novelist and the appreciative heart of a generation that took nothing for granted.

But it's not always easy living with a man who cast a shadow as wide as any Oregonian: War hero. Olympic track coach. Guru to Steve Prefontaine and other UO running greats. Pioneer of jogging. Quiet philanthropist. And inventor of the waffle-soled running shoe on whose wings Nike took flight. "We didn't have an awful lot of personal time together," she says.

But she learned to share him. And he learned to involve her.

"You're sitting at the table where Nike was all but born," she says, once we're back at her assisted-living apartment in this north-central Oregon town of 460. "I remember sitting at it when Bill, John (Jaqua) and 'Buck' (Phil Knight) would be hammering things out."

Sometimes she was asked to take notes. "I always felt like a midwife. I remember writing this $500 check and saying: 'Now, what am I doing this for?'"

She tells you of the two having waffles on their deck above the McKenzie River and Bill saying, "That's it!" He could make a rubberized running-shoe sole from a waffle iron.

"It didn't surprise me. He was forever using my hair dryer to peel off glue from shoes."

But, mainly, she tells you not of mountain-top moments — say, life with Pre — but those hidden in the canyons: How it was she, not he, who proposed. How the multi-family camp trips at Cultus Lake included a little boy named Dave Frohnmayer, now president of the University of Oregon. And how, though he had plenty of both, Bill cared little for the limelight or money.

"Attention," she says, "bothered him like flies."

And yet, whether taking on the U.S. Olympic Committee or the Bhagwan Shree Rajneesh, the man couldn't help but attract it. She remembers how, as the Rajneesh cult morphed like an insurgent military group in the '80s, Bill huffed: "They've got Wasco County, but they're not taking Wheeler."

The Bowermans owned considerable land just across the John Day River from "Rancho Rajneesh," and when "the war," as Barbara calls it, ended, Bill wondered if they should sell. Barbara wouldn't hear of it. "That," she says, "is my Picasso."

And so it was that in 1998, the couple moved back to the land they both loved, where Bill had spent the first eight years of his life.

Barbara didn't cry that Christmas Eve when he died. But, later, she saw the paper on the doorstep with the headline about his death.

"I thought of all those boys he'd coached who were going to read that headline," she says. "Then I cried."

Typical others-first Barbara.

Beauty in the shadows.

August 16, 2005

A soldier's life

HE WOULD eventually become the father to seven children and the grandfather to nine. He would become the youngest board member of the American Stock Exchange. He would serve as CEO to a handful of major fishing tackle companies, including Fenwick and Garcia.

But on the first Tuesday of the year 2000, Ralph Lafferty would sit in his home in the south hills of Eugene and, at age 81, remember not what he had become, but the reason he was alive to become anything at all.

It was Christmas Eve 1944. Lafferty was a 26-year-old captain in the Army's 2nd Battalion Headquarters of the 86th Infantry, 10th Mountain Division, which had just landed in Naples, Italy. Like some others in the division, Lafferty was a Eugene boy. He had been a yell leader and swimmer at University High and an ROTC student at the University of Oregon.

After college, he trained for three years, much of it in the Colorado mountains, to prepare for offensives such as the one he would soon join: Allied troops sweeping north against Germans in the rugged Apennines Mountains.

For now, Lafferty watched little Italian boys dive for coins thrown by U.S. soldiers into the Bay of Naples. They must be freezing, he said. A fellow soldier — a buddy of his named Bill — scoffed. They're tough kids, he said; they can do anything.

The 86th Infantry spent the winter about 300 miles north, in a mountainous region near Livorno. March arrived: Showtime. The 86th headed north, leapfrogging with other regiments against German forces. Allied casualties were high. And the fighting was getting fiercer.

On April 14, 1945, a major Allied offensive began. Early on, a commanding officer at an observation point had been hit and Lafferty was called forward to replace him.

The mountainous area was littered with land mines — "S" mines about the size of a can of beans. Touch one and, like a fireworks display, the can popped up about 20 feet and exploded, spraying hundreds of marble-sized steel balls.

Lafferty arrived to a division pinned down by German machine-gunners. The commanding officer, though still alive, had a bullet through his jaw. Mortar fire rained down.

Suddenly, Lafferty was hit in the arm. A soldier grabbed Lafferty's hand and tried to pull him up, but Ralph felt as if the arm, now limp, wasn't even his. He lay there for about an hour, then, with two others, tried to make a break.

Boom. A soldier had triggered a mine. A guy next to Lafferty — he remembers him only as "Sgt. White" — was dead. The shrapnel hit Lafferty in the legs, buttocks and foot. He didn't know it at the time, but he also suffered a punctured lung.

"Can't move," Lafferty told another soldier who had survived.

Help came two hours later. A litter was thrown together using an army raincoat. Lafferty was carried two miles to a makeshift medics' post. He was wrapped in a blanket and shot with morphine. Then, medics went on to the other wounded.

A temporary hospital had been set up in a school, back in the village of Pistoia, about 20 roadless miles away. Jeeps were few and far between. Lafferty didn't know the extent of his injuries; he did know that he needed to get to that hospital somehow — and fast.

He waited. Minutes became an hour. Two hours became three. He heard talk of an available Jeep, but nobody came for Lafferty.

Then, oddly, he heard a familiar voice: It belonged to his buddy, Bill, a guy he'd seen only once or twice since they'd watched the little boys dive for coins on the day the soldiers had arrived. Bill, a major, was bullying a private, trying to commandeer the Jeep himself. But majors didn't drive Jeeps; majors were driven around by privates.

Not this time, Bill said. He helped get Lafferty's litter strapped to the Jeep, hopped in and drove off. He zigzagged his way to Pistoia, where Lafferty found himself in a school hallway. "This man needs blood!" someone yelled. He was taken to a classroom-turned-operating room. He saw a garbage can. It was filled with arms and legs.

He was operated on by a Dr. Pat Burford, a man who got only the most serious cases, a man who, years later, Lafferty would visit — and thank — in St. Louis.

But after Lafferty recovered and went home, after he got on with a life that has continued for nearly 55 years since that day, the one he credits for saving his life is the man who commandeered that Jeep and raced him, cross-country, into the good doctor's hands.

"If I hadn't gotten there when I did, I wouldn't have made it," Lafferty says. "And I credit Bill for that. He always was a take-charge guy. It was just a case of Bowerman being Bowerman."

January 9, 2000

10.

Losses

A life too short

HOW DO I EXPLAIN Mario Miranda, the young man from *The Register-Guard's* 20Below News Team who died Friday in a car accident?

Think of every pants-sagging, cool-walking, like-ya-know-talking teenage stereotype you can think of. That's exactly what Mario Miranda was not.

He would walk into our monthly 20Below meetings — I'm the skipper of this motley crew — in slacks and a button-down shirt.

"It took me two years just to get him to wear a shirt that didn't have buttons," said Bob Nardo, a longtime friend of Mario's and a senior at South Eugene High.

Last summer, Mario went to stay with his grandmother in California and, once settled, called Bob.

"How goes it?" Bob asked.

"Great," Mario said. "Grandma has CSPAN-2!"

Mario Miranda had a passion for America and conservative politics. He started Elmira High's Young Republicans Club.

Not surprisingly, his views often ran counter to those of his 20Below teammates. In 1998, when we asked new team members who they would like to share a campfire with, answers included Janis Joplin, Bob Marley, Bruce Lee and John Lennon. Miranda chose Ronald Reagan.

He was 18 going on 63. He was so mature that at 20Below meetings I sometimes got the feeling he was the only adult in the room, including me.

He was William F. Buckley Jr. with pizza breath. He was Alex Keaton on the old "Family Ties" sitcom, a conservative in a world of liberals — but without Keaton's cockiness.

Mario's conservativism wasn't the stuff of in-your-face bumper stickers and obnoxious talk radio. It was, he believed, simply the best way of making a great country greater.

He was modest, intelligent and, given the political currents he swam against, courageous. He didn't waffle when stating an opinion but neither did he lord his opinions over his peers. He did more listening than talking.

I sensed he liked the other students and they liked him, partly because he was so unconventionally proper and partly because he was so quietly committed. "He cared about the world more than anyone I know," Nardo said.

Each of our five columnists is mentored by an adult at *The Register-Guard.* I was Mario's mentor. He was a good writer, not great. But he would not only accept criticism, he would thank me for it. He desperately wanted to improve.

Last spring, he wrote a piece on the young man who began the high school fund-raising pageants for the Children's Miracle Network; one CMN organizer said it was the best story she'd ever seen on the guy. A Great Debate in which Mario argued against tighter gun control measures triggered more response than anything we've ever run in 20Below.

Politics came easily for him; humor did not. He had that Bob Newhart way about him; he was funny because he was so serious.

"I am young, Hispanic, compassionate, sensitive, non-Protestant and certainly not rich," he once wrote. "In fact, after I pay the $70 for my Advanced Placement history class credit, I will have a net worth of $7.50."

Sometimes, I'd kid him about what a great baseball name he had, and pretend I was announcing him: "Now batting, Marrrrio Mirrrrrrrrrrrrranda!"

He'd smile that awesome smile of his. But he much preferred "Senator Miranda." "I can think of no job better than that of a legislator in the U.S. House or Senate," he once wrote.

Mario had a few teenage traits. "He was a burger-and-fries guy," Nardo said. And he had seen the original *Star Trek* movie 15 times. But he collected autographed pictures of politicians, not baseball cards.

"Seriously, he had literally hundreds of pictures of political leaders," Nardo said. "He would write them all the time. Last year, we took a road trip to California and just like some guys talk baseball trivia, we talked political trivia. He could name names of senators from all the states, just like that."

After graduation this spring, he planned to attend the University of Oregon. Just a few days ago, Nardo tried to talk him into applying to American University in Washington, D.C., but Mario told his pal, "I don't want to spend my entire life in Washington, D.C."

Mario Miranda was a cool kid. Not because he was conservative, but because, liberal or conservative, he cared. He cared about wanting the world to be a better place, and he did something about it.

The last time I saw him was after our 20Below meeting on Jan. 6. He came up to me in his typical serious style and said, "Thanks for your feedback on my column. Is there anything I can do to get better?"

No, Mario, nothing. Nothing at all. You did just great.

January 23, 2000

Goose music

DALLAS, ORE. — On a grassy butte rising above the Baskett Slough National Wildlife Refuge, friends gathered to remember Rich Guadagno on Saturday afternoon.

Ten miles west of Salem, it was the place he loved most. A small wooden observatory sits above 2,500 acres of grasslands, Oregon white oak and marshes that draw thousands of Canada geese, whose distant call never ceased to thrill the man.

Goose music, he called it.

As manager of the refuge for the U.S. Fish & Wildlife Service, Guadagno, 38, had lived alone on the site from 1992 to 2000, before accepting a similar position at Humboldt Bay National Wildlife Refuge in Northern California.

But in September he flew back East to help celebrate a grandmother's 100th birthday. His Newark-to-San Francisco return flight was one most Americans — and certainly the 125 people at Saturday's ceremony — won't ever forget: United Airlines Flight 93.

Said his girlfriend, Diqui LaPenta, of Arcata, Calif.: "The last words I said to him were, 'I love you. See you Tuesday,' "

But that Tuesday shattered lots of lives, LaPenta's among them.

Along with 44 other passengers, Guadagno died after the plane was hijacked by terrorists and turned toward Washington, D.C. When a group of passengers apparently rushed the hijackers, the plane crashed in rural Pennsylvania.

Ask anybody who shivered Saturday atop Baskett Butte and willed their grief-numbed lips to sing *Morning Has Broken*: Guadagno was among those who rushed the cockpit. "When we heard the news about what had happened, we knew, we absolutely knew," said Judy Brunkal, whose family had grown close to Guadagno.

"He wasn't about to let terrorists fulfill their ill-fated plan," said his former supervisor, Jim Houk. "His finest hour was his last. He gave his life to prevent a greater national tragedy."

And yet Guadagno's life, say those who knew him, was never about being in the spotlight.

"To be called a hero would have embarrassed him greatly," LaPenta said.

And so it was that those who came to Baskett Butte dwelled not so much on how he had died, but on how he had lived: with great passion for people, plants, birds, photography, astronomy, gardening, guitar playing, bird-watching, Italian food and animals, particularly his dogs, Raven and Lady Hawk.

They remembered a man who didn't care much about money and things, but could make a friend before the two had finished their second cup of coffee.

"He had the gift of making everybody around him feel like they were his best friend," Eric Coombs said.

The family of a local state police officer he worked with all but adopted him, the man's kids calling him "Uncle Rich." When the man's daughter got married in New Mexico, the family was stunned to see Guadagno show up.

They remembered a man who loved the natural world.

"Everywhere we look from up here, we see his legacy," Houk

said. "From the visitors' kiosk to 600 acres of restored wetland to restoring endangered species habitat here on the butte."

He guarded the refuge like a pit bull; he was, after all, a federal law-enforcement officer. He once arrested a sign-shooter — while unarmed and out on a jog.

And yet, if he could unleash his inner pit bull, he was usually as laid back as a goose on an updraft.

Birdwatcher Bill Tice told of being summoned to Guadagno's office after another Fish & Wildlife officer had apprehended him for being in an off-limits area. Tice, scared, felt like a fifth-grader being called into the principal's office. Instead, Guadagno wanted to know what kind of birds he was seeing. Anything good?

"We talked for an hour," he said. "If you ask me, we should re-name this place Guadagno National Wildlife Refuge."

Actually, that was discussed. But most agreed that Rich wouldn't want that; it would call too much attention to him. And so they settled on naming the lookout above the butte in his honor, complete with a plaque and a freshly planted Oregon white oak.

Those who had gathered sang a handful of songs — Raven, his dog, chimed in nicely on *Imagine* — and the service ended with *Amazing Grace*. When it was over, people headed down the butte, carrying programs with a Nelson Henderson quote that fit the oc-casion well: "The true meaning of life is to plant trees, under whose shade you do not expect to sit."

The sun was low above the Coast Range and, in the distance, you could hear it: goose music.

November 18, 2001

Gone: 20,451 years of life

IN MAY, which ended Friday, *The Register-Guard* reported the passing of 20,451 years of life from our midst. We lost 282 people.

This is the kind of thing you learn when you keep a database of the paper's obituaries for a month, which I've long thought of do-ing and finally did.

We lost Pearl Martin, 85, of Cottage Grove, who used to make quilts for the Eugene Mission, and Claudeen Naffziger, 67, of Eugene, who was orphaned as a little girl but went on to become a high school class valedictorian, a psychologist and an author.

Fifty-one percent of those who died were males, 49 percent females. In age, they ranged from 108-year-old Maria Tino of Eugene to 4-day-old Ashlyne Benson of Springfield.

Two 10-year-olds and a 6-year-old died, but the average age at death was 72.5. Those born in the 1910s and 1920s comprised 48 percent of the deaths, followed by those born in the '30s (11 percent), '40s (9 percent) and '50s (6 percent).

We lost Roger Anderson, 53, of Springfield, who once won the Portland Marathon's wheelchair division, and James Lawson Jr., 54, of Cottage Grove, who served three tours of duty in Vietnam. Three.

Those who died left behind 416 children, 909 grandchildren, 1,005 great-grandchildren and 69 great-great grandchildren.

Nearly four in 10 died of "age-related causes," nearly three in 10 of cancer and nearly one in 10 of heart failure. Strokes, Alzheimer's, diabetes, asthma, emphysema, influenza, kidney failure — all took lives.

Accidents claimed nine people. In 16 cases, relatives chose not to disclose the cause of death. In a couple of cases, the cause of death was unknown.

We lost Monna McCormick, 85, of Springfield, a former Timber Bowl waitress who once won a lawn mower in a poetry contest sponsored by a local radio station, and Joseph Morse, 89, formerly of Eugene, who founded Morse Brothers construction and gravel company.

Most who died came here from somewhere else. Only 11 percent were born in the Eugene-Springfield area, 28 percent in Oregon.

Interestingly, 14 of the deceased — people, not percent — were born in Oklahoma, ranking it, along with Washington, second behind California in non-native births. Other high-ranking states of birth were Texas, Iowa and Idaho, with nine people each, and South Dakota with eight.

Regionally, the West Coast (55 percent) was the birthplace of most, followed by the Midwest (28), South (9), Rocky Mountains (8) and East (5). Five percent were born outside the U.S.

We lost Steve Overton, 47, of Eugene, a former hell-raiser who had cleaned up his life before being killed in an automobile accident, and Rosalie Baker, 77, of Springfield, who helped build B-17s and B-29s during World War II.

The average deceased person had lived in this area 36 years. Fifteen people who died had been married for more than 60 years. Thirty-three had no services.

Occupations leaned heavily toward the blue-collar side. Of the 282 people who died, only about a dozen had white-collar jobs. The largest single job category was "logger/millworker." "Homemaker" was the most common job listed for women.

Beyond that, the people's jobs ranged from ministers to mechanics, teachers to tree planters, farmers to pharmacists. A few were doctors and nurses. A few ran service stations. A few drove trucks.

We lost Robert Norman, 70, of Eugene, who once sang in front of President Dwight Eisenhower as a member of the Air Force Choir, and Craig Reimer, 36, a former Eugene man who played electric guitar in San Francisco coffee house bands.

Forty-seven of those who died were listed as having served in the military; six helped build World War II ships and planes.

They were Baptists, Mennonites, Buddhists, Catholics, Congregationalists, Jewish — and everything in between and beyond.

Their interests were across the board: panning for gold, writing music, walking dogs, sewing, dancing, reading, beachcombing, bowling, woodcarving and watching "Wheel of Fortune." They coached youth baseball and volunteered at the Oregon Country Fair.

More fished, hunted, golfed, gardened, rooted for the Ducks and "enjoyed spending time with family" than any other single "hobby."

We lost Alvin Ray, 69, of Eugene, who drove a truck 1.7 million miles for Bi-Mart without an accident, and 10-year-old Dixie Bradley of Veneta, who was "trying to master the hula hoop" before dying May 8 from injuries sustained in an auto accident.

One month. Two hundred and eighty-two deaths — and yet what an incredible amount of life.

June 2, 2002

The risk of reaching high

IN THE AFTERMATH of Saturday's *Columbia* space shuttle
tragedy, my sister and I find ourselves thinking about the same
odd thing: the Oregon Trail.

She is immersed in writing a book (*A Heart for Any Fate*) based
on the experiences of the King family, for whom Kings Valley, west
of Corvallis, is named. And I'm forever trying to find meaning for
the present in the past.

We meet, then, in sibling synchronization over the phone,
though soon our imaginations take flight to 1845 near what's now
Cascade Locks. It's here, Linda Crew writes in her book, where the
family is approaching the final leg on its 2,000-mile journey.

Like the astronauts, the Kings, too, are on the *Columbia* — not
in a spacecraft, but on a raft being carried by a river that is far
tamer now in its post-dam years than it was in 1845. They're almost home.

Then, suddenly, they're gone.

Though some family members survive, John King, his wife, Susan, and two babies drown when a wagon slips off and disappears
into the river.

Pioneers, whether they're 19th-Century travelers in wooden-
planked schooners or they're 21st-Century travelers in $3 billion
space shuttles, live — and die — on the edge.

We stare at the replays on television, the white contrails against
the blue Texas sky, and think: This can't be happening. Then, we
begin analyzing and re-analyzing and further analyzing how this
possibly could happen.

But we can't hide from the truth that centuries of time have
shown: Those who push the limits — those who dare to go where
others dare not — often pay the price.

Should we be shocked at this death in the sky? Certainly. Should
we grieve for those who are dead — and the loved ones they left?
Deeply. But we shouldn't believe this was some sort of historical
anomaly that no other people have faced.

For the courageous, it comes with the territory. It always has. It
always will.

When people reach high enough for honorable things — for the
heavens or for the promised land or for freedom — a price is asked.

Nothing good comes for free.

Death came for 19th-Century slaves who sought the freedom they deserved.

Death came for those who hid Jews in Nazi-controlled Europe in the 1930s and 1940s.

And Saturday, death came for those willing to be catapulted into orbit for the good of science and discovery — the good of humankind.

We forget, sometimes, historical context.

We live in a world of such technological proficiency — my crashed computer notwithstanding — that we've almost come to believe we're invulnerable. That the default format is: Everything works. All the time. But not in a world that blends risk and fallible human beings.

We don't stop to consider how few lives (17) the U.S. space program has lost; before Saturday, shuttles had safely completed 88 missions since the *Challenger* explosion in 1986. By contrast, disease alone killed about 10,000 Oregon Trail pioneers in the 1840s and 1850s.

We've been so acclimated to grand accomplishments that our inevitable failures seem inconceivable, like a straight-A student who gets a B.

And, what's more, Saturday's "failure" wasn't some obscure accident that will make Page 3; instead, the Columbia's contrail streaked the Texas sky, like a skywriter's lament, for all to see.

In 1843, the diary of one pioneer said: "A very bad road. Joel J. Hembree son Joel fel off the waggeon tung & both wheels run over him." And so death came to a 6-year-old pioneer boy, the lone sign of tragedy being another grave along the Oregon Trail. No headlines. No CNN. No nonstop analysis.

The trail to promised lands are always wet with tears. On the immigrant ships, the bodies of those who died en route to "the golden land" — America — were buried at sea. On Omaha Beach, the bodies of American GIs sunk into the sand or were pulled out by the tides. In Texas, the remains of the astronauts fell from the sky.

Death comes in different ways for the courageous few who refuse to settle for the world as it is. But such people have much in common.

Never mind that the space shuttle *Columbia*, based on its 12,500 mph speed at its explosion, could fly the route of the Oregon Trail in about 9.6 minutes. The men and women who climbed into that craft 16 days ago were no different from the family who climbed onto that raft 150 years ago.

As onlookers to Saturday's tragedy, we'll never forget those words, "The space shuttle is gone." We should never forget the seven who gave their lives. And yet like the pioneers on the river Columbia, we must honor those who are gone by doing what they'd do:

Climb back on the raft and continue the journey.

January 2, 2003

The $17.04 check

WHEN A SECRETARY at Shasta Middle School was opening contributions to the school's Tree of Giving campaign earlier this month, one struck her as odd.

The check was for $17.04. A note with the check tried to explain it. But halfway through, the secretary stopped reading. The tears made the words too blurry.

The story begins in 1991 when Shasta teacher Zall Villanueva, who began the school's annual drive to contribute to Valley River's yearly fund-raising event, was teaching at Wyatt School outside Harrisburg. In his fifth-grade class, he had a student named Chase Whitham.

Chase, whose family owned a blueberry farm near the school, was the self-appointed class clown. He was the kid who once ate a peanut butter and jelly and worm sandwich — for a quarter. Who, while on recess one Halloween, had a student rush to get "Mr. V" and report that Chase had hurt himself.

"I ran out and there he was, blood on his face — fake blood, as it turned out," Villanueva says, chuckling.

Chase was one of those kids who'd be driving Villanueva nuts one minute, then making him laugh the next. True, nobody spent more time after school that year than Chase. But it's also true that, when Villanueva challenged the class to get involved in Valley River's Tree of Joy project, Chase led his team through the mall to buy a Christmas present for a needy child with the $25 he and other team members had raised by mowing lawns and washing cars.

"He was a good-hearted kid," Villanueva says.

"Mr. V was always trying to get the kids involved in something, to think of others," says Laurie Whitham, Chase's mother.

At the eighth-grade graduation ceremony, Chase thanked Mr. V for teaching him — and putting up with him.

Chase went off to high school, first at Harrisburg High, then at Marist. Villanueva later left Wyatt for Shasta. The two saw each other here and there.

Then, a few years ago, Villanueva heard that Chase had joined the Army, that he was headed for Iraq. He sent Chase postcards.

Chase, 21, was part of the Stryker Brigade in Mosul, Iraq. He sprinkled his service with touches of levity, was rarely without a smile and didn't forget Mr. V's challenge to think of others.

"His buddies told me there was one very quiet, withdrawn soldier who didn't speak much English because he was Laotian," Laurie Whitham says. "The guys called him 'D.D.' Chase pulled him out of his shell. Got him interested in lifting weights, making him feel included. And he opened up and started speaking more."

Then, the unthinkable: Last May 8, after a handful of hot, tired soldiers from the Stryker Brigade slipped into a murky swimming pool in Mosul, an electrical jolt suddenly shot through the water. Stunned soldiers crawled out. It was D.D. who noticed that Chase was missing. He jumped back in to save his pal.

Too late. A pump had shorted out, sending an electrical current through a water pipe near Chase. D.D. survived. Chase did not.

After her son's death, Laurie Whitham met his Army buddies at Fort Lewis, Wash., when they returned from Iraq.

"D.D. said Chase had been like a brother to him," she says. "He risked his own life to try and save my son."

Amid their grief, Laurie and her husband Mark had to tie up knots left unfinished by Chase's death. Among them: paying off his pickup and closing his bank accounts.

His checking account balance was $17.04.

It only seemed right, Laurie figured, to send it to what's now the Tree of Giving. It's what Chase would have wanted.

And so, taking out a pen, a mother gave away all her son had left to give.

December 14, 2004

A lesson too late

AS SOON AS I heard the news of his death March 26, I remembered the playground incident. Actually, I wish I could forget it. But sometimes our childhood choices — even when we factor youthful naivete into the forgive-me column — stay with us longer than we'd like.

It was sometime in the early '60s. He and I were elementary-school classmates.

I remember them as good times: Line soccer. These cool new things called skateboards. Mr. Brown reading *Black Like Me* and *The Lion, the Witch and the Wardrobe* to us after recess.

But I doubt my classmate would have remembered them as good times. Looking back, he seemed lonely. He lived with his grandmother because his parents had died when he was small. I couldn't tell you who his friends were.

I never remember there being an "inner circle" in our class; as I recall, that was more a junior high and high school phenomenon. But in his eyes, I believe, there was such a circle. And he clearly saw himself as outside looking in.

Why else would he have come up to me on the playground that day and made me the offer: a dollar to play two-square with him at recess.

Our classroom economy was based on trading cinnamon sticks, baseball cards and those good-smelling erasers that we used to scrunch between our noses and upper lips. Thus, an actual dollar bill — real money — had incredible value. Greed won out; I accepted.

I was the better player but didn't humiliate him; I remembered who had buttered my bread.

That night after dinner, I rode my Schwinn to the Cornet 5 & 10 store. I found one of those 100-man bags of army men and was headed for the cash register when I heard the familiar voice of my mother. Just my luck.

"What are you doing here?" she asked.

You can't hide from a mother; I didn't even try. Her eyes riveted to the army men and I was at the truth-or-lie crossroads.

"How do you plan on paying for those?" she asked. "You don't have any money."

When you're 10, it's not easy hiding dirty money. I didn't even try, slipping the dollar bill out of my pocket. She asked where I'd gotten it.

Maybe I was feeling guilty. Maybe I realized I was toast. For whatever reason, I told the story about the boy at school paying me to play two-square with him.

I didn't get the army men. Instead, I got a lecture from my mother about why I shouldn't have taken the money. And why I should have played two-square with him — because he was a kid looking for a friend.

I gave him back the dollar the next day. Not long thereafter, our family moved and I transferred to a new school.

Years later, he and I wound up at the same high school. I sometimes saw him out in the parking lot, sitting on the front of his car, having a smoke with other guys sitting on their cars and with the girls who had bleached-blonde hair, dark at the roots. He always wore a black leather jacket. He was what we called a "hard guy."

He grew up, married, had a son and worked much of his life at an auto parts store. The obit said he enjoyed four-wheel driving.

It didn't say how he died but I know. The Linn County sheriff's office confirmed what I'd already heard through friends: He killed himself. He drove out into the woods and swallowed a bunch of pills. He left a note.

I don't know why he took his life. But I will always wonder if he was as lonely as a grown man as he was as a young boy. And I will always wonder if his life might have turned out differently had people like me befriended him for the right reasons, not the wrong.

I think of that haunting Janis Ian song from the '70s called *At Seventeen:*

> *To those of us who know the pain*
> *Of valentines that never came,*
> *And those whose names were never called*
> *When choosing sides for basketball ...*

I don't ever recall this boy being bullied or bad-mouthed; I just recall him being one of those whose names were never called.

I think of teenagers today, some so desperate to belong — and so angry they don't — that instead of pulling out a dollar to rent a friend for recess, they pull out a gun to make classmates pay a far higher price.

In our two-square and four-square games, we sometimes called for "do-overs" — say, if a ball landed on the line and we couldn't agree whether it was "in" or "out."

After reading my classmate's obit, that's what I yearned for: a do-over — a chance to go back in time and tell the kid to forget about the buck. *You serve.*

Alas, life rarely affords such chances. Instead, it can only beckon us to learn from our shortfalls — the times we were asked to choose sides. And we wrongly chose ourselves.

April 8, 2001

One little candle

THE WORLD SAID goodbye to Clayton Swenson on Wednesday in a funeral at England's Eugene Memorial Chapel. But Megan Swenson, his 12-year-old granddaughter, already had done so — in her own way.

She remembers a man who built a tree fort for her and her brother, Jake. Who took them crabbing at Depoe Bay. Who was there to celebrate birthdays, holidays — "all that stuff," she says.

"He was a really creative person," says Megan, a seventh-grader at Monroe Middle School.

"All the grandkids caught their first fish with Grandpa," says Steve Swenson, Megan's father and Clayton's son. "For Megan, that was Fall Creek, eight years ago."

Clayton Swenson, 74, was a retired Navy man who started showing signs of Alzheimer's disease about four years ago. His wife, Elizabeth, died last spring after a stroke.

"He used to be really talkative," says Steve, who heads up the Eugene police Special Operations Division, "but he hasn't recognized anyone for months."

He had been at the Veteran's Hospital in Roseburg, but his condition worsened. A month ago, the Swensons moved him to the Green Valley Care Center in Eugene so he could get advanced care. Family visits were difficult. The man was like a statue.

"Nursing homes have a feel about them — not really uplifting,"

Steve says. "I understand people are doing their best, but the homes are definitely God's waiting room."

That's what led to his idea. "What would you think," he asked Megan, "of playing the piano at Grandpa's nursing home?"

Those of us who remember ourselves at age 12 imagine being asked a similar request. And rolling our eyes. Or pointing out that we're busy that day, whenever that day might be.

"I'd like to do that," Megan said.

On a Sunday morning, Sept. 28, Steve and Megan went to Green Valley. A number of residents, in wheelchairs and walkers, were watching "Dennis the Menace" reruns in the garden terrace dining area. Some were asleep, heads slumped forward.

"This one lady tapped me on the shoulder and said she wanted me to help her," Megan says. "I said, 'What do you want?' She said, 'I want you to take me home.'"

Megan sat at the Lowrey upright — she had brought no music — and started playing *The Entertainer* for the handful of people.

A few smiles creased the faces.

She played a song that she had remembered from her elementary school graduation, *One Little Candle*, about how "*if everybody lit just one little candle / What a bright world this would be.*"

People began clapping. "They were like plants who hadn't been watered in a while," Steve says. "This was water."

Some who had been down the hallway wheeled themselves closer to the girl at the piano. Soon, about 20 people were gathered. Someone asked who she was. "I'm Clayton Swenson's granddaughter," she said.

"Small world," a resident said. "He lives right here in this same place!"

"Actually, he's sitting right over there," Megan said, proudly pointing to her grandfather.

She played a couple of songs she had written herself, including one called *The Gift*.

She looked at her grandpa. His eyes were locked on her. He was tapping his foot. "We hadn't seen that in quite a while," Steve says.

The 45-minute session ended. The residents went back to their lives and Megan to hers.

A few days later, Steve Swenson got a phone call: His father had taken a turn for the worse. He died last Saturday morning.

The news hurt, Megan says, but something eased her pain. "I'd gotten to say goodbye to him with the songs," she says. "I think he knew who I was. I could just tell."

In such moments do candles burn their brightest.

October 16, 2003

The Book of Psalms

HE BOUGHT IT at a Trappist monastery outside McMinnville — a paperback book of psalms.

On a yearly pilgrimage, he'd heard the monks passionately reciting these words rooted deep in the land of Israel and so plunked down $3.45, hoping the words might also move him.

They did.

Nearly every morning since that day in the early '80s, Les Corey awoke at his Cottage Grove home and spent an hour alone reading *The Psalms: A New Translation from the Hebrew Arranged for Singing to the Psalmody of Joseph Gelineau.*

He read. He meditated. He prayed, inspired by the 150 Old Testament songs that scholars say were written between the 10th and second centuries B.C.

"They go back to the days of (King) David, and yet I find them so applicable," says Corey, who attends Our Lady of Perpetual Help Catholic Church in Cottage Grove. "They remind me of who I am, where I am and what I am. They remind me of the gift of existence. They're a tremendous gift from the Jewish community."

And they went with him wherever he went, which is a considerable distance. Corey, 75, is a retired Cottage Grove High School social studies teacher and loves to travel to the lands he once only taught about from books.

He and his wife, Ellie, also a former teacher, have been to such places as China, Thailand, Hungary, Italy, Costa Rica, Mexico and Russia. The book accompanied him on every trip, even one to Israel he made in 1982 as a Fulbright Scholar.

"The book probably has more than 150,000 miles on it," Corey says.

It has scribbled notations on many of its pages: favorite psalms, lines to remember, "Prayers for Peace."

He remembers one morning when he was flying toward Russia

and how the sun was bursting through clouds below just as he read "the heavens proclaim the glory of God" (Psalm 18, or Psalm 19 in many other versions).

Then, on a later trip, he reached for the book. But it was gone.

It happened last November. The Coreys had taken a TWA flight from Portugal to New York, changed planes and were headed to Portland when Les realized it: He'd left *The Psalms* in the magazine pouch on the other plane.

No sense in trying to track it down, he figured; it was long gone, probably in some airport trash bin. After all, it was only a $3.45 paperback.

Still, Corey missed it. "It was almost like losing a friend," he says.

Back home, he scoured bookstores for a similar book, but it was out of print in that compact size. He bought a larger one, but it wasn't the same. No scribbled notations. No dog-eared corners. No crinkled cover, weathered by journeys around the world — and journeys within himself.

Life went on — more than three months of it. Then, last Monday, a weathered 7-by-11-inch padded envelope arrived at the Corey household with the oddest of return addresses: Israel. Specifically, Jerusalem.

The Coreys knew nobody there; what could this be? In a moment, Les opened the package and held it in his hands: his book.

"I was shocked," he says.

A letter accompanied the book. "Dear Mr. and Mrs. Corey," it began, "you are probably wondering how I have your book ..."

To say the least, thought Les, since it was left on a plane that had left Lisbon and landed in New York. How did it wind up in Israel?

"A friend of mine," continued the letter, "has a son whose father-in-law works with one of the airlines here in Israel. He often gets bags filled with books that people left behind on the plane. Since he is a Hebrew speaker, he passes along the books to my friend who is an American (as are we). After she took the books that she wanted, she gave the bag to me and I noticed your book which was filled with notes, etc. and I figured that it was probably not something that you were happy about losing. Happily, your name and address were in the book.

"I hope you haven't been without it for long — I have no way of knowing if it was left behind last week, last month or last year. Sincerely, Rivka Freudenstein."

Since talking to the Coreys, I've been unable to reach Rivka Freudenstein.

"Whoever she is, she must be a very sensitive person," Les says. "Reminds you of that Anne Frank quote about realizing there are good people out there in the world."

He's writing Freudenstein back.

"Something tells me this isn't the end of the story," Corey says. "Of all the places that plane could have gone from New York, why Israel? It's almost like salmon returning to spawn. The psalms returned to their homeland!"

March 4, 2001

Broken wings

Blackbird singing in the dead of night
Take these broken wings and learn to fly
— John Lennon/Paul McCartney

You wake up one morning and your world is in order: Husband. Daughter. Dog. Career.

In Eugene, you all pile into the Subaru to head for work at Pleasant Hill High, where you're an English teacher and your husband is a guidance counselor.

The two of you are worried about a possible war in Iraq. But the previous night, 2-year-old Olivia was so tired she was asleep by dinner and so you had the rare opportunity to just talk. And what you talked about was this: being compassionate to others in a world that often isn't.

Now, you're on Highway 58. Patrick is at the wheel. Patrick your best friend, the guy you met at the University of Oregon when your black Lab, Runa — the same dog now in back — got lost and he offered to help find her. Adventurous Patrick who leads the family on totally unplanned summer trips across the country, laughing as he says the names of states backward. Now entering Odaroloc! Patrick who is now giving you a hard time because it's March 17,

2003 — St. Patrick's Day — and you're not wearing green.

Olivia is in back. Olivia, the little girl who strikes up conversations with total strangers. Who loves dancing and doing puzzles with you on Saturday mornings. Who fears only one thing: school mascots. Thinks the Pleasant Hill billy goat is Godzilla with horns. Runs in terror from the Oregon duck.

The dashboard clock says 7:45 a.m. You turn to look at Olivia. Suddenly, Patrick's panicked voice: "Oh, my —"

The sickening sound of metal on metal. The jarring impact. The eerie quiet ...

You wake up one morning and your world is in order. Then suddenly you're at a hospital and Dr. Mary Budke is telling you something you can hardly comprehend. They're dead: Patrick. Olivia. Runa. Just like that — gone.

Katie Barr tried to stay at Pleasant Hill. She returned two weeks after the accident. Returned after summer vacation.

But Oct. 10 was her last day. She wrote a letter for the school newspaper to explain why she was abruptly leaving the place she loved.

"Patrick and I had an ongoing dialogue about what makes a good teacher," she wrote. "My reply was always that a good teacher is content, bringing experience, joy and hope to the classroom. I want to continue to be that teacher, but as it stands right now, I need to reclaim some of these qualities for myself."

It is about the most difficult thing she's ever done, she tells you later: leaving students who gave her a new black Lab, Elmo, and devoted a couple of weekends to fortifying her back yard so the dog wouldn't escape. Leaving teachers and administrators who brought meals, lent shoulders to cry on and listened.

But Patrick McCurdy worked at the school, too. "I already miss him as a friend, as a husband and as the father of my daughter," she says. "I can't miss him one more way. I feel like half a person now. And I can't be the teacher I want to be without finding that other half."

So she's selling her house. On Friday, Barr, 35, plans to get in her Subaru Outback with Elmo and head south to the San Francisco area to be with family. And after the holidays, who knows? Probably a Patrick-esque road trip east — no itinerary, just a quest for discovery in unexplored places, perhaps passing through Odaroloc, Sionilli and Wen Kroy en route. And maybe a return to Pleasant

Hill come fall.

"Everything that means something to me is gone," she says, "but the human spirit has some incredible ways of helping us cope. Patrick and Olivia and Runa gave me so much. Now I have to find those gifts again."

And so you wake up one October morning and leave, not to forget what you've lost, but to remember what might be found.

October 26, 2003

Love on Court 3

IN TENNIS, it's best to practice with a partner who's slightly better than you. Someone who challenges you but doesn't pulverize you. Someone who stretches you but cares more about improving your game than proving his or her own game.

And so it was for John and Carole Duran, folks say.

He was the slightly better tennis player but she was the go-getter who attacked the net regardless of the activity: rock hounding, jewelry-making, baking, fishing, roller-dancing, skiing or twanging her electric guitar. In most pursuits, she led, John happily followed.

"They brought out the best in each other," said Tom Greider, owner of Willow Creek Tennis & Sports Center, where the two were members.

Tennis drew them together. They met in August 1995 on Court 3 at Willow Creek, where Carole was playing in a senior masters tournament.

Three months later, the two were married on Court 3 at Willow Creek. They wore tennis outfits. A minister pronounced them "doubles partners for life."

But Saturday afternoon, Carole Duran was eulogized on Court 3 at Willow Creek. She died last Sunday in a scuba diving accident in Hoodsport, Wash., on the Olympic Peninsula. She was 54.

"I saw something in these two people that I didn't even know existed," Rosemary Redmon told the crowd of about 150 people on the indoor court. "I've never seen two people so in love with each other."

If not love at first sight, it was a reasonable facsimile. John had been divorced for 18 years, Carole had never married. He was 47, she 49.

Lonely and considering moving to Arizona, John saw her playing in the tournament and was smitten. That night, he showed up late for a tournament banquet. He hurriedly grabbed a seat; it was right next to her.

Carole was talking about rock hounding near Prineville. "How often do you and your husband go there?" John asked. She told him she wasn't married.

Only a week later, after a handful of dates and hundreds of vollies, he proposed at The Mission restaurant. She said yes with the speed of her killer backhand.

Once married, the two were inseparable. These were not people in snow-white sweaters with the arms tied around their necks. They lived in a single-wide mobile home in west Eugene. She was a veterinarian technician; he's a dietary manager.

"Blue-collar tennis players, a feel-good couple, always together," said Greider. "They were the couple you'd want to show your kids to say: 'This is what it can look like.' "

But they weren't the couple you remember from high school — so infatuated with each other that they ignored everyone else. They meshed their lives with family and friends.

"When you were single, the two of you lived good lives," said Lydia Duran, looking at her brother. "Together, you lived great lives."

On the court, they often teamed up for doubles. "They were never as concerned about keeping score as about their love of the game," said Mike Backus, a doubles partner of John's. "That's the lesson of John and Carole — loving what you do and the people you're experiencing it with."

Last month, Greider saw the couple in the gym: they were playing one-on-one basketball. Next thing he knew Carole was asking about using her roller skates on the floor.

Go, go, go — that's how they lived. "Carole could do more in a weekend than most people do in a month," a friend told the gathering. That's why she and John were in Hoodsport; they'd taken up scuba diving last fall.

"She loved diving," said John. "On Saturday she'd gone on her first night dive and was the only one of us to see this octopus. She had so much energy — and shared it with others. And, oh, she had this smile ..."

Early Sunday afternoon, the two were among four students — along with an instructor — trying their first 100-foot dives. At the bottom, John and Carole exchanged "OK" hand signals. But on the way up with the rest of the group, Carole got in trouble. Results of an autopsy are still pending. She drowned; *how* hasn't been determined.

As the rain pelted the roof Saturday, more than a dozen people stepped to the microphone and paid tribute to — as John described her — "the woman of my dreams."

"On and off the court, they strengthened each other's weaknesses," said Greider. "Just like a good doubles team, the sum of their parts was better than the two individuals alone."

So now what? If Saturday's service offered any encouragement for John, it was to not play the rest of the game on the baseline, lobbing back whatever shots life might send.

Instead, the consensus seemed to be this: keep attacking the net — just like Carole had done, from the first point to the last.

February 4, 2001

11.
Time

One hour of time

YACHATS — I crawl out of my bag Sunday morning and realize two things changed while I was sleeping: The blimp-like log I stuffed in the fireplace to heat the cabin during the night is now the size of a Hostess Twinkie. And the gods of time — technically, the laws of the land — have given me an extra hour.

What a gift. One full hour. Sixty minutes. Free. Thanks to the undoing of daylight-saving time.

Oh, I know there's no such thing as a free hour; I know it's really only the hour we lost last April that's finally slinking home — the Prodigal Son of time, back after having been squandered by people, say, watching an entire "Jerry Springer" show.

But it feels like it's free. It feels like the time I found a wadded-up $10 bill in my pickup's ashtray, tucked there for some emergency. I hadn't gained a thing, but it sure felt like it.

So I hit the beach for a morning run to contemplate time, specifically an hour of time — and try to slow the rust of middle age in the process.

As I plod along, I realize I'm in the midst of an extraordinary hour even now. It's cold. An overnight frost has dusted the shore pine and salal. Clouds cling to the foothills of the Coast Range — the valley, I later learn, is socked in — but the sky along the coast is Windex clear.

It is, I realize, the weather god's makeup call for last summer's "coast crud," those days when the valley baked in sunshine while the coast shivered in fog. Suddenly, the geographic tables have been turned and I decide this will be my extra hour, an unexpected gift, particularly because the sand is still tattered with the remnants of Saturday's daylong rain.

If you're going to get extra time, you could do worse than an almost-windless, cloudless hour on the Oregon Coast. The air smells particularly "crabby." The beach is almost deserted. And the sun beams down with the orangeish glow of a Springfield streetlight.

Who could ask for more?

The purist, of course, will harrumph that I'm wrong in thinking this could qualify as my extra hour. That came at 2 a.m., the official time to "fall back."

I can't accept that. Who wants to be given an extra hour while they're sleeping? You get it, but you don't even know you got it. In my mind, this yearly gift is a must-be-present-to-win proposition: To enjoy the reward you not only have to be awake, but actually aware of the hour.

I beckon the poet William Blake from horizons afar:

To see a world in a grain of sand
And a heaven in a wild flower,
Hold infinity in the palm of your hand
And eternity in an hour ...

Preach it, Bill. Here was a guy who, if they'd had daylight-saving time two centuries ago, wouldn't have settled for taking his gift while lying down — asleep.

Here was a live-for-the-hour guy who understood the value of being in the present.

Here was a guy who wasn't going to fall asleep every evening with the remote in his lap.

We only get so many of these hours, you know: 24 per day, 8,760 a year, 613,200 if we live to be 70. Like snowflakes, no two are alike, unless you're working a cannery belt or listening to Phil Collins. At any rate, the supply is limited.

So it's important to notice what's happening around you in that hour: how the sandpipers and their pipe-cleaner legs juke left, right, stop and go as if they're the Audobonian equals of Duck running back Onterrio Smith. How the surf is tinted orange from the sun and how the driftwood is still floating out at sea, waiting for the season's first big storms to wash it ashore.

Ah, but I think, it's not enough to just notice the hour. We must seize it. We must do more than admire the set, but get up on the stage. We must — enough of me; I spy Sir Walter Scott brooding on the rocks just north of the Adobe Motel:

"One hour of life, crowded to the full with glorious action, and filled with noble risks, is worth whole years of those mean observances of paltry decorum."

By the time I return from my run, I'm as energized with inspiration as I am drained of strength. It is time, I realize, for glorious action! I shower and drive to Yachats.

It is time for a noble risk; you never know if you're going to get your paper when you put in that $1.25, but it's a chance I must take. I can't wait till Sunday night to read about the Ducks' win over the Cougars.

Finally, it's time to ignore paltry decorum, i.e., a middle-aged body that even running can't save.

"Can I help you?" asks the woman at the bakery.

"Yes," I say, seizing the hour with glorious gusto. "I'll take a cream cheese Danish."

October 30, 2001

And miles to go

IN HIS APARTMENT at Washington Abbey, the clock ticks, but you wonder if Robert Clark even hears it.

Not because his hearing has gone bad, which it has, but because the man seems so blessedly willing to ignore time's demands. The ex-University of Oregon president, now 93, first stepped on campus 60 years ago this month as a speech professor. He has been retired for 28 years. He has been without his wife, Opal, for 10.

But, a lover of poetry, he will not go gentle into that good night. He reads with a magnifying glass the size of a salad plate and apologizes for forgetting names and dates. But by my third visit

I'm convinced his humility exaggerates such weaknesses.

Clark still speaks with the well-measured cadence of the learned man he is. He remembers the population of Maywood, Neb., near where he was born in 1910 (300), the anti-Vietnam War fervor on campus in 1969 ("I didn't have a honeymoon") and his salary when forced to retire in 1975 ($38,000).

His is a quiet rage against the dying of the light. Not the stuff of senior skydiving, but of writing and going to the symphony and taking mile-long walks by himself.

His coffee table looks like it belongs at the Eugene Public Library: dozens of history, nature and literary magazines. His apartment is decidedly bookish, accented with art and family photos.

Thin, with wispy white hair, Clark is academia's John Wooden, a man who exudes a quiet dignity. But his soft-spokenness hides a courage that he tapped often in the controversial '60s and '70s. While president of San Jose State, he stood up to then-California Gov. Ronald Reagan, who wanted to fire striking faculty members — and won.

At the UO, amid the tumult of car bombings and protests — some on his front lawn — he stood up to then-Gov. Tom McCall, who wanted to send in the National Guard. Clark dug in, not wanting to risk further escalation.

"McCall wet his pants and backed off," says Keith Richard, the ex-UO archivist. "Clark was one of the better presidents. He faced problems that no other president faced and kept the place under control."

But, against his wishes, he was forced to quit in 1975; mandatory retirement then was 65. The university offered Clark an office. He politely said no, choosing instead a cubicle at the library where he could study.

He researched, wrote essays and books and served on scholarly boards. Now, he does less of everything, but writes for Washington Abbey's newsletter, reads often and still observes the natural world with a child's imagination.

"It's frustrating, forgetting so much of what I once knew," says a man who once received a Guggenheim Fellowship. "Wild flowers, for example. I used to remember all their names."

We talk of what brings him joy — having so many family members in Eugene who "spend more time with me than I deserve." What grieves him. "Losing my wife. Never gotten over that." What he thought of *Animal House*, the 1978 movie that included scenes from his old office. "Four stars as entertainment, none as an honest commentary on the university." And what frustrates him. "I used to be able to read so fast, remember so much."

Finally, we talk of poetry. He shows me collections of poems he reads from each night, including a 1943 book by Robert Frost.

"*Whose woods these are I think I know,*" I say, suddenly back in high school English.

A sparkle softens his eyes.

"*His house is in the village though,*" he adds with zest. "*He will not see me stopping here / To watch his woods fill up with snow.*"

He continues reciting the poem, like a gymnast performing a flawless routine. I nod my approval.

On the wall, the clock keeps ticking. But, for now, President Clark hears only the silence of the woods, so lovely, dark and deep.

July 10, 2003

Wasted on the way

WHEN CROSBY, Stills & Nash walked casually onto the stage Monday night at the Cuthbert Amphitheater, it was like running into an old high school classmate after 30 years.

On one hand you're glad to see them; how can you forget that night in 1969 when you first heard the magical harmony of *Suite: Judy Blue Eyes?* On the other hand, you're thinking: What's with the gray hair and paunch?

I'd seen David Crosby, Stephen Stills and Graham Nash at the Hult Center in the early '90s, so it wasn't as if I expected Stills to still be wearing that old Los Angeles Rams jersey and Nash to still have dark hair. I'm a student of the aging process myself, recently flunking my Butte to Butte midterm.

Still, don't a lot of us subconsciously expect our heroes of yesterday to somehow be frozen in the time in which we remember them best?

Such subliminal thinking — that, say, Crosby should still be a stocky 29 instead of a portly 61 — has warped into a prejudice on my part: I've laughed at longtime rockers like CS&N for staying on stage too long.

Shouldn't they unplug their amps and retire to their La-Z-Boys and Clappers? Shouldn't — to contradict a Crosby song — they cut their hair? Shouldn't they quit before their stagehands have to shuttle in oxygen tanks instead of guitars?

Monday night's concert changed my thinking. These guys shouldn't be chided for still making music. They should be applauded.

Not only because they still have the magic, but because they're doing what we all should be doing: taking whatever gifts we have as far as we can take them.

Musicians shouldn't be expected to play at the level they did 30 years ago anymore than runners should be expected to keep running sub-40 10Ks. But where's the nobility in hanging it up if you don't have to? Is the world a better place if the trio stays home and watches "Jeopardy" or if it leads 4,500 people of all ages, sizes and colors in an exhilarating singalong of *Our House?*

Sure, some of CS&N's sweet harmony didn't make the trip from the '70s. After a mix-up on *The Leeshore,* Crosby said to Nash, "Did I leave out a verse?" And the ultimate sign of aging came when a fan up front suddenly flashed her breasts to the band. Nobody on stage seemed to notice.

Still, as the concert continued, I sensed that what was happening here — despite a few misguided fans — was something special. It was like a reunion of sorts where everybody, after getting over the fact that nobody is 18 anymore, relaxes and just has fun.

Crosby, looking Santa-like with his long, white hair and reddish face, showed up in a short-sleeved shirt and slacks, as if he'd just wandered in from a Santa Monica wedding.

Nash, like Crosby — 61 and barefoot — looked like some thespian whose makeup artist aged him just before the show. His hair and goatee have gone gray and white, but he remains thin, cool and collected.

Stills, 58, looked like a pony-tailed biker from the neck up and one of the *Cocoon* geezers from the neck down, a billowy floral shirt hanging almost like a mu-mu over his shorts, his spindly legs anchored to — egad — penny loafers.

Never mind that the group's bass player, Eugene native David Santos, couldn't have been out of diapers when CS&N first got together in 1968. These guys can still play music.

When singing *Guinnevere* in the gathering darkness, Crosby brought the crowd to hushed reverence, his frizzy, fan-blown hair silhouetted blue by the lights. Stills' high-pitched guitar solos must have broken dishes in Noti. And standing between his edgier mates, Nash was his usual understated but warm self.

"What a lovely evening," he said with his subtle British accent, "and we get to share it with you."

That's what this is all about, I realized: three-part harmony between musicians, songs and fans. It's about memories. And it's about living our lives so we don't someday look back and — in the words of a CS&N song — lament all the "time we have wasted on the way."

July 24, 2003

Fountains of youth

THE AMERICAN Association of Retired Persons this week launched its new magazine, *My Generation*, which is the journalistic equivalent of Barbara Bush showing up to the inaugural ball in go-go boots.

Prunes are history; the industry recently won approval from the Food and Drug Administration to call them "dried plums," a more boomer-friendly term that supposedly won't conjure up thoughts of the gut-level reason someone might be eating them.

Now, *Eugene Weekly* has bumped up the type size of its print. "It's cheaper," the editors told readers, "than inserting 31,000 pair of reading glasses in our paper."

Everywhere you look, the hard, cold reality is staring baby boomers in our sagging faces: We're getting what used to be known as "old," but which boomers will undoubtedly relabel something more palatable, such as "youth deficient."

I find the baby boomers' refusal to go gentle into that good night laudable and laughable.

Laudable because I admire people who live with gusto to the end; there is something delicious about opening the trunk of your 74-year-old mother's car and finding a pair of swim fins.

Laughable because it's just so positively boomer-esque — this sense that, with enough rationalization, marketing spin and positive thinking, we can avoid the inevitable.

The bottom line: Death happens. It is no respecter of designer labels. Give it whatever boomer euphemism you want — "life-challenged" or "pulse-impaired" — but death ultimately will claim the boomer generation as certainly as it has claimed every other generation.

Given that reality, we boomers would be best to approach death — and the inevitable physical deterioration that precedes it — not with fear or dread, but with grace and humor.

For example, you have to love that TV commercial — can't think of the sponsor; must be having a "my generation" moment — where boomers are picketing in front of a store. When cops pull up and hand them their written Miranda rights, the protesters keep re-positioning their cards as if adjusting trombone hand slides; bad eyes.

Having recently taken up the, uh, trombone myself, I could relate — as could many boomers, I'm sure.

The oldest of the nation's 78 million baby boomers — born between 1946 and 1964 — began turning 55 last month. From here, the generation will become a smaller portion of the population until the last boomer dies — probably after being electrocuted at age 119 while playing an electric guitar upside-down in a hot tub.

"Baby boomers will not willingly give up the pleasures they had in youth," John Scroggins, the editor of *The Food Channel* newsletter, says in *American Demographics* magazine.

This, after all, is a generation that's big on comfort, ease and getting its own way. When we crowded the elementary schools, more schools were built. When we began having children, disposable diapers were invented. Now that we're nearing retirement age, we fully expect the world to continue catering to us.

Only now we're fighting one of Quixote's "unbeatable foes" — the relentless march of time. Mortality. The Big "D."

Desperate to serve their most important client, businesses are doing what they can: enlarging the type. Renaming the prunes. (What? No related Web page: gonow.com?) Even giving us a retirement magazine that looks like *Rolling Stone* on hemorrhoids.

The sale of skin creams, suntan lotions and hair coloring is surging as boomers do battle with aging. "This generation of ours refuses to believe it's getting older," says Betsy Carter, new editor-in-chief of *My Generation.*

Fine, but try telling that to your 55-year-old stomach after a couple of cheese enchiladas.

Bottom line: No amount of whistling in the dark is going to stop the aging process; it's the boomers' Kryptonite. But it's also a natural part of human existence — and our time would be better spent accepting that than soaking up infomercial fountains of youth.

We need to wake up and smell the liniment oil. Rage against the dying of the light, sure, but also realize that even rage has its limits — like wearing Spandex, for example. Realize it's OK if we can't equal our 1990 Butte to Butte time; it's enough just to run. Understand that seasons change; it's in the script.

"Youth is the gift of nature, but age is a work of art," author Garson Kanin wrote.

To confirm that, I need look no further than a host of pre-boomers I know who are aging with great humor and grace — people in their 60s, 70s and 80s who don't have time to worry about wrinkles, finding the latest e-mail elixir — LOSE 20 POUNDS BY THE TIME YOU FINISH THIS SENTENCE!!! — or psychological wounds they might incur should they eat — gasp! — a prune.

They're all too busy living.

February 8, 2001

Running downhill

ON THIS, THE day of Eugene's 29th annual Butte to Butte race, I offer you a runner's life:

At age 15 to 20 you look in the full-length mirror and think: I can run fast.

You flex your quads and mentally dare Pre to race you in anything over a half mile.

You run daily doubles all summer long. On your cannery job, you incessantly ponder the 440 splits that will take you under 4:45 in the mile.

You not only keep a daily log of your workouts but make a color-coded bar chart of your weekly mileage, entitled "How Shin Splints Affect My Running."

You want to grow up and be *Runner's World* editor Joe Henderson. In the meantime, you consider moving to Australia and training with distance guru Percy Cerutty, running all day long in loose sand. Could it get any better?

You run a marathon — a 9 a.m. start, in late July, in Newberg, with not a single aid station. (Who knew?) When you finish, exactly four people are on hand — you have the photo — and one is a runner puking out his guts.

You don't even get a measly shirt, just a certificate with the word "marathon" misspelled "marathan."

At age 25 to 30 you look in the full-length mirror and think: I can run.

You flex your new Nikes and dare the high school punks to stay with you. (They stay with you only for the first half mile, then leave you in their Central Oregon cinder dust.)

You run every few days, not wanting your workouts to get in the way of your new job.

When it comes to tracking workouts, your motto is: If it feels good, log it.

You want to grow up and be Alberto Salazar.

You compete in road runs that draw 5,000 runners. Each time you run, you're given a shirt. What a cool concept!

At age 35 to 40 you look in the full-length mirror and think: I can — hey, what happened to the mirror? You learn your two little boys broke it while playing bathtub hockey.

You flex and promptly pull your left quadricep.

You decide to get your aerobic workout by playing noontime basketball. The movie folks are right. You can't jump. Or, for that matter, dribble or shoot.

You now chart your workouts on a computer, but the technology changes so fast that your floppy disks, roughly the size of a Little Caesar's medium-sized pizza box, won't work on your new setup.

The logs get lost in the technological shuffle.

You want to grow up and avoid prostate cancer.

You do the Hood-to-Coast race two years in a row and the next year get stomach cramps during the pre-run meal. Your team leaves you in a parking lot in Sandy and you face the true loneliness of the long-distance runner: having to call your wife and ask her to drive two hours to pick up her pathetic husband.

You have so many road-running shirts that you can't get your dresser drawer open.

At age 40 to 45 you look in the full-length mirror and think: I can run — but I can't hide. For the first time, every french fry you eat shows up somewhere on your body.

You think about flexing and then think, naw.

You work out on the stair machine at the office while reading magazines full of Viagra advertisements.

You go to bed at 11 p.m., read for eight minutes, fall asleep, wake up at 6 and start working. Who has time to keep a stupid workout log?

You don't want to grow up, period.

You run the Butte to Butte, but three minutes slower than the previous year, and get beat by your friend the former chain-smoker who took up running the previous month.

While painting the house, you realize your paint rag is a 1983 Seattle Seafair 10K shirt. You begin pawning off the others at garage sales.

At age 45 to 50 you look in the mirror and think: We need a new mirror. This one makes me look frumpy like my father did at this age — and I don't look like that. Do I?

You don't even think about flexing.

Instead of working out on the stair machine, you double-click that "LOSE 20 LBS. OVERNIGHT!" e-mail and briefly consider paying $69.99 to wrap your body in 10 yards of hot, cheese-coated Saran Wrap.

To avoid growing up, you fixate on the past, dreaming of the sands of Australia, as if you were the guy in Hemingway's *Old Man and the Sea*.

You run the Butte to Butte but get beat by two firefighters in full gear, a woman who's pushing her day-old baby in one of those three-wheel Baby Joggers and a friend whose previous longest run was to the bathroom from his living room.

Ah, but as the body fails the mind sharpens: For the first time, you pass on the shirt.

July 4, 2002

The up side to 50

Once, while talking to a Boston hotel desk clerk, I asked whether a parking garage she'd referred to as being "next door" was east or west of the building. "It depends," she said, "on which direction you're coming from."

Hmmm.

That incident comes to mind as, amid my life journey, I ponder pitching my tent at age 50 — starting today. I know the truth: that there are certain fixed realities that no amount of ignorance — this clerk lives in what Oliver Wendell Holmes once called "the thinking center of the continent" — or no amount of rationalization can change.

We're born. We grow older. We die. And yet how we grow older isn't nearly so firmly rooted, meaning the clerk's comment actually works for me, if not geographically then personally.

When it comes to aging, a lot does depend on where you're coming from.

A friend of my mother's husband died last week at 85 — while windsurfing in the Cook Islands. Meanwhile, I've taught a few 21-year-old college students who seem already resigned to life as a meaningless wait for who knows what, their faces locked in that half-bored/half-angry expression of unhappy campers in a really long postal line.

I know an 85-year-old woman who's hard to reach because she's outside gardening, at the spa or playing golf. And I know 30-something people who are far more passionate about some group of "survivors" on a TV reality show than about living their own adventures.

All of which suggests that age means little. And attitude means much.

Culturally, I'm supposed to dread this day, as if it signifies life's shot clock is off and I'd better do something with that basketball — quick!

"What's it like?" asks a colleague, as if I were involved in a near-death experience. It's like — no big deal.

If my math is correct, we each lose one day per day — the same rate for the 80-year-old as for the 40-year-old and the 20-year-old. It's like Fern Ridge Lake being drawn down inches a day in the fall;

the water level gets lower wherever you are on the lake. The only difference is that some of us have less water beneath us.

I'm not trying to be curmudgeonly about this. While I don't understand the dread factor of turning 50, I absolutely welcome the humor. It's fun chiding a soon-to-be-50 friend about his having been offered the senior discount at Burger King — years ago.

It's even fun to be the "chidee"; my sons, for example, think it hilarious-bordering-on-pathetic that I am DVD-impaired.

The most secure people I know, some in their 70s and 80s, laugh constantly about growing older.

I think of a 70-year-old Eugene woman who's been through half an alphabet of medical problems — arthritis, breast cancer, Charcot's bone disease, diabetes, etc. — and yet lives with a sort of Marla Runyan "what-me-worry?" staying power.

She jokes, reminisces about the past, plans for the future, laughs, cries. Best of all she lives with a sort of a childlike zeal that reminds me of this: The people to be pitied aren't the ones who are turning 30 or 40 or 50 or 60, but those who, regardless of their ages, aren't content with wherever they are.

On Saturday night, at a simple five-person family party, I was given three gifts, one of which was — wouldn't you know? — a DVD.

The gift was a photo chronology — dozens of pictures of me, mainly with family and friends — of my half-century of life, complete with music. And when it was over — odd, but the photos got blurrier as I watched — I was reminded of this: Our age isn't what really matters about our journeys. It's the people who have shared it with us — and molded our attitudes in the process.

That's where I'm coming from — at the blessed age of 50.

February 3, 2004

Ducking into the night

THE LATE-NIGHT call jolted me awake. It was from the Lane County Jail. Donald, a collegiate mascot I know, was in the slammer after ruffling some feathers at the Wild Duck. I posted bail and took him to IHOP on East Broadway to dry him out.

"Coffee, black," I told the waitress. "And one really, really, really long straw."

"And for the duck?" she said.

"That *is* for the duck. I'll take your Breakfast Sampler. Eggs over easy."

I handed back the menu, looked at Donald and slowly shook my head sideways.

"So what's going on? Last time I saw you, you were frolicking at Mac Court — like mascots are supposed to — after the Ducks won the WNIT title. Now, this."

"Sorry, I — ."

"Sorry? The cops said when they arrived you'd knocked two guys out cold with a tae kwon do kick and were standing atop the bar, singing Sinatra's *I Gotta Be Me* — and all you say is 'sorry'?"

He stared off toward some nothingness beyond me, the slightest mist in his egg-sized eyes. "Everything's closing in on me," he said. "I guess I just quacked."

"You mean you cracked."

"Whatever. English isn't easy for ducks. My French is better."

He slurped his coffee. I've heard quieter dental suctions.

"So exactly what's closing in on you?"

"Frohnmayer choosing the new, sophisticated 'O' as the university's official symbol; you're not gonna see me bursting through that baby like I did through that old, collegiate 'O.' And Washington State trying to sweep the name 'Wazzu' under the rug. Don't you see? The world is changing. Sophistication is in. Levity is out."

"So?"

"So — I'm history. Canard grille."

"What?"

"Grilled duck, stupid. It's French. The university is slowly phasing me out. I can see the handwriting on the wall, but I can't see my image anymore on the Autzen Stadium walls. Too many symbols, they say, obscure the message. And I'm the odd duck out."

"No," I said, "you're a duck with decades of history around here. There's something to be said for tradition, you know."

"You can buy off tradition with bean dip," he said. "Look at Reser — and formerly Parker — Stadium. Charlie Parker wound up with a plaza named after him. A stinkin' plaza!"

"Come on, a donor kicks in some bucks, they name the stadium for him; welcome to the real world, Donald. But nobody's replacing you. You're an institution, as much a part of Eugene as roof fungus or old growth hippies."

"Wake up, Rip," he said. "College sports aren't your father's Oldsmobile anymore. The administration is running a new offense. They're sending me long — on the mother of all fade routes. It's one thing to be attacked by opposing fans — ."

"Yeah, I heard about the basketball incident in Vegas a while back. Did you really rip off your head and punch the guy?"

"Hey, someone tackled me. But, again, that was an opposing fan. It hurts when your own folks have you in their sights."

"What are you talking about? Everybody loves you. You're cool. You strut. You ride on the back of that motorcycle. You —"

"I'm Disney. I'm a percentage of every T-shirt sale blown away into their corporate coffers. I'm a liability."

"You're unique. What other mascot is Disney-based? And, look at the bright side, you've avoided the PC controversy. You could be a Seminole Indian."

"Safe for now," he said, "but I have nightmares about PETA riding in on its high horse with charges of cruelty to birds."

"It'll never happen," I said. "PETA doesn't ride horses. Animal abuse."

The duck threw down his hands, like he does after a bad call, then, arms folded, stared off in space again.

"It's like they're clipping my wings," he said. "Sure, I'll still be around for games, but you won't see much of me elsewhere: on shirts, sweatshirts, hats. Hey, I need room to fly. I gotta be me."

I listened as he continued and began to finally understand. "When we played at UCLA last fall, there was a disagreement over where I was allowed to stand," he said, "so they temporarily stuck me in a security room." His ample lips starting to quiver. "Then I heard them, the chants from our section: 'Free the duck! Free the duck! Free the duck!' "

He gulped, then sniffed. "When I came back into the stadium, you'd have thought I was Joey himself. The cheers thundered. It was my finest moment."

I picked up the check and we said our goodbyes. The duck headed toward campus.

"Hey," I called out to him. He turned. I lifted my fist in a show of solidarity. "Free the duck!" I said and watched him gently nod, turn and waddle into the uncertain night.

April 28, 2002

12.

Ties that bind

Who's sorry now?

ARLINGTON, Va. — I saw her two tables away at a Women in Military Service for America luncheon. Could it be her? Naw. She couldn't look that good after all these years, could she? I mean, I don't look that good after all these years — and 42 have passed since I fell in love with her.

Besides, what would she be doing here? What does she have to do with the military? But, then, what was I doing here? What do *I* have to do with the military?

"And now," the emcee said, "I'd like to recognize a woman who's been so supportive to women in the military: Connie Stevens!"

My heart fluttered like baseball cards in the spokes of my old Schwinn. As she stood to the applause of hundreds, I remembered that magical moment in 1962 when I came home from Emery's IGA Foodliner in Corvallis, clutching the first 45 record I'd ever bought. I was 8 years old. And in love for the first time.

The song on that MGM record — nobody remembers flip side songs — was *Vacation*.

"Put away the books, we're out of school / The weather's warm but we'll play it cool / We're on vacation, havin' lots of fun / V-A-C-A-T-I-O-N in the summer sun."

The song is seared into me like a read-only file permanently fixed on the hard drive of my heart.

As the clapping faded, I looked at her. She glanced at me, almost as if she knew me. Sure, I was a married man but there was no turning back: When this luncheon was over, I wanted my photo taken with my arm around Connie Stevens.

This puppy-dog love is not my nature. Famous people are no different from you and I: just rich, more beautiful, more powerful and more often to be stopped in public by some doting jerk who says something stupid that begins "When I was a kid ... ."

None of which would dissuade me from meeting my 1962 heart-throb. I hatched a plan in my mind: Let the Southern women in their flashing red, white and blue flag-pins get their cheesy photos, then swoop in with more dignified Oregon aplomb.

After 10 minutes, she shook the giggly gadflies and strode purposefully toward the exit, with just enough of a sideways glance to suggest she knew I was coming. And would welcome me as if she, too, had been waiting for this moment.

I handed my camera to a stranger with orders to shoot on sight. Showtime! "When I was a kid," I blurted, "you were my favorite singer! How about a photo?"

I put my arm around Connie and smiled big. She put her arm around me and smiled, too.

"Your song *Vacation* was the first 45 I ever bought!" I gushed.

There was a slight pause, the kind of worrisome pause you get when you first see the little beach ball on your Macintosh spinning and realize your computer is locked up.

"You must mean *Sixteen Reasons*," she said, forcing a smile. Her touch on me weakened. "I didn't do *Vacation*."

Oh ... my ... gosh. I had mistaken Connie Stevens for another '60s singer, Connie FRANCIS, my true heartthrob! The beach ball kept spinning.

"Uh, yeah, right, of course, *Sixteen Reasons*," I stammered.

My smile twitched on and off like a wire-shorted lamp. Hers dimmed considerably. The woman with my camera couldn't get it to work. Dead battery.

In a moment, Connie was gone, out the door. And out of my life. Forever. I bent over and buried my head in my hands.

I knew she knew. That's what hurt. She knew it was another woman for whom my heart had fluttered. And yet she had the dignity not to say a thing.

The poet John Donne pondered "for whom the bell tolls." But what did he know? He never made a jackass out of himself like me.

I ponder this: "How do you un-ring a bell?" You can't, I've dediced. You can only hope, in this case, that Connie Francis doesn't hear about my two-timing ways — and, when we someday meet at last, she welcomes me home in the summer sun. And, this time, the camera works.

June 4, 2004

Luke and Katie

H E FIRST NOTICED the little red-haired girl back in Mr. Ford's first-grade class — Room 1 — at Yolanda Elementary School in Springfield. It was the 1990-91 school year.

She first noticed him the same year. What she noticed was that he was holding her hand while Mr. Ford read from the book *Shiloh*, not that she exactly objected to the gesture. Boy germs were, yuk, boy germs but, well, Luke was Luke.

"I remember telling them, 'No, no, no, first-graders don't get to hold hands,'" says Dennis Ford.

But like water seeking its own level, love finds a way. On this, the day before Valentine's Day, the Luke Barr-Katie Kisor story reminds us so.

In her first-grade diary — I saw it with my own eyes — Katie drew a picture after that incident. It looks like a couple of ants having a picnic while "Mr. Ford" stands in the distance like the Statue of Liberty. "When Luke held my hand!" reads the caption.

"They were these two precious kids," recalls Marie Hinkle, the school health assistant then and now. "She had red hair. He was blond."

But tide and time wait for no tykes. Soon, first grade was over — and second and third.

One night, Luke and his mother, Jeannie, watched a "chick flick" in which a young man takes a train home to see his true love. Later, Jeannie walked into Luke's room. Her fourth-grade son was holding a photograph he'd framed of Katie.

"Someday, mom," he said, "that's going to be me on that train, and Katie's going to be there to meet me."

Jeannie and her husband, Mark, started calling their young romantic "Charlie Brown" because he liked the little red-haired girl but was afraid to talk to her. Not that he didn't find other ways to show his affection. Once, he punched out a playground bully who was pestering her — and wound up in the principal's office.

Soon, though, Katie had grown so much taller than Luke that it appeared he was the one who needed defending.

"I want Luke to ask me out, but he hasn't yet," Katie wrote in her diary as a fifth-grader.

What "ask me out" means in fifth-grade lingo is: *Hands off, everyone else, he's mine*. Not that she shared such feelings with Luke. Instead, she thrashed him in a game of "mercy," in which participants try to bend back each other's fingers until one person screams in agony.

"I won him," she told her diary.

He liked her competitiveness. She liked his.

"I've never told him I like him a lot and it wouldn't be unusual if we went out together forever and then got married," she wrote in her diary. "I know it sounds sort of unusual saying this at my age and I'm only 11 years old. I want to kiss him so bad but I don't have the guts."

His "journaling" was less detailed. He carved her name into his dresser with a pocket knife.

At Briggs Middle School, the two remained "pals" but went their separate ways.

"Where's 'Luke the Drifter?' " Katie's grandfather would kid, referring to a name from a Hank Williams song.

Oh, he was still around. But he'd bagged his brazen first-grade hand-holding ways for a more subtle approach.

"I'd walk out on the porch on Katie's birthday or at Christmas or Easter and there would be a present from Luke," remembers Katie's mom, Lauri.

Then, of course, there was this romantic overture: On a dare from Katie, Luke — with pal Peter Bauer along for support — showed up in the middle of her cul-de-sac and danced the hokeypokey for her.

"He was absolutely in love with her," says his mom Jeannie.

Obviously he was in love with her. Why else would one dance the hokeypokey in the middle of a cul-de-sac? As the song says: That's what it's all about.

Time passed. High school came. As juniors, the two remained "just friends." Then Luke, hanging around after a Thurston High wrestling practice, saw Katie practicing with the girls' basketball team. She invited him to come watch a game.

"I started going to all her games, then her softball games," says Luke.

They went to the junior-senior prom together and had a great time. Weirdly, though, that scared Katie.

"We'd just been pals to that point and I didn't want us to lose our friendship," she says.

In her April 23, 2001, diary entry, Katie referred to a number of guys. "Then there's Luke," she wrote, "the one I've always talked about .... I like him a lot ... To tell you the truth, I'm pretty sure he's the right one. I've always known that deep down in my heart. And I hope he feels the same way."

In the summer of 2001, before their senior years, she realized he did feel the same way. They first kissed after a twilight raft trip down the McKenzie River. Then — why should this surprise us? — they named stars for each other. They decided they were more than "just friends."

"We'd been praying that she'd find just the right person," says Lauri Kisor. "She did."

The two graduated from Thurston High last spring and are now 19 years old.

Recently, Luke told Katie he wanted to swing by Yolanda to see their old first-grade teacher, Mr. Ford. "He has some picture of us he wants us to see," he told her.

When Mr. Ford took his class — Room 1 — outside for recess, Luke bent on one knee and, in the very classroom where he first held Katie's hand 13 years ago, looked into her eyes.

"Katie Kisor," he said, "will you marry me?"

At first, she was too stunned to answer.

"We'd turned on the intercom because we knew what was happening and wanted to listen," says Hinkle, who'd gathered with other staffers in the office.

"Then we decided it was too personal so we shut it off. But I wanted to. You couldn't find two better people. With all the depressing news around, this is nice."

Mr. Ford came back in the classroom. "I admit, my eyes leaked," he says. "I've known them for years. You hear of high school sweethearts who get married, but first-grade sweethearts?"

By the way, the little red-haired girl was there to meet him at the train station. She said yes. The wedding is set for Sept. 6 at Dorris Ranch.

February 14, 2003

L. J.

AS YOU MAY know, I'm a great proponent of the winning-isn't-everything philosophy.

But, I confess, such thinking is more easily embraced while sitting at a computer than while sitting in the grandstands of your son's state high school semifinal baseball game, knowing if Sheldon High makes one more out it plays for the state championship.

Alas, it was not to be.

As a Lakeridge batter swatted a run-scoring hit to right field Wednesday, my son's youth sports career ended and, along with it, my career as a youth sports parent.

But every season offers its lessons and this final season offered me an important one: Trite as it may sound, it is just a game. Like most good lessons of life, I learned it the hard way:

It was March 7, and my son, Jason, was due home from baseball practice any moment. Good news, I believed, awaited him in a letter; I was fairly sure it was an acceptance to Linfield, his college of choice. He burst through the front door.

"Hey, you got — "

"Coach's wife has cancer," he said, his voice breaking, tears in his eyes.

To complicate matters, Lisa Johnson — she and Ben are both 34 — was eight months pregnant. She had been experiencing severe stomach pains and, knowing cancer ran in the family, had gone to see a doctor earlier that day.

Afterward, she had come straight to Ben's practice session. He was hitting infield, just reaching to catch a ball tossed to him from catcher Jon Powell, when he saw her by the backstop. He looked in her eyes and just knew.

He left the practice and never returned.

He needed to be there for Lisa, he realized, and for his 6-year-old daughter, Jordyn, and for his unborn son. So he took a leave of absence as a coach and PE and first aid teacher.

As if working out an adoption, he helped find a coaching replacement: Jim Fryback, a veteran from Springfield High. It was an interesting recommendation given that although both coaches know baseball inside and out, they have strikingly different styles.

Johnson is a toe-the-line guy, Fryback easygoing. But Johnson believed this team had great potential, and believed Fryback's experience could help his guys reach it.

On the Sunday after learning of Lisa's cancer, I saw Ben at a stadium work party. He hovered like a mother leaving for a business trip, wanting to make sure the house was in order.

He told me he needed to get out of the way and let Jim run the show. This, he said, was a special team; it could go the distance at state. And Fryback could help make it happen.

Sheldon opened its season two days later, about the time doctors induced labor on Lisa. She gave birth to a healthy boy, Blake. Sheldon beat Mountain View, 7-2, even though some players hadn't even figured out Fryback's signals yet.

Two days later, doctors removed a mass of cancer nearly the size of a baseball from Lisa's intestines. Hers is an aggressive cancer — high-grade lymphoma.

Ben literally lived at the hospital as Lisa began the first of three intense rounds of chemotherapy. Between rounds, Lisa and Ben showed up April 16 for a game against Churchill — Sheldon's 11th straight win. Lisa had on a fishing hat — she'd lost her hair — and was holding Blake. She looked tired, but exuded the sort of peaceful nature I've always seen in her. Ben looked uncomfortable, sitting in the stands instead of the dugout.

He and Lisa celebrated their 10-year wedding anniversary May 18 not with sips of champagne at a nice restaurant but with drips of chemo at Sacred Heart Medical Center. By then, Sheldon was 18-3 and preparing for the playoffs.

In their first game, the Irish rallied from a 2-0 deficit to beat Wilson 5-4 in extra innings. Next, they hung on to edge Gresham 2-1, then came from 3-1 down in the last inning to beat Sprague 4-3.

It was the first time in 28 years that Sheldon had made the semifinals; 80 teams had started the season, four were left. Then came

Wednesday's heart-rending loss — the sixth Sheldon game in a row decided by a single run.

Looking back at a spring he'll never forget, Ben says he's pleased with the job Fryback did and proud of the team. "It was," he says, "the best team I never got to coach."

When my son looks back at this season, I hope he remembers the lesson of never giving up; Lakeridge's impressive comeback was similar to a handful Sheldon had made itself.

I hope he remembers the levity Fryback brought to the ball park.

But, above all, I hope he remembers a shamrock patch on his game jersey with the initials "L. J." on it and a coach who left for all the right reasons — reminders that in the grand scheme of things, it is just a game.

June 3, 2001

New man on board

FERN RIDGE LAKE looks different as I arrive Wednesday night for the first sail of the year. For example, it has water. The drought is over. A new season has begun.

But something else is different. As I walk down the dock, my 75-year-old mother — the sailing purist who insists on bringing in the boat under sail, not engine — is sitting in the cockpit as expected. But there's a man with her, and he's not my father.

He's not the guy who dreamed of this 22-foot boat with my mom decades ago, the guy who sailed it with her for 13 years.

Today marks the first Mother's Day I've experienced when my mom has a new man in her life. After 60 years, she's dating again. And they're not just passing notes in some Oasis class. This is serious.

My father died in 1996. So, until now, the last time my mother had taken up with someone new was the fall of 1942. It's a little different the second time around. Her suitor is 84, not 19. But love, like water, has a way of finding its own level.

Though they'd known each other casually, they officially "met" last October at Richey's Market in Corvallis. Bob, a retired professor of forest science at Oregon State, had lost his wife of 60 years to cancer in August. He was, he says, in that "black hole" after the initial shock. He looked sad.

"So I gave him a little hug," mom recalls.

About a week later, she was driving home and thinking to herself: I'm ready for something new in my life. She and my father had been married 50 years and a day when he died unexpectedly. Since then, she had traveled, taken classes, volunteered — the problem wasn't emptiness. It was loneliness.

When she got home, a message was waiting on her answering machine. It was from Bob. "I wanted to thank you for the hug," he said. She sent him information from a grief support group she'd attended and said if he ever needed to talk, feel free to call. He did, but she was out.

Then some hiking friends bailed on her. "I figured, 'What do I have to lose?'" So she called Bob and they hiked Bald Hill together. She thought: "This is a nice guy." He thought: "This is quite a woman."

For the second hike, she made soup — "just in case he might want to come back to the house for dinner." Later that night, the phone rang at my sister's. "He did?" my sister said into the phone, then turned to her family. "Bob stayed for the soup!"

He liked her zest for life. She liked how he was sure enough about himself to let her lead at times — unlike some guys she'd sailed with who insisted on taking the tiller when she wanted to dock the boat herself, sails up.

E-mail updates from my sister started shooting my way. And I started wondering: Who is this guy and exactly what are his intentions? And why doesn't my mother e-mail me anymore?

They cooked dinner together, baking a salmon Bob had caught. They watched the Civil War football game on TV. Goodness, they started renting videos and cuddling! Hello, mom, remember me — your only son?

Finally, it was time: time to meet the children. She met three of his four. He met my sister, then later me.

It was, I admit, weird seeing my mother with another man. But when we shook hands, he put his free hand atop our two. I liked that. He was far younger-looking than I expected, well tanned, sort of forest science's answer to William Holden. He drives a 2000 Volvo, plays the banjo and hunts ducks.

When we were parting he put his arm around my mother. "I want you to know," he said — and his eyes got misty — "that I think this is one wonderful woman."

"As long as you keep believing that," I told him, "I don't think we'll have any trouble. Still, have her home by midnight, OK?"

She's never home anymore when I call. She went to Hawaii with Bob and his family. "It's like our lives are a baseball game," says mom, "and we're going into extra innings."

But the big question: Would Bob pass mom's all-important sailing test? Though he'd been in the Navy in World War II, this was different. This was a windy night on Fern Ridge. This was being on board 22 feet and 13 years of memories that belonged to this woman, her son and a man now gone.

An hour later, with Bob and Mom sharing the tiller, I know the answer. I'm focusing the camera on them. The sun, low above the Coast Range, tints their faces in orange. I click the shutter and their smiles confirm it: He's passed.

As the sun dips lower, mom guides the boat gently into the slip, sails up, no engine. She and Bob step onto the dock and celebrate with a kiss — just like that, right in front of me.

"I can't get over how you brought her in like that, Marolyn," says Bob. "Perfect."

On the other side of the boat, fastening a line, I smile inside. The drought is over. A new season has begun.

May 12, 2002

The Shedd Cafe

SHEDD — I'm only halfway through my breakfast Friday morning at the Shedd Cafe when I realize it: I've stumbled upon a lost tribe.

There's no suit-and-cell-phone crowd here, cramming down franchise specials while racing off to palm-pilot appointments. Instead, a handful of 70-plus men in plaid shirts and farm caps sit at one table. Mostly 70-plus women sit at another, each group melded by stories thicker than biscuits and gravy.

"This place is a cross between 'Ozzie & Harriet' and 'The Twilight Zone,' " says John Huddleston, who runs the lone restaurant in this unincorporated town on Highway 99 East, about 30 miles north of Eugene.

For starters, these folks own the place. Yep, a few years back, when the cafe owner died and the locals were faced with no place to go for coffee, 21 of them pooled their bucks and bought it for $60,000, then leased the restaurant to Huddleston.

"We had to," says 78-year-old Darrell Dannen. "This is all that's left of Shedd."

The cafe is a vanilla box decorated in vintage-car models, Coca-Cola posters and American flags: heavy on ryegrass farmers and Beaver believers; light on ties, heels and Ducks.

"It's like an old whittlin' bench where guys gather to talk," says Lee Chandler, whose husband, Richard, is known as "The Colonel."

She's virtually the lone Duck fan. "We let one in just to say we're integrated," quips Don Wirth, a farmer in knee-high rubber boots.

The history in the Shedd Cafe lingers like the smell of bacon. "They bring in pictures of themselves when they were in fifth-grade together," says Huddleston. "Or talk about the time a barnstormer came through town and they got free rides."

Most grew up, and still live, within a dog's bark of the cafe. Dannen's house was built by Frank Shedd himself, a Union army captain in the Civil War whose land claim gave birth to the town named in his honor.

"Do I live around here?" says 95-year-old Vernon Roberts. "Oh, no." But time and distance mean different things to these folks than to most. "I'm from Peoria." That's five miles away.

In the same way, Barbara Lewis calls herself a newcomer. "I've only been here 40-some years."

A while back, a customer was lamenting that he was feeling his age — 73. "That's nothin'," said Roberts. "I've been married long as you've been alive." It's true. He met his wife, Ruth, in one-room Shedd High in 1924. "Sat right behind me. Smiled every time I turned to look at her."

Ross Sprenger, 83, arrives; he has built his own carousel and railroad (2-foot-wide track). "Well, here he is, right on time — it's the colonel," says 80-something Grant Lindsay as in walks Richard Chandler as if cued by a stagehand. He flew more than 100 missions in World War II and Korea.

"We get a lot of real heroes here," says Huddleston. "Folks who survived the Depression. People who worked hard all their lives and didn't ask anything of anybody."

As the Elvis legs swivel on the clock, the stories pile up like a trip through a buffet line: Hunting. Fishing. The time Roberts, in the '30s, rode a motorcycle through town while standing on its seat.

Some are about people no longer here. "We've lost a lot of folks," says Wirth. "Hank, Hazel, Ross Sprenger's wife, Lucille ... ."

Ruth, the wife of 95-year-old Vernon, is no longer behind him as she was back at long-gone Shedd High. Instead, she's in front of him, chatting with other women about everything from ag auctions to this Saturday's barbecue fund-raiser to raise money for library books.

A waitress, seemingly out of nowhere, begins passing out pineapple upside-down cake.

"Linda made it fresh last night," she says.

Soon, they go their separate ways. And I go mine — back to the city, back to the world of convenience stores, tailgating drivers and fast-food restaurants where conversations don't often get beyond "for here or to go?"

The Shedd Cafe, I realize, isn't the lost tribe. We are.

April 29, 2003

The language of love

A MAJOR REASON the divorce rate has quadrupled since 1970, many marriage therapists say, is a failure to communicate.

In a world of e-mail, instant-messaging and cell phones — a world where communicating has never been physically easier — lots of husbands and wives split up because they can't find a common language to work through the inevitable challenges of life.

Which brings me to an outdoor wedding I watched Saturday that buoyed me with hope.

Jincy Schar, 28, married Robbie Roberson, 24, on the tree-shaded lawn of the country home north of Eugene where the bride grew up and always dreamed of being married.

I've never seen a wedding that drew more people — 500. A wedding that required so much Kleenex. And, above all, a wedding that featured the bride and groom using sign language to exchange their vows.

Jincy Schar, you see, can't hear. And, until recently, Robbie Roberson couldn't sign. But on an afternoon in which even the wind seemed to hush for the ceremony, the two became husband and wife.

Some in the "nonhearing community" believe that deaf people should marry only deaf people; a "hearing person," no matter how sensitive, they believe, can't truly understand life for someone who can't hear.

Some in the "hearing community," meanwhile, believe that marrying someone who's deaf is to ask for an unnecessary burden; why start with a relational obstacle when you don't have to?

But, frankly, Robbie and Jincy Roberson don't care about the cultural forces. They care about each other. About their common faith in God. And about, well, swing-dancing and such.

"It's not about one person hearing and one person not," says Jincy, who talks but with limited inflection. "The most important thing is the people involved, the commitment."

Yes, at times they get frustrated with the barrier, but mainly when Jincy feels lost among Robbie's "hearing" friends and vice versa. "We help each other out," Jincy says. "We won't give up. We don't believe in divorce."

"I communicate with Jincy better than with anyone I've ever met," Robbie says. "She's made it easy."

They met in 1999 through common friends. And that's all they were at first: friends. But one thing led to another and suddenly Robbie, wanting to know Jincy better, found himself driving north on Interstate 5, practicing the sign-language alphabet. "By Albany, I was signing the words I saw on billboards," he says.

"What impressed me about him was his heart," Jincy says. "He was kind and caring."

"Beyond her looks, what captured me was her spirit," Robbie says. "She's special. Those 500 people didn't come to see me."

Jincy, a 1993 graduate of Sheldon High, graduated from Cal-State Northridge and from the Western Culinary Institute in Portland. She is a private chef.

Robbie, a 1996 graduate of Springfield High, is the business development coordinator for U Lane O Credit Union (now Oregon Community Credit Union) and a guy who can ruin scrambled eggs.

He isn't a chef.

Their wedding was the perfect blend of tears and laughter. The laughter got an early start at the rehearsal when Jincy, with some people in the back saying the microphones needed more volume, yelled — well, as loud as she can yell: "What are you guys, *deaf?*"

During the next day's ceremony, the tears flowed with the softness and steadiness of Oregon's winter rains:

When Jincy's father, Jason, walked his daughter down the aisle — in total silence. (It was the idea of Jincy's maternal grandmother, Donna Gehrke, to honor her granddaughter and all that she's overcome. All you could hear was the sniffling of a proud father.)

When a soloist sang Frank Sinatra's *All the Way.*

And when the two signed their vows to each other. (Though neither saw each other's vows beforehand, both had communication among their pledges. Robbie drew some laughter when he signed, "And I am honored to call you my husband and best friend.")

Once pronounced husband and, er, wife, the two headed down the aisle arm-in-arm, a '57 Thunderbird waiting in the distance. The audience burst into wild clapping, some by striking their hands together, some by shaking their hands above their heads — sign lingo for clapping.

The three-piece jazz band struck up Benny Goodman's *Sing, Sing, Sing.* And Jincy and Robbie started swing dancing, right there in the aisle, then segued to a dip and, finally, to a dramatic kiss.

In any language, that said it all.

August 8, 2002

Angel of Shooter's Pub

AT SHOOTER'S PUB & Grill, a River Road bar where a mounted deer head is flanked by dozens of photos of guys posing with big fish, Kayleen Johnston first overheard the news: Dick's wife needed a kidney.

Kayleen, a bartender, waitress and self-appointed sergeant of arms — "I don't like drunks"— knew Dick Morgan as little more than a retiree who came in weekday afternoons to play video golf and sip pounders of Coors Lite. She didn't know his wife, a Merrill Lynch client associate, in the least.

"How do I find out if I'm a match?" she said.

Huh?

"Just like that," fellow Shooter's worker Nancy Hubbard says. "No hesitation at all."

But you don't even know this woman, someone told her. What if you give her one of yours and your remaining one goes bad? "What are you thinking,' said John McCauley, a Shooter's regular. "And just when I thought I knew you."

But who, really, knew Kayleen Johnston? Knew about her spending the first 18 years of her life in either an orphanage or a foster home? About having a baby at 16? About the rape — and hanging out a fourth-story window to avoid a repeat attack, but not being able to hang on? About having surgery after the fall to save her life and fuse her spine together?

Who knew about the automobile accident, the hysterectomy, the demons of drugs?

"This body," the 45-year-old woman says, "has been through a lot. Twenty years ago, I shoulda been dead."

But now, she was offering a total stranger life — or at least life without dialysis.

"It's what I wanted to do," says Kayleen, who lives outside Junction City. "And I'm a determined person. You grow up in an orphanage, you learn you won't get anything unless you try very, very hard."

She's terrified of needles. But, in late 2003, she went in for her blood test and proved to be a match.

"When I first met her," Jeanne Morgan of Eugene says, "I told her I couldn't believe she was willing to do this for me. I just hugged her."

As part of a further test, Kayleen had to pee into a plastic jug, whenever nature called, for 24 hours. She drove the sample to the lab in her '89 Ford Bronco.

But happily-ever-after stories have never been her strong suit, so it was no surprise when the doctor delivered the bad news: Kayleen had too much protein in her urine. Disqualified.

On one hand, it was the perfect "out": She had made the noble effort and yet someone else was putting a kibosh on the idea. Glory without sacrifice. And no longer facing three months without a paycheck while she recovered from a surgery.

But any one-too-many customer who's had Kayleen pry the car keys from his hands knows the woman rarely takes no for an answer.

"Let's fix it," she told Dr. Brian Jones. "This woman's life depends on it."

To even have a chance of reducing the protein in her urine, he told her, she would need to stop smoking, change her diet and cut back her drinking. Kayleen stopped smoking, changed her diet and cut back her drinking. And, oh yes, quit taking the pain medication for her back.

The bartender, who earns $8 an hour, even lied so she could give away a kidney to a woman she didn't know. Kayleen was given a monitor to measure her blood pressure every 20 minutes. Also, she was asked to keep a log of how much she was exerting herself at each juncture.

"If I knew my blood pressure was high, I'd just write something like, 'Took dog for walk,' even if I was sitting still."

Kayleen was re-tested. This time, she got the thumbs-up as a donor. She and Jeanne went to Portland last summer for tests at Oregon Health & Science University and a party afterward to introduce Kayleen to Jeanne's extended family.

Bad news again: Doctors discovered Jeanne, 57, had heart problems; she would need to begin dialysis until her condition improved.

"It was yet another opportunity for her to bail," Jennifer May, a co-worker of Jeanne's, says of Kayleen. "But she didn't. That's what's so amazing."

Instead, she grieved for the woman she didn't know. "She was so depressed at the party," Kayleen says. "I felt so bad for her."

Finally, the transplant was back "on" for Jan. 18. First, the what-to-expect talk from doctors and social workers: "The sawing of my ribs, the laying out of the intestines. After a while," Kayleen says, "I just said, 'Enough. Let's do it.'"

They did it. Jeanne remembers the two women, side by side on gurneys, before their surgeries. "I just told her I was praying for the two of us," she says.

Four days later, the two saw each other for the first time since their surgeries: Both tired. Both sore. Both relieved.

"The fantastic part was when we learned the kidney had kicked in right away," Kayleen says. "I'm like, 'Yes!' "

On the sixth floor of the US Bank Building, Merrill Lynch employees greeted the news with guarded optimism. At Shooter's, more than a few beers were hoisted in honor of their very own Kayleen. "In my mind, she's a hero," says McCauley, among those who questioned her decision.

"I consider it an honor," Kayleen says. "I mean, how many chances do you get like this? I've made a lot of bad choices in my life. This is a good one."

Though not home free — the first few months are critical for a transplanted kidney — Jeanne is expected to return to Eugene on Friday from Portland. Kayleen has been home for three weeks but isn't expected to return to her job at Shooter's for nearly two more months.

She walks slowly, like someone whose body has been through a lot. Which, of course, it has. Only this time, it's a good sort of pain.

"I got a thank-you card from Jeanne yesterday," says Kayleen, who had to have three ribs broken during the procedure. "Said she wished she could have my rib pain so I wouldn't have to have it. Made me cry."

And this from a woman so toughened from the past that tears don't come easily.

"You hear talk about there being no angels anymore," says Blaine Werner, who works with Jeanne at Merrill Lynch. "But here's this woman ... "

The angel of Shooter's Pub & Grill.

February 17, 2005

Love at its deepest

ON A RECENT Saturday evening, I found myself among hundreds of other guests at an outdoor wedding in north Eugene. I had rushed through post-Duck-game traffic, was emotionally drained and frankly wasn't primed to be inspired by much of anything beyond a cold drink.

But this evening was about to remind me that inspiration comes at the oddest times and places. Not necessarily when you expect it. And not necessarily from a pulpit, a poet or a two-dollar greeting card.

In this case, it came from outside a port-a-potty.

Beyond wind-whipped balloons that threatened to hammer the groom, the wedding seemed almost heaven-made: just the right touch of pomp, humor and spiritual leavening, all played out on a grassy spot backdropped by a small lake. A slight smell of blackberries wafted across the crowd.

The young bride and groom arrived at the makeshift "altar" to the accompaniment of music written by a brother of the groom. The two said vows they'd written themselves, promising to love each other in sickness and in health, in good times and in bad.

They kissed. People broke into applause. Balloons rose in the air. And the bride and groom all but floated down the grassy aisle toward the rest of their lives — after a less-than-quick stop at the festive outdoor reception that followed.

That's when it happened. After a pit stop in the Honey Bucket, I stepped out to find a man and a woman, both of whom looked to be nearly 80, next in line. It was, I realized, Pat Chase and her husband, Lowell, whom *The Register-Guard* had featured a few years ago in a story about men who'd flown World War II bombers.

Pat was in a wheelchair, having suffered a stroke a few years ago. Lowell looked a tad shaky, not being in good health himself.

But he bent over to help his wife up and out of her chair. Slowly, almost as if part of one of those old Tim Conway comedies where the actor plays the shuffling old man, the two worked together for the benefit of one.

I held the door open, wondering if I should help further. The people in line waited patiently, perhaps wondering the same thing. Perhaps thinking, as I was, that we were in the midst of something strangely special.

We were witnessing love at its deepest level. Not People-magazine, what's-in-it-for-me love. But true love.

Mr. Chase put his arms around his wife. He lifted her to her feet with such dignity and respect, as if she were precious china that would break if he were to let go.

"I've got you," he said.

Mrs. Chase put her arms around his neck. She looked at him with such trust and admiration, as if he were still the 21-year-old tenor that she, a piano player, had met at the University of Oregon School of Music after the war.

The moment froze in front of me like a photograph. Because in 1946, you see, the Chases had been that 20-something couple down by the lake. They had said their vows, promising to love each other in sickness and in health, in good times and in bad.

And now, 57 years later, they were still making good on that promise.

In a world where promises have become cheap, where a marriage has only a coin-flip chance of lasting, where too many people flee marriages when the good times end, the scene wasn't one of futility, but of hope. Not one of shame, but of honor.

Soon, a daughter-in-law of the couple, Lynn, arrived on the scene to help Pat inside. No balloons rose into the air. Nobody broke into applause. But I sensed we'd all witnessed something important about promises to keep.

With the problem resolved, I left. I headed back to the reception, where I watched the carefree bride and groom twirl on the dance floor. And hoped they would still be leaning on each other once the music stopped.

September 28, 2003

13.

Our house

We don't own our pets

WHAT A ludicrous idea, this recent attempt to convince the Eugene City Council that people with pets be referred to as "animal guardians."

And what an equally ludicrous idea for the council to stick with its policy of referring to such people as "pet owners."

Anybody with a brain larger than that of a Chihuahua's knows neither label fits.

We don't own pets. They own us. And we don't guard pets. We clean up after them.

Having lived with dogs and cats for most of my life, I recommend that the City Council officially refer to people with animals as "pet hostages."

This phrase better expresses the obvious truth that people living with pets give up their basic four freedoms — sleep, money, quiet and the right to unshredded sofa arms — to cater to some four-footed, conniving ball of pitch-pocked fur, giving it whatever it wants at whatever hour and at whatever cost. (Not that I'm bitter.)

They have us wrapped around their little paws, these creatures great and small and smelly.

Take the dog owner being dragged by a leash. Who's in charge here? Take the dog owner carrying a plastic bag full of — let's just come right out and say it — doo-doo. Who's in charge here?

Or take our cat. (Better yet, take all four. E-mail me at bwelch@guardnet.com.)

They have two basic purposes in life, these fickle felines: to go "out" and to come "in." After years of mulling these two basic instincts, I finally understand their deeper meaning: Cats want outside so you'll have to get up from whatever you're doing and let them inside. They want inside so you'll have to get up from whatever you're doing and let them outside.

That's it. The urge has nothing to do with what's outside or inside; they couldn't care less. They just want to remind you that they own you. It's a game with simple rules: They always win. You always lose.

This in-and-out instinct is as basic as the salmon's need to spawn, the main difference being that if you ignore them, salmon won't claw through the 1x4 molding around your front door and reach their fins inside and brandish them at you in anger. Or worse, go to the back door and shred the screen like Gentle Ben on meth.

As the "pet hostage," you either meet their demands or pay the price. They say "meow," you say "how high?" They say "feed me," you say "right away!" They say "I'm going to hurl right in your lap," your spouse says, "Oh, poor baby" — and she's not referring to you.

There's more. One afternoon I was walking through the dining room when I had to step over a cat that was stretched out on the hardwood floor, fast asleep. This didn't bother me. What bothered me was that I'd never seen this cat before in my life. And it was sleeping after having sucked up our cats' food like an Oreck Upright.

To which I wanted to say: "Can I get you some decaf — perhaps an after-dinner mint?"

It isn't enough for our cats to hold us hostage, they now invite the neighbor cats over and let them humiliate us.

Where is our cats' sense of indignation? Of duty and honor to protect the home turf? I want our cats to hiss at this bewhiskered slacker. To get their hair up on end. To flatten back their ears in grim defiance and do that fake-punch thing, a la Rocky. Instead they yawn and go take a nap.

Cats nap for one simple reason: to rub it in. To remind you that as you rush off to your life of responsibilities and deadlines, they are sleeping. And when you return from a hard day's work, they are still sleeping, often in the same position. It's a control thing. Subtle, but powerful. You work. We sleep. Ha, ha, ha.

When they sense you might be starting to believe that the house actually belongs to you, they sharpen their claws on the arms of a chair, the animal equivalent of having someone not only smoke in the house, but flick ashes on your Duck football guide.

One cat, with all the aplomb of some teenage tagger, hops up on your desk and — editors, I'm sorry, I didn't want you to find out this way — sprays on your list of work phone numbers. Our oldest cat went so far as to be hit by a bus — just to score sympathy points and ding me with a $400 bill for the metal plate the vet put in her.

All of this is to say: You are helpless in my paws. I am cat, hear me meow. Hear me scratch on the door with an incessant stop-start pattern more annoying than a single mosquito in a tent. Smell the calling card I left on your variable-speed drill out in the shop. See me each month in that PetSmart line on the Visa bill; yes, we can cost that much!

So against such a daily assault, why, you ask, do I have cats in the first place? Simple. I want to stay married. And every now and then, I confess, when I see a cat curled up in front of the fire or stretched out in a spot of sunlight or purring at the foot of the bed, I think to myself:

I'm glad I'm theirs.

April 20, 2002

In hindsight ...

When trying to decide whether to share about my recent colo-noscopy — not to be confused with my columnoscopy, which would refer to my editor giving me a really, really thorough annual review — I was influenced by two things:

One was knowing Katie Couric, the NBC "Today" show host, had undergone a colonoscopy before TV cameras. Goodness, if she had the guts to show pictures, I figured, I can at least write words.

The other was hearing of folks I know who'd had the exam

— and learned they had cancer. And, thus, a chance to beat it.

The American Cancer Society reports that although everyone over the age of 50 should get a colon cancer testing, only about 44 percent of us actually do.

I learned that the displeasure of having a small camera stuck where the sun don't shine is overblown. Before the procedure, some suggested a colonoscopy is the medical equivalent of a Duck fan enduring a 50-21 loss to the Beavers: painful and humiliating, with too much enemy trespassing into one's end zone. Naw, it wasn't that bad. And, at times, downright funny.

"Good luck on your muffler inspection," one friend e-mailed.

Another, a poet, gushed forth words of eloquence, rewriting Robert Frost's *Stopping By Woods on a Snowy Evening*. Appropriately enough, it began: *"Whose colon this is I think I know / He's now past fifty and so ... ."*

And so there I was Wednesday night, after a day of drinking nothing but clear liquids, trying to work up the courage to drink something called Fleet Phospho-Soda, not to be confused with a regular soda. Judging by the TV commercials, when you drink a regular soda, life erupts into a cacophony of fun: you're Jimmy Hendrix playing electric guitar. You're windsurfing a 10-foot wave. You're surrounded by bikini-clad women.

When you drink Fleet Phospho-Soda, you erupt, period. You're Mount St. Helens. You're riding a 10-foot wave. Your wife suddenly decides she needs to do some last-minute Christmas shopping, even though it's only Dec. 15. The cats start scratching madly on the door to get out and, because you're locked on target, finally break a window and flee, screaming madly.

But, mixed with apple juice, this people's Drain-O doesn't taste as bad as everyone says. Honest. And the stuff works. All evening my stomach rumbled like high Cascades thunder. I became as predictable as Old Faithful.

At some point, my younger son popped in for a visit. "Sorry," I said, "I gotta run." In more ways than one.

Finally, it was show time; I could tell because I was lying on a gurney next to a TV screen on which my nether regions were about to make their cinematic debut. A poster of a waterfall — how fitting — hung on the ceiling.

Among a zillion questions, my doctor asked me to tell him the type of exam I was here for, a precautionary measure that probably began soon after some patient with a sprained wrist got the surprise of a lifetime.

The nurses did a good job of making me not feel like a scared man in a backless hospital gown. The intravenous sedation took hold. I stayed awake, but it was as if I was suspended in time, not like Emily in *Our Town*, returning from the dead to see her 12th birthday. More like Bob in *My Tush*, returning from his 118th trip to the bathroom to see his large intestine.

"You have a really nice colon," I remember a nurse telling me, an obvious pickup line. I ignored her. In fact, near as I can tell, I ignored everything: time, space and reality in general.

The good news is that I never felt a thing during the procedure. Nothing. The better news is that all was quiet on the polyp front. "You won't need another one of these tests for 10 years," my doctor told me.

My exam — it took about half an hour — had begun at 11:15 a.m. I was home by 1:30 p.m., blessedly eating for the first time in 40 hours. That, frankly, was the most difficult part of the whole procedure: not eating.

So give yourself a chance to live longer. Have the foresight to allow a doctor some hindsight.

December 19, 2004

Where the time goes

IT HITS YOU, for the first time, about a month ago. Your 22-year-old son asks for an edit job on something he's written, as he's done often over the years.

Only this one is different. As you begin reading, the words grow blurrier and blurrier. Then you realize why:

You're reading your son's wedding vows.

It's one of those Judy Collins, "who-knows-where-the-time-goes" moments, as real as it is cliched. One day you're fixing his spelling on a "How I Spent My Summer Vacation" piece for Miss Sofie's fourth-grade class, the next day you're helping polish his "How I Want to Spend the Rest of My Life" piece for his wedding.

You realize this is actually going to happen: After a wedding reception, that little kid is going to hop in a sports car with a young woman and you're going to be standing there in the exhaust, holding environmentally safe bubbles in one hand and a stack of Visa receipts in the other.

You recall that your other son is off to college in the fall and so this means the trio is breaking up: Crosby, Stills & Nash each going solo, the wedding nothing but a metaphorical "just a song before I go ... "

You remember that coed softball moment from earlier this summer, you at the plate with an 0-and-2 count and your soon-to-be-married son — with just a hint of fear in his voice — yelling "just meet the ball, dad." (Striking out in coed softball is like being skunked while fishing a trout hatchery.)

For an instant, as your knees shake ever so slightly, you say to yourself: How did it come to this? Only yesterday I was a Midget League All-Star and, suddenly, I'm 47, down 0-and-2 and experiencing the humiliation of my own son yelling at me those same Little League eye-on-the-ball cliches I used to yell at him.

And you want to say: Hold everything. Nobody ran these changes by me. Everybody back to your original positions.

But then, you get a fiendish look on your face and think: I'm not losing a son, I'm gaining office space. You imagine the already-approved three-way trade that will provide you with a home office all your own — and library shelves to be named later.

What's more, you think about gaining a beautiful daughter-in-law — someone who sees in your son the same qualities that make it hard for you to let him go. You think how she brings out the best in him and he the best in her. (And realize that your fistful of Visa bills pales compared to what her folks ponied up.)

Finally, after returning from your brief Mr. Toad's Wild Ride Into Mid-Life Insecurity, you suddenly see this wedding as a grand adventure that you shouldn't miss. So you hop on board.

You stop worrying that the ceremony will be more disastrous than Dan Rather's new hairdo.

You relax and marvel at the changes in protocol compared to your own wedding more than 25 years ago. In 1975, couples couldn't register for gifts by computer, nor did they get cool stuff like a case of Mountain Dew and a new basketball net, as your son did. (All you remember getting is an olive-green crock pot and enough fondue sets to invite the entire Woodstock crowd over for chocolate-covered strawberries.)

Two days before the wedding, you invite 15 guys over to barbecue burgers and give your son advice on marriage. It's risky business, you realize, but the results are phenomenal, including an old high school friend who comes from Portland with a visual aid he's made out of PVC pipe and nylon ribbon — sort of a "Tool Time" tribute to the emotional differences between men and women.

Your home becomes The Groomsmen Hotel, large bodies tucked into small rooms like those sea lions on the Newport Bay docks.

Friday: golf by day; rehearsal and dinner by night. (Only the finest for this upscale crowd: pizza.)

Finally, the day arrives: Saturday's wedding ceremony is perfect in all its imperfection. Afterward, gusty winds topple table centerpieces for the outdoor reception, but nobody seems to care.

So intent are you on trying to enjoy everything — and to capture it all — that you wind up offering a toast with a microphone in one hand and a video camera in the other.

Darkness descends. And suddenly your son and new daughter-in-law are running beneath a cathedral of golf clubs and climbing into that sports car and are gone in the night, just as you knew they would be.

Back home, there's an envelope addressed to you and your wife. It's from him — a thank-you note, complete with a Burrito Boy gift certificate.

As Sunday's rain falls outside, you read it again. Not as his editor; those days are gone. But simply as his father.

Again, the words get blurry. But this time, it's a blurry you feel blessed to know.

July 31, 2001

Second wind

CORVALLIS — Since last May, when I wrote about my 75-year-old mother falling in love with an 84-year-old man, a number of you have asked for an update.

Both had lost spouses — my mother six years ago after 50 years of marriage and her new suitor 16 months ago after 60 years of marriage.

We last left them dockside at Fern Ridge Lake, where Bob Tarrant had passed the Marolyn Welch School of Sailing test: Instead of letting his male ego shove her aside and grab the tiller, Bob had watched in wonder as she'd guided the 22-foot boat safely into its slip — without having to use the motor.

Last Saturday night, the two raised their sails for good: They got married in a small Episcopal Church chapel in front of 34 family members.

I never thought I'd walk my mother down an aisle and, along with my sister, Linda Crew, "give her away" to be married. I never thought a woman from North Dakota who I'd never seen before would wrap me in a hug and say, "You must be my new stepbrother!" I never thought I'd see my mother drive off to a honeymoon at the coast with a man in a car whose back window was soaped with "Just Married."

But every now and then, like a sailor caught in the doldrums, a warm breeze suddenly musters itself to fill our sails. And for my mother and Bob this is such a breeze — a "second wind," if you will.

When learning that my mother was getting remarried, a few people expressed concern. "Are you OK with that?" they asked.

How can you not be OK with the idea of a kind, honorable man — even if he was among the 1937 Oregon State students who caravaned to Eugene to gloat after the Beavers' 14-0 Civil War win — seeing the wonder of your own mother? Or the idea of two people being the answer to one another's loneliness?

Some worried about their ages. It's painful losing a spouse, they'd say. Aren't they setting themselves up for a second dose of sorrow? Who knows how much time they have left?

Hey, who knows how much time any of us has left?

Mom and Bob's philosophy is simple: Every day together is a day they wouldn't have had together if they'd played it safe. In short: What's the joy of sailing if you never leave the dock?

And so there they sat, one autumn day, meeting with a minister about the wedding.

"Would you like some premarital counseling?" he asked.

"Well, given that we have 110 years of marital experience between us," Bob said, "I think we'll pass."

Not that they, or their families, had plied these waters before. I mean, do you throw a bachelor's party for an 85-year-old groom?

We passed on that idea. The two families, in a sort of grown-up "Brady Bunch" scene, met in the church's fellowship hall an hour before the ceremony to get to know one another. Bob has four children, 58 to 47; five grandchildren; and four great-grandchildren. (How many kids get to see their great-grandfather get married?) My mother has two children and five grandchildren.

After photos and small talk, we headed into the chapel. I'd been in a fairly light mood — as the minister explained the logistics of the ceremony, I had, like a football referee, signaled that Team Tarrant would kick off and Team Welch would receive — but as my mother and I started down the aisle, everything changed. There was Bob, waiting at the altar. His eyes were red with tears.

That choked me up. Mom had to reach hard for the words "til death do us part." "When you're 19 and getting married," she later told me, "you don't think of that. Now you do."

The families clapped and hooted when the two were introduced as husband and wife. Then, after the church bells rang — mom insisted on bells after not having them back in 1946 — the families gathered at a bed-and-breakfast for a celebratory dinner.

We offered toasts, the most memorable coming from Bob. Paraphrased, he said that the little numbers behind our names — our ages — don't mean squat. What matters is how we live.

I like his thinking. It goes along with the card my wife, Sally, and I made for the two, replete with words from the English poet George Chapman:

Give me a spirit that on this life's rough sea
Loves t' have his sails fill'd with a lusty wind,
Even till his sail-yards tremble, his masts crack,
And his rapt ship run on her side so low
That she drinks water, and her keel plows air.

As a gift, crystal or china or a crock pot just didn't seem right, so we went with something more appropriate:

Matching sailing gloves — for the voyages ahead.

December 3, 2002

Letting go

YOU ARE THE BOWS," Kahlil Gibran once wrote, "from which your children as living arrows are sent forth."

On this, my 25th Father's Day, the verse hits a bull's-eye with me in an odd way, the Lebanese-American philosopher having not been much of a football fan and my latest challenge as a father involving exactly that.

Last fall, Jason, my 22-year-old younger son, informed his mother and me that, despite having never played a single down of organized tackle football, he planned to play for a local team in the National Nineman Football League.

At first, I assumed this was one of those bad ideas that, like the ill-fated Apple Lisa computer, would go away on its own. But he persisted. He had dreams of being the living embodiment of all the computer football players he'd invented and thumb-toggled to glory over the years. I had nightmares of paralyzing injuries.

We sparred for months — "Some of these guys have played Division 1 football," I blurted at one point, "and you weigh 150 pounds." But hadn't I taught him to think big and take risks? he countered.

Yeah, but ... .

Ultimately, he prevailed. He earned a spot on the Eugene Knights. "I might play tailback," he said as the spring season neared. "My teammates call it the pinata position." I didn't laugh.

The first game arrived. Adjacent to the Mohawk High field I saw one of those monster pickups that you could hold a tailgate party beneath. "That probably belongs to the linebacker who's going to tackle Jason," I told Sally, my wife.

"Stop being so negative," she said.

A few dozen fans were on hand. Parents. Girlfriends. The players were mainly in their 20s and 30s. It was sort of KidSports meets *The Longest Yard*, that Burt Reynolds movie about the prison football team.

Jason looked like one of those pipe-cleaner figures you made back in second grade. Skinny. Easily bendable. I looked at the guys on the other team. They looked big, a few with beer guts that folded over their pants like the top of a bran muffin arching over the bake cup.

The game began. I didn't want to watch.

Jason played mainly wide receiver and cornerback, making five tackles and recovering a blocked punt. You'd have thought he had made a game-saving interception. He jumped up and flapped both arms in the air to pump up our estimated crowd of 16.

The Knights lost 28-6, but the only stat that mattered to me was this: one (number of games Jason had played without sustaining a life-altering injury).

In the second game, he caught a pass over the middle, shook a tackle and headed up the sidelines. Suddenly, I leapt to my feet and started screaming encouragement. He went 55 yards before being dragged down. Hey, I thought, that was my son! Our son.

The Knights lost 70-0. In fact, they would lose all seven of their games. But in one, a kid named Jason Welch intercepted two passes, made eight tackles and caught a 30-yard touchdown pass. In another, he caught two TD passes, one a 95-yarder. Beyond bumps and bruises, he never got hurt.

My favorite moment was seeing him, in game five, score the first touchdown I'd ever seen him score.

Afterward, we had a barbecue for players and parents in our backyard. The players laughed and joked and ate what must be a Nineman record number of chocolate-covered strawberries. A 270-pound lineman requested, and was given, my wife's recipe for coconut pecan brownies. I watched Jason describe, in detail, his TD catch.

On his own, he had proven something this season that he needed to prove to nobody but himself. Earned some respect. And found a place to belong.

Part of fatherhood, I've realized, is protecting our children. And part is letting them go their way. "You may house their bodies," writes Gibran, "but not their souls."

As the archers, we sight the target and launch an arrow. Cringing. Hoping. Praying. And then find ourselves, at times, amazed that it's landed where it needs to be — even if it wasn't where we were aiming.

June 20, 2004

The drinking fountain

CORVALLIS — We'd come, my mother and I, for one last look at the place where it all began.

At Corvallis High's main office on this mid-June afternoon, we told a secretary why we were here. Around us, chaos abounded. Not only was this the last week of school, but this was the last week of school in this building ever.

A new building was being completed. Soon, the original CHS, which opened nearly 70 years ago, would be torn down. Boxes were scattered, the office lost in a clutter of past, present and future.

In another area: mementos that people had purchased to remember this place — lockers, doorknobs, classroom flags and the like.

"Can we help you?" a secretary asked.

As my 78-year-old mother told the story, a couple of others in the office started half-listening. She told about how, in the summer of '42, at the first back-to-school dance, she had met him. She was a 15-year-old junior. He was an 18-year-old freshman at Oregon State College.

They met at the south drinking fountain outside the gym. The band was playing a new Glen Miller song called *At Last.* My mother even remembers the line being sung when their eyes first met: "You smiled and then the spell was cast."

Now, as she continued with her story, others in the office stopped what they were doing and listened.

After a few dances, she continued, he walked her home to her house at 33rd and Van Buren. Could they see each other the next night?

It was an invitation that ran head-on into one of her parents' cardinal rules: Thou Shalt Not Date College Men.

"But, mom," she pleaded the next day, "he's not a college man. Technically, he doesn't register until tomorrow."

Her parents were stiff, letter-of-the-law types; they had an odd respect for technicalities. Her mother paused.

"OK," she said, "but just this once."

"Just this once" — after the man's service in World War II was over — turned into a marriage that lasted 50 years and a day. And led to my sister and me.

Which is why we had come back to the school where my mother and father had met. And, in 1972, from which I had graduated.

We had come to see the south drinking fountain outside "the old gym." To take photos of that spot. To say goodbye.

By last week, the old gym and the drinking fountain were gone.

You probably have places like that in your past. Places that, oddly, seem more important the farther away from them you get.

You live in a house for years and return to see it. But it's gone.

You work at a business for years and return to see it. But it's gone.

You play in a field for years as a child and return to see it. But it's gone.

It feels almost like a death. In Bend, recently, I saw an empty lot where once had been the newspaper office at which I'd worked. It made me feel forgotten. Insignificant.

Though we might not demand much of the world, maybe that's all we ask: that someone notice we were here.

You meet a stranger at a drinking fountain. You endure a war to get married. You have two children. Build a photography business in your basement. Survive a car wreck than nearly kills you both. Welcome grandchildren. And, in retirement, name your dream sailboat *At Last*.

Then, the day after you've celebrated your golden wedding anniversary, one of you is suddenly gone. And yet time marches on, threatening to forget that the two of you ever *were*. Now, after a wrecking crew's work, the place where you met is even gone.

But nobody can take away the memories, though, at times, they ask a price.

In this case, $78.13.

That's how much we paid for the south drinking fountain outside the old gym at Corvallis High. It now sits in our backyard, soon to be incorporated into some sort of flower arrangement — or inset into our wooden garden shed.

To remind us of where it all began.

July 24, 2005

Our new Oregonian

MAYBE YOU'VE experienced it: one of those "whoa" moments when you're reminded that in the book of life, you've ventured far beyond the preface. I just had one.

I was staring at a photograph of a middle-aged man holding a day-old baby. A 20-something man stands beside them.

That would be my son. The middle-aged man would be me. And the baby I was holding — well, that would be my first grandchild, Caden Grant Welch, born at 2:34 a.m. Monday.

Thus begins the sixth generation of Oregonians in our family.

Cade's first scream in the night — I heard it from a Sacred Heart hallway — was the sweetest thing I've heard since two similar screams from a Bend hospital 25 and 23 years before.

And so on this Mother's Day, I celebrate not only the woman who gave birth to me and the woman who gave birth to my sons, but the woman who deepens the plot of our family's story: Susan Anderson Welch.

I remember her first official "meet-the-parents" dinner at our Yachats beach cabin. With teenage sons around, Welch dinners at the coast could get rowdy; thus, moments before we sat down — and, with Susan in the other room — I slapped a verbal warning label on The Fam: No funny stuff.

It's a testament to the respect I command that the first grape was fired about 12 seconds after the blessing. I don't know who hurled the opening pitch in this festive food fight; I only know this: Susan's retaliation is now the stuff of family legend, a five-grape barrage that left me with one distinct thought: She's a keeper.

In July 2001, Ryan and Susan were married, leaving us a thank-you note and a $10 gift certificate for Burrito Boy, the kind of thing that makes parenting all worthwhile. Then, last summer came the news: Susan was pregnant.

As the birth date neared and Susan bulged, I found myself looking at my daughter-in-law with a sense of awe: Somewhere in there, I thought, is a new generation.

We soon saw digital and video images of what we learned was a little boy. But if technology had changed in the last few decades, some things had not. "I'm hoping he'll come before Saturday," Ry said. "I wanna take him to Oregon's spring football game."

Ryan did take him — but in a carrying case named Susan.

The call came the next night: Sunday. They were headed for the hospital. Game time.

At 1:59 a.m. Monday, Dr. Julie Haugen tied her surgical mask and entered Room 201. From the hallway, we "cheap-seat" family members would hear the contractions well up — along with encouragement from bed-side coaches — then subside. It was like listening, on the radio, as the Ducks football team struggled to punch it in from the 5 yard-line.

"Push, push! Great, Susan! Almost there, girl! Ahhhhhhh."

Third and two. Long pause.

"Push, push — so close. Oh, oh, oh! There's the head! Ahhhh-hhh."

Fourth and inches. I looked at Susan's father, Wally, and wondered what it must be like to hear the pain of your exhausted daughter at such a moment.

"Here we go! Oh, my gosh! Here he comes!"

I knew we'd scored when Ryan broke into tears, but I awaited the official signal.

And then it came: Caden's cry in the night.

A new generation. A grandson. A little boy who might someday carve castles in the sand at Yachats.

Like autograph-anxious fans, we of the Hallway Gang waited for the signal to come on the field and, when given the OK, joined the revelry. Cameras flashed. Cell calls were made. Hugs and high fives were exchanged. The commotion reached such a pitch that a nurse politely flagged us for excessive celebration, the patient next door needing some sleep.

We calmed down. I leaned over and looked at my grandson face to face, humbled by how small he was. Humbled at the miracle of new life. Humbled to be so blessed.

People headed for the exits. In the soft-light room, Caden was wrapped in a blanket and placed in the waiting arms of his mother, my hero.

I didn't lose it then. That would come seconds later when she spoke her first words to her son. Words of wonder, tinted with the slightest touch of uncertainty. Words I will never forget.

"I'm your mom."

May 8, 2005

Acknowledgments

Author Jean Rhys is right: Life is a lake fed by many streams. And so it is with a book. Many help give it life.

Thus do I offer thanks to Jim Godbold, for taking the risk in 1989 to hire me at *The Register-Guard* even though another editor — long since departed — wanted the guy from Colorado.

To Publisher Tony Baker and Editor Dave Baker, for giving this book the green light.

To Dave Lieber, columnist at the Fort Worth *Star-Telegram*, for convincing me to package a book of columns.

To Eugene outdoor writer Bill Sullivan, for helping me understand how to do it.

To my *Register-Guard* editors Margaret Haberman and Jim Murez, who made my initial drafts better. To copy editors who corrected my mistakes. To R-G sports editor Ron Bellamy, who allowed me ample sports turf and even occasionally joked, "Whataya got for us today, Welch?"

To Tom Penix, Ryan Welch and Jason Welch, for taking far too many late-night calls about graphic design and computers.

To Pat Armstrong and Paul Neville, fellow writers who continually encouraged me.

To Dean Rea, who not only gave me my first full-time job but, along with his wonderful wife, Lou, copy edited this book.

To my late father, Warren, who taught me to love Oregon's outdoors. And to my mother, Marolyn, who taught me to follow my dreams.

To my wife, Sally, who, when I'd decided not to apply for the columnist job, said, "Go for it. I don't want you looking back when you're 80 saying, 'I could have done that.'"

And, finally, thanks to *Register-Guard* readers, who have inspired me with your stories, sharpened me with your constructive criticism and encouraged me with your words.

ALSO BY BOB WELCH

AMERICAN NIGHTINGALE
The Story of Francis Slanger,
Forgotten heroine of Normandy

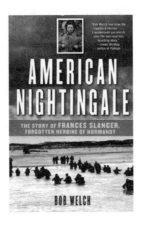

"A stirring story of intense personal devotion."
— PUBLISHERS WEEKLY

"Enrich your life and read this touching story."
— JAMES BRADLEY, AUTHOR OF FLAGS OF OUR FATHERS

"Has the golden cast of 'Saving Private Ryan'"
—BOOK BABES

"A heartwarming story for all ages."
—BOOKLIST

Atria, a division of Simon & Schuster
Hardcover $22.
Softcover $14.
Available at bookstores and at www.amazon.com

ALSO BY BOB WELCH

WHERE ROOTS GROW DEEP

Everyone leaves a legacy.
The only question is: what kind?

"Makes us want to touch the world and change the way we'll be remembered in it."
— JANE KIRKPATRICK, AWARD-WINNING NOVELIST

"Any reader will sense the rhythm of life as told through simple yet profound stories."
—THE HON. SEN. MARK. O. HATFIELD

"Filled with wisdom and hope."
—SANDRA ALDRICH, AUTHOR

Harvest House
Softcover $12.95
Available at www.bobwelch.net
or by e-mailing info@bobwelch.net

BOB WELCH AS A SPEAKER

*"Hands down, the most impressive speaker
we have heard in years. The response
was nothing short of remarkable."*
— ALEX RANKIN, ARCHIVIST,
BOSTON UNIVERSITY

*"Stimulating, engaging, captivating ...
one of the highlights of the conference."*
— MIKE MONOHAN, EXECUTIVE DIRECTOR,
UNIFORMED NURSE PRACTITIONER ASSOCIATION

*"There wasn't a dry eye in the room ...
one of the most inspiring and entertaining
events the medical society has sponsored."*
— CANDICE BARR, EXECUTIVE DIRECTOR,
LANE COUNTY MEDICAL SOCIETY

*"He took the time to engage us,
which in turn made his address that much
more powerful. I highly recommend him."*
— TRACY SIMS, FORMER PRESIDENT,
OREGON ASSOCIATION OF COLLEGE REGISTRARS
AND ADMISSIONS OFFICERS

CONTACT INFO

Phone: 541-517-3936
Email: info@bobwelch.net
Website: www.bobwelch.net
Mail: P.O. Box 70785, Eugene, OR 97401